Encyclopedia of English Period Furniture Designs

José Claret Rubira

Sterling Publishing Co., Inc. New York
Distributed in the U.K. by Blandford Press

Library of Congress Cataloging in Publication Data

Claret Rubira, José.
  Encyclopedia of English period furniture designs.

  Translation of: Muebles de estilo inglés.
  Includes index.
    1. Furniture design—England.   2. Furniture—England—
Drawings.   I. Title.
TT196.C5813 1984   749.22   83-24149
ISBN 0-8069-7830-9 (pbk.)

Translated by Alice Hobson

Edited and designed by Barbara Busch

Copyright © 1984 by Sterling Publishing Co., Inc.
Two Park Avenue, New York, N.Y. 10016
The material in this book was originally
published in Spain under the title,
"Muebles de Estilo Inglés," © 1982 by
Editorial Gustavo Gili, S.A.

Distributed in Australia by Oak Tree Press Co., Ltd.
P.O. Box K514 Haymarket, Sydney 2000, N.S.W.
Distributed in the United Kingdom by Blandford Press
Link House, West Street, Poole, Dorset BH15 1LL, England
Distributed in Canada by Oak Tree Press Ltd.
% Canadian Manda Group, P.O. Box 920, Station U
Toronto, Ontario, Canada M8Z 5P9

CONTENTS

PUBLISHER'S PREFACE

Given the extent of the British Empire, it was perhaps inevitable that English furniture design had such a far-reaching influence. But even if the Empire had never extended beyond the shores of Great Britain, the beauty and practicality of English furniture would have assured it a place in museums and homes throughout the world.

Historians, furniture makers, restorers, decorators, set designers and students—all those who wish to identify a piece or authenticate a design—will find in the following pages a pictorial history of English furniture design from the Tudors to the Victorians. There is also a section dealing with American Colonial and—a rarity in books published in the English-speaking world—a section on English Minorcan furniture. Although England's control over Minorca was brief and intermittent, its influence in the area of furniture design was as extensive and long-lasting as in North America.

English furniture design "travelled well" largely because of its extraordinary adaptability—frequently to environments totally different from those for which it was originally intended. The furniture is as comfortable to live with in the warm climate of Minorca as it is in the rigors of a New England winter.

It is a furniture that also adapts readily to quite different life styles. Although some of the very large pieces require large rooms, the bulk of English furnishings will fit as gracefully into a small urban apartment as it does into the stately homes of England for which it was originally intended.

There is another unique quality to English furniture which is perhaps a part of its adaptability. It is the only furniture to be found in museums which it is possible to envision children clambering about and living with.

Tudor-Stuart   Queen Anne

Tudor   Jacobean   William and Mary   Queen Anne and George

Cromwell   Charles

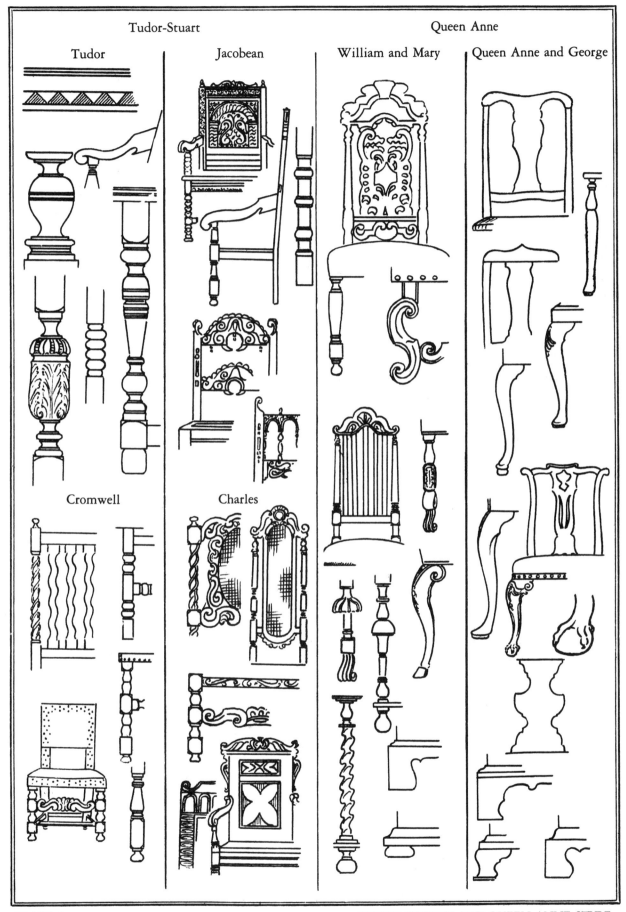

PLATE 1.   TUDOR-STUART AND QUEEN ANNE STYLE.

5

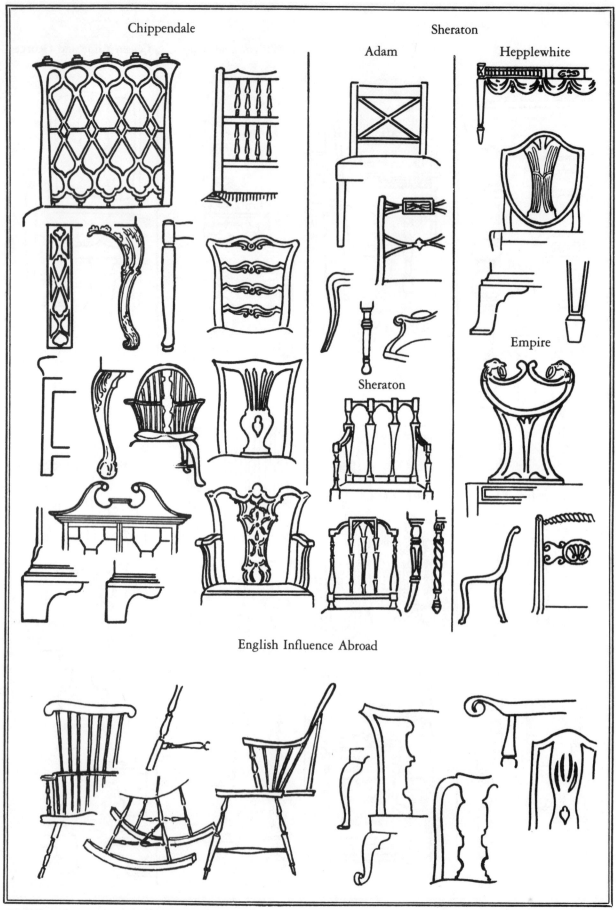

Chippendale

Sheraton

Adam

Hepplewhite

Empire

Sheraton

English Influence Abroad

PLATE 2.

ENGLISH FURNITURE STYLES.

6

PLATE 3.   TUDOR-STUART STYLE (architectural features).
1 and 2. Oak panels, period of Henry VIII. Layer Marney Hall, Essex.   3. Oak Panel, 1535. Costessey Hall, Norfolk.   4. Receiving room with oak panels, Manor House, Upton Grey, Hampshire.   5. Ceiling section with simple mouldings. Layer Marney Hall, Essex.   6. Ceiling section with delicate bas-relief. Chastleton House, Oxfordshire.

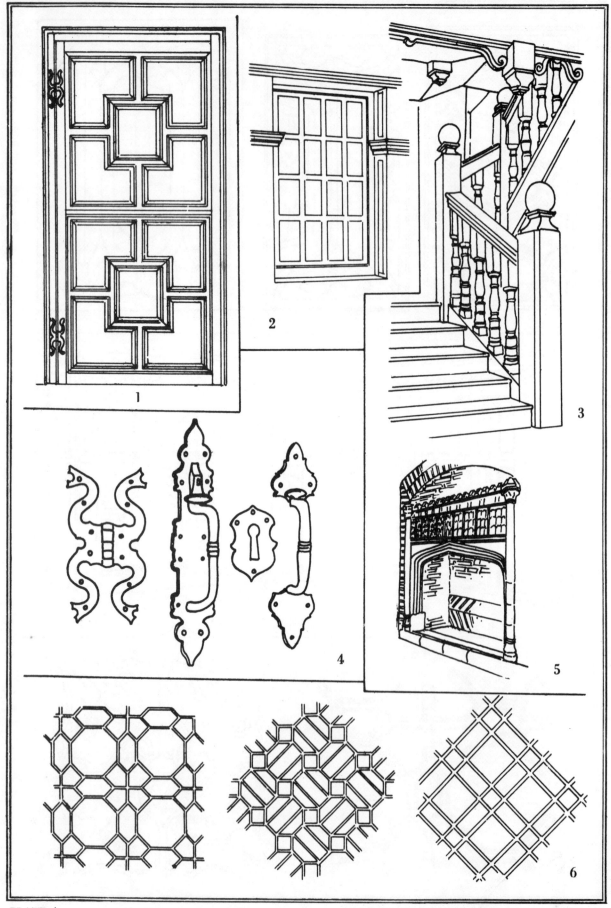

PLATE 4.   TUDOR-STUART STYLE (architectural features).
1. Door with panels from the period of James I. Lynsted, Kent.   2. Window from reigns of Elizabeth I and James I.
Powis Castle.   3. Stairway section from reigns of Elizabeth I and James I. Mance House, Upton Grey, Hampshire.   4. Hinge, escutcheon plate and door pulls from the period.   5. Fireplace, second floor of Tattershall Castle,
Lincoln County.   6. Three geometric forms used for window panes in Elizabethan period.

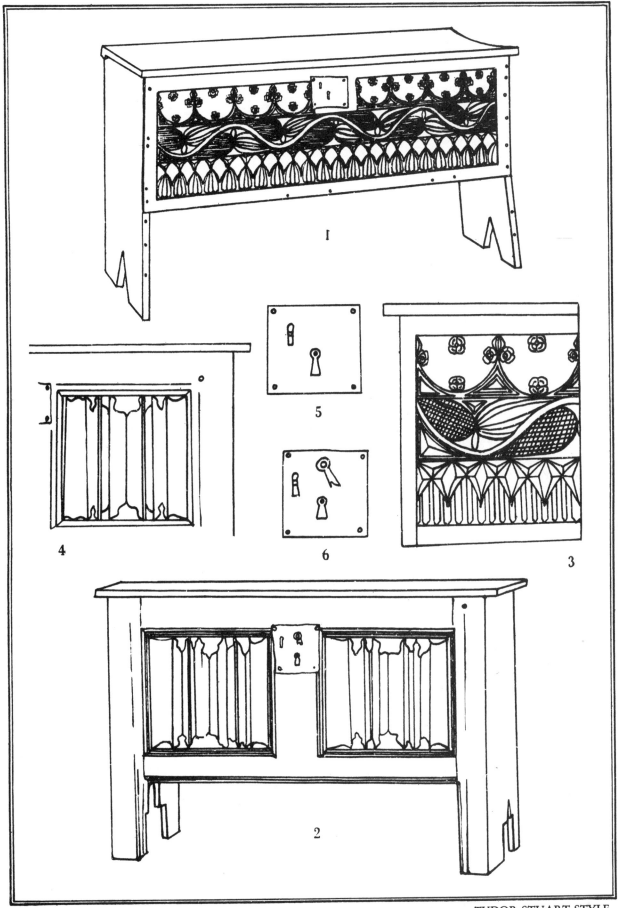

PLATE 5.   TUDOR-STUART STYLE.

1 and 2. Simple chests from the 17th century.   3 and 4. Decorations on their respective panels.   5 and 6. Escutcheon plates.

Victoria and Albert Museum.

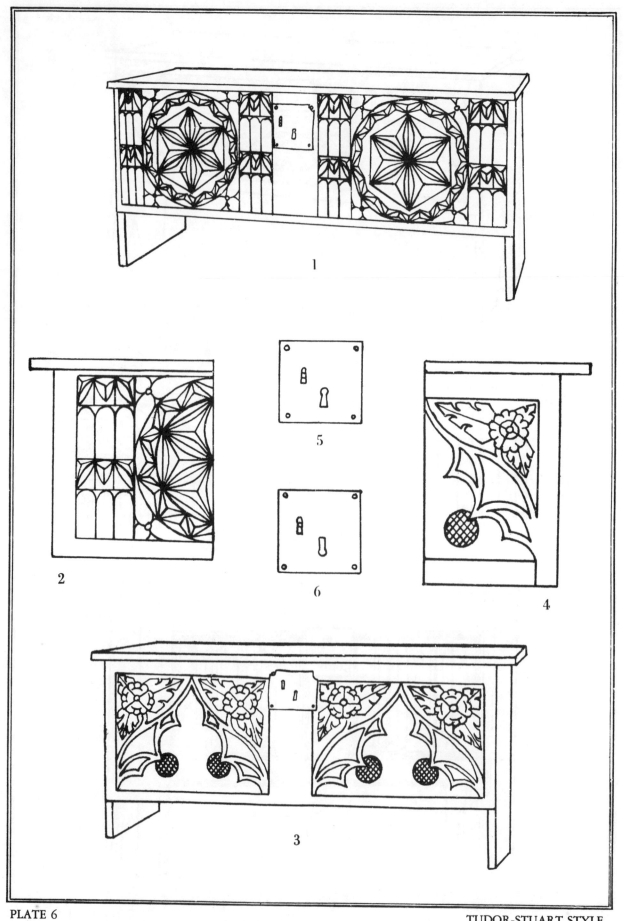

PLATE 6

TUDOR-STUART STYLE.

1. Chest from the 15th century.   2. Detail of same.   3. Chest from the early 16th century.   4. Detail of same.
5 and 6. Escutcheon plates.

Victoria and Albert Museum.

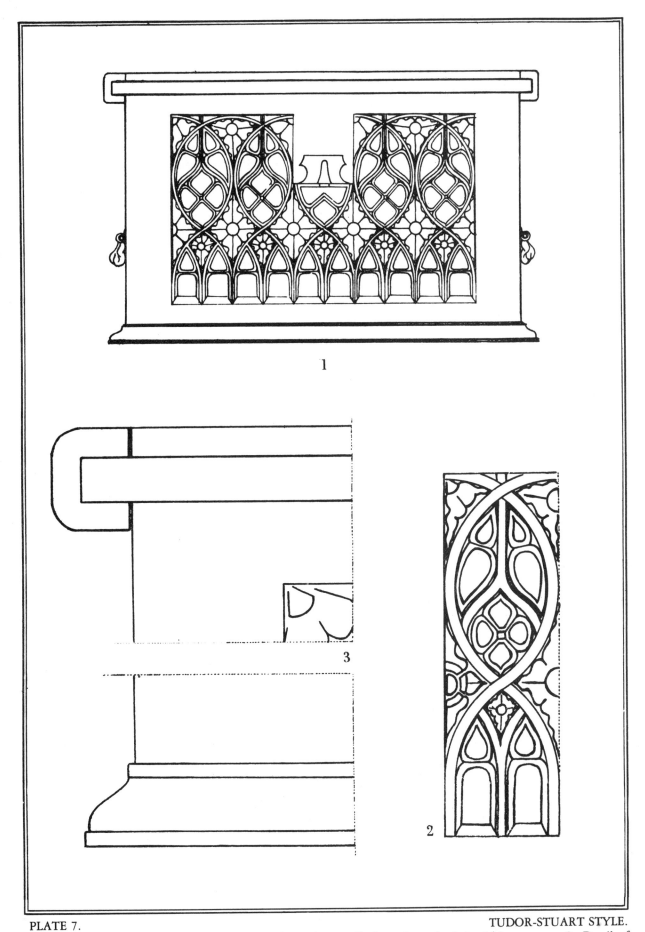

PLATE 7.   TUDOR-STUART STYLE.
1. Gothic chest from the 16th century, with decorative motifs from the end of the 14th century.   2. Detail of decoration.   3. Upper and lower mouldings.

Private collection.

PLATE 8.   TUDOR-STUART STYLE.
1. Chest with type of decoration called Romayne work.   2 and 3. Detail of decorative panels.   4. Moulding on the
lid.   5. Escutcheon plate.

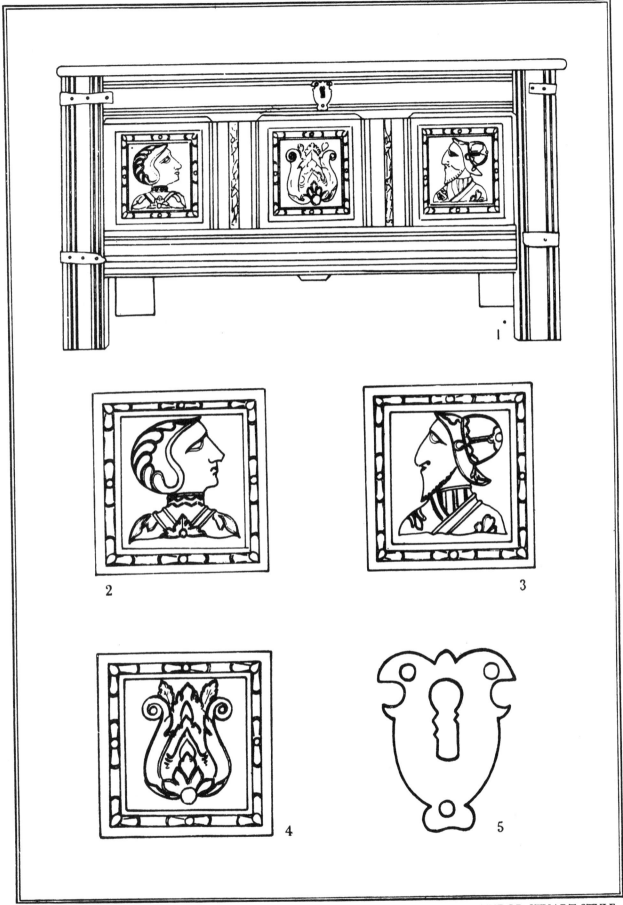

PLATE 9   TUDOR-STUART STYLE.

1. Chest with Romayne work, from the 16th century.   2, 3 and 4. Details of panels.   5. Escutcheon plate.

Victoria and Albert Museum.

PLATE 10.   TUDOR-STUART STYLE.
1. Chest from the first half of the 17th century.   2. Detail of the side panels.   3. Detail of the central
panels.   4. Decoration on the uprights.

Victoria and Albert Museum.

14

PLATE 11.
1. Chest from the 17th century.   2 and 3. Decorative details.

TUDOR-STUART STYLE.

Victoria and Albert Museum.

PLATE 12.

TUDOR-STUART STYLE.

1. Chest from the 17th century. 2. Decoration on upright. 3. Decoration on socle. 4. Detail of panel. 5. Detail of upper frieze. 6. Rosette.

Victoria and Albert Museum.

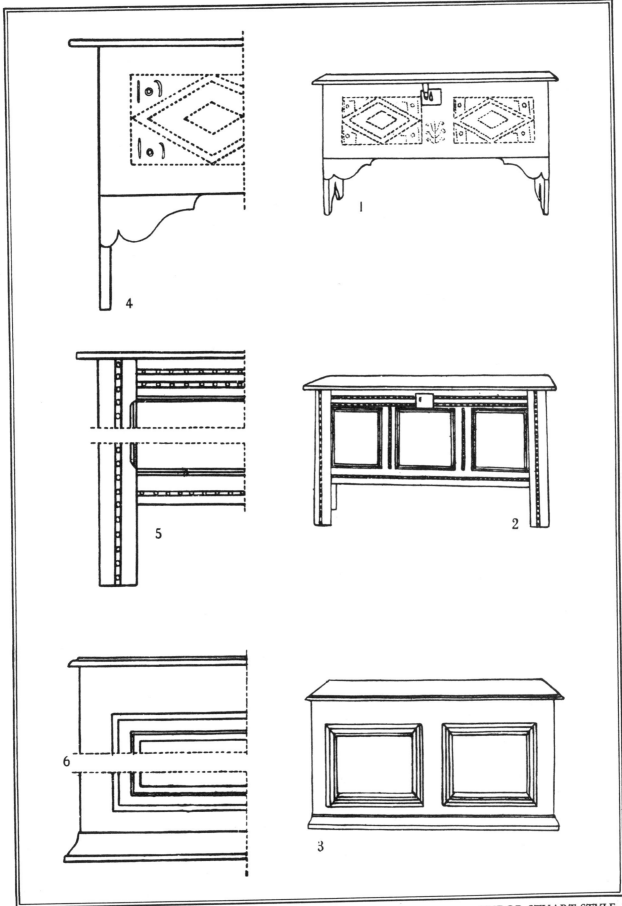

PLATE 13.
1, 2 and 3. Simple chests from the 17th century.   4, 5 and 6. Details of same.

TUDOR-STUART STYLE.

Private collection.

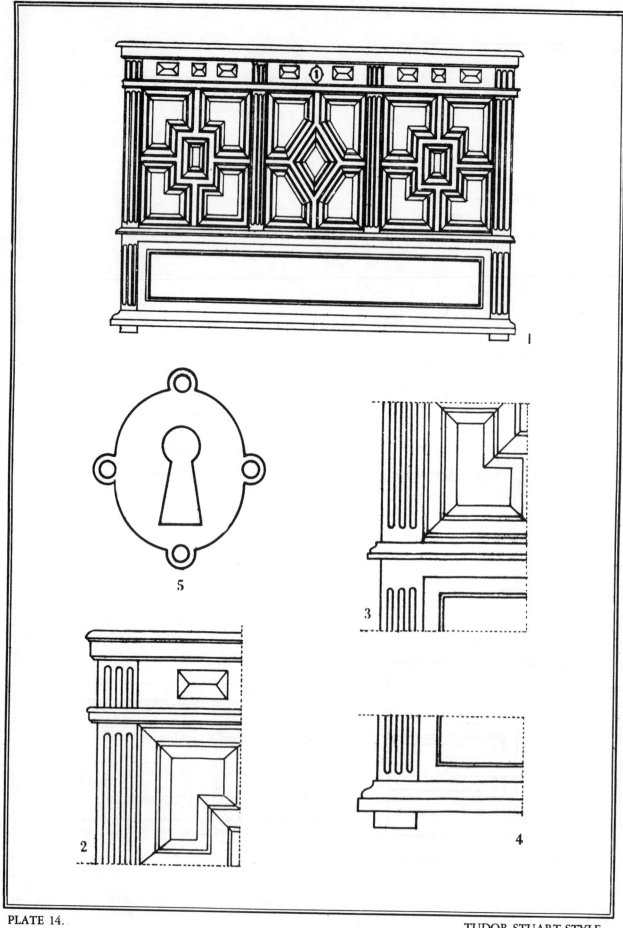

PLATE 14.

1. Jacobean chest from the 17th century.   2, 3 and 4. Decorative details.   5. Escutcheon plate.

TUDOR-STUART STYLE.

Private collection.

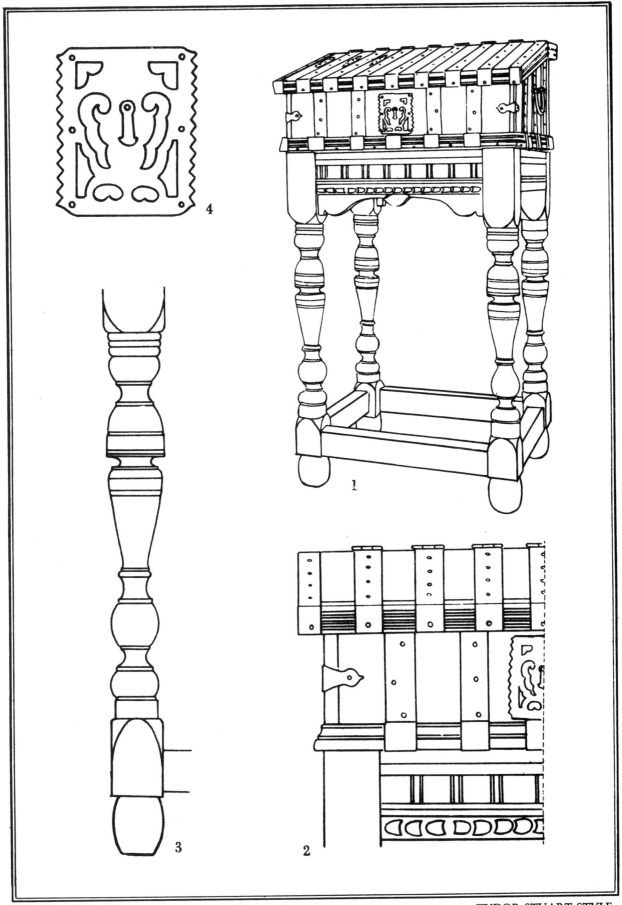

PLATE 15.   TUDOR-STUART STYLE.
1. Box for the Bible, with pedestal table.   2. Detail of box.   3. Leg.   4. Escutcheon plate.
Victoria and Albert Museum.

PLATE 16.
1 and 2. Boxes for the Bible, 17th century.   3, 4, 5 and 6. Decorations on same.

TUDOR-STUART STYLE.

Victoria and Albert Museum.

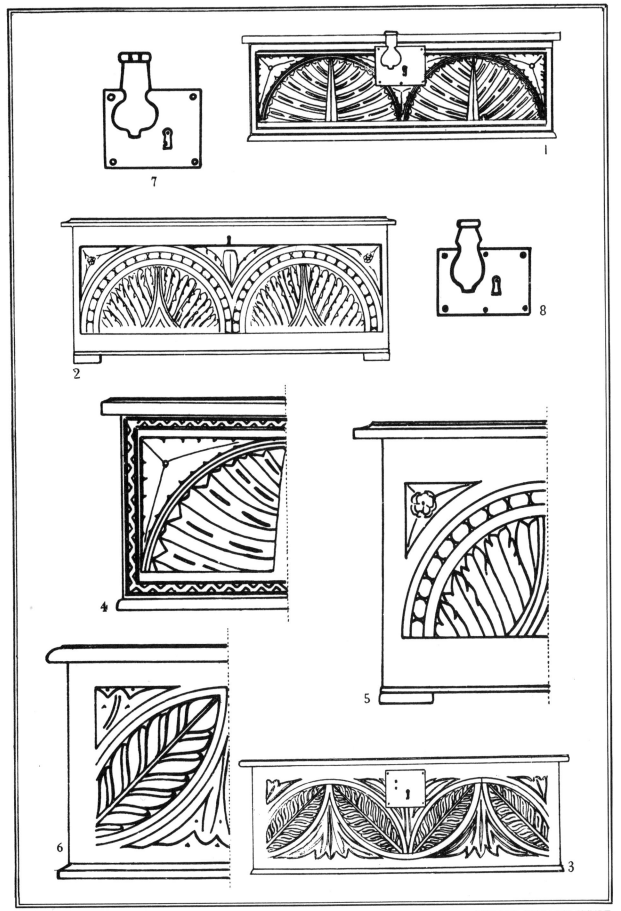

PLATE 17.   TUDOR-STUART STYLE.

1, 2 and 3. Bible boxes, end of 17th century.   4, 5 and 6. Decorations on same. 7 and 8. Iron hardware.

Private collection.

PLATE 18.   TUDOR-STUART STYLE.
1. Bible box, with pedestal table.   2 and 3. Decorative detail and leg of same.   4. Box for Bible with owner's name.   5. Decorative detail.

Private collection.

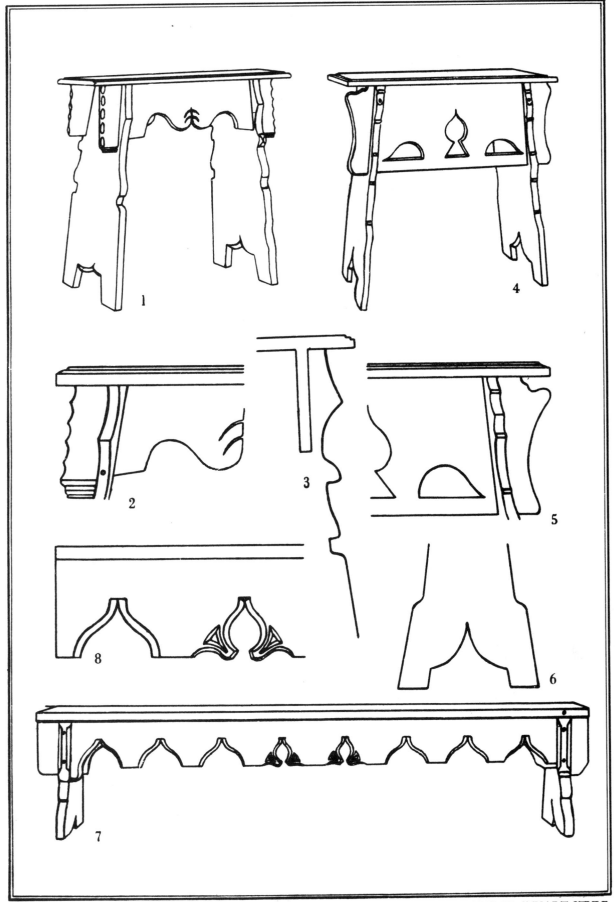

PLATE 19.   TUDOR-STUART STYLE.
1. Stool from the end of the 15th century.   2 and 3. Details of same.   4. Stool from beginning of 16th century.
5 and 6. Details of same.   7. Bench from 16th century.   8. Decoration on bench.

Victoria and Albert Museum.

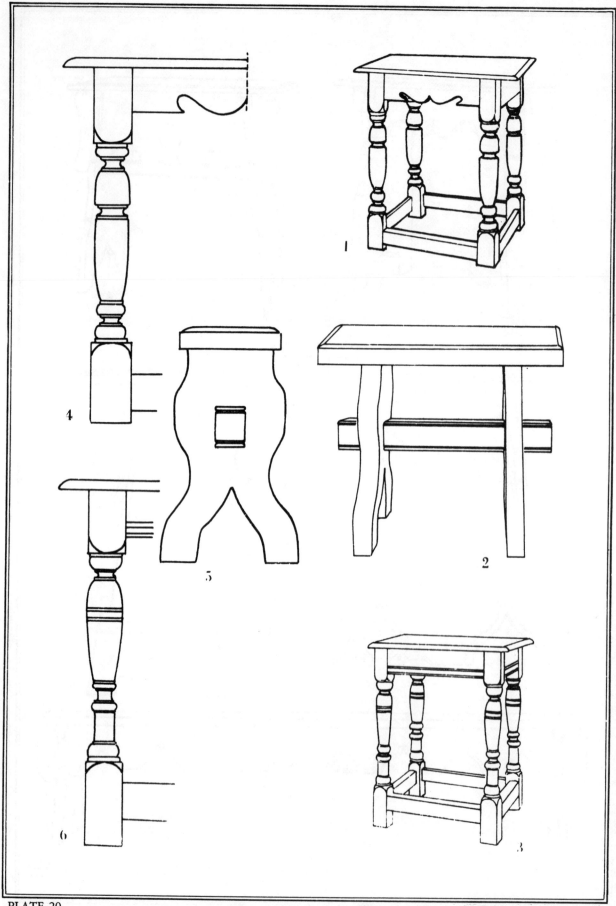

PLATE 20.

TUDOR-STUART STYLE.

1, 2 and 3. Stools from 17th century. 4, 5 and 6. Details of numbers 1, 2 and 3, respectively.

Charterhouse School, London.

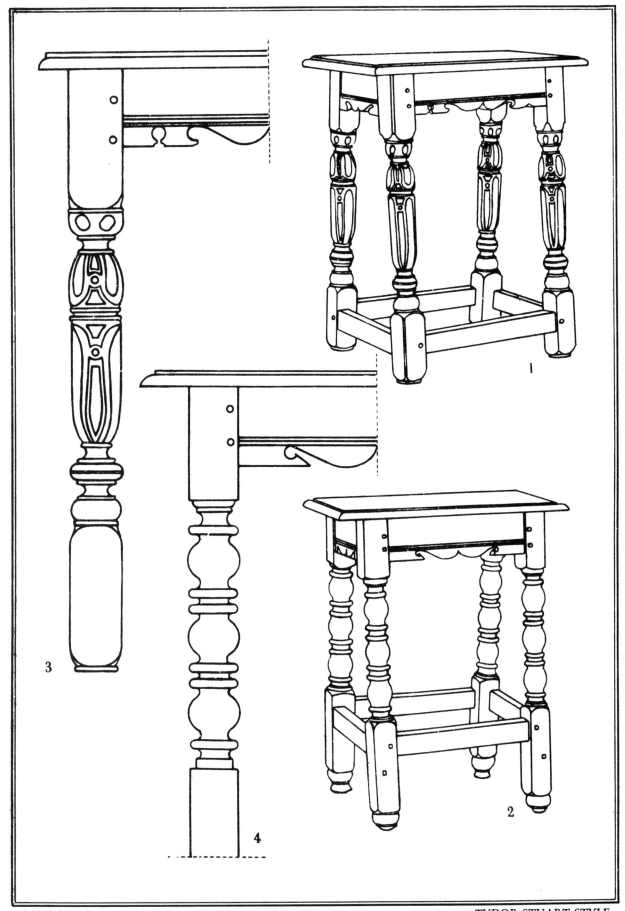

PLATE 21.   TUDOR-STUART STYLE.
1 and 2. Stools from the 17th century.   3 and 4. Detail of legs and profile of numbers 1 and 2, respectively.
Victoria and Albert Museum.

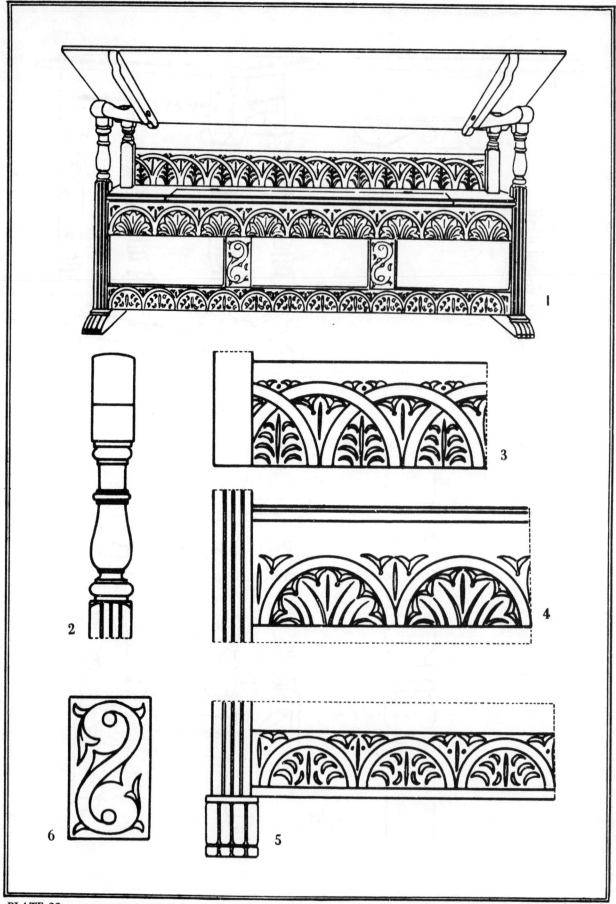

PLATE 22.   TUDOR-STUART STYLE.

1. Table bench from the 17th century.   2. Detail of upright.   3. Detail of frieze on back.   4. Detail of upper crosspiece.   5. Detail of lower crosspiece. 6. Decoration on rail.

Victoria and Albert Museum.

PLATE 23.

1. Bench from early 17th century.   2. Detail of lower back panels.   3. Detail of upper back panels.

TUDOR-STUART STYLE.

Private collection.

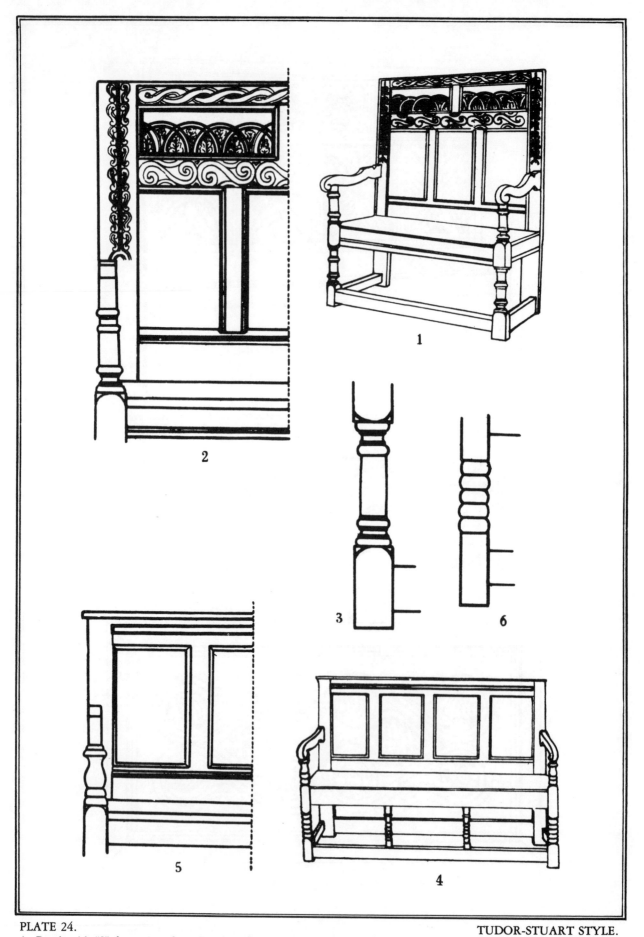

PLATE 24. TUDOR-STUART STYLE.

1. Bench with "S" decorations from the 17th century. 2. Decorative detail of same. 3. Detail of front legs. 4. Simple bench from 17th century. 5. Detail of back. 6. Detail of front legs.

PLATE 25.   TUDOR-STUART STYLE.

1. Armchair with Romayne motifs; 16th century.   2, 3 and 4. Decorative details.   5. Turned chair; 16th century.   6. Detail of its structure.

Private colleciton.

PLATE 26.   TUDOR-STUART STYLE.

1. Armchair from the 16th century; with "guilloche" design on back.   2. Decorative detail.   3. Armchair from 16th
century.   4. Detail of back.

Victoria and Albert Museum.

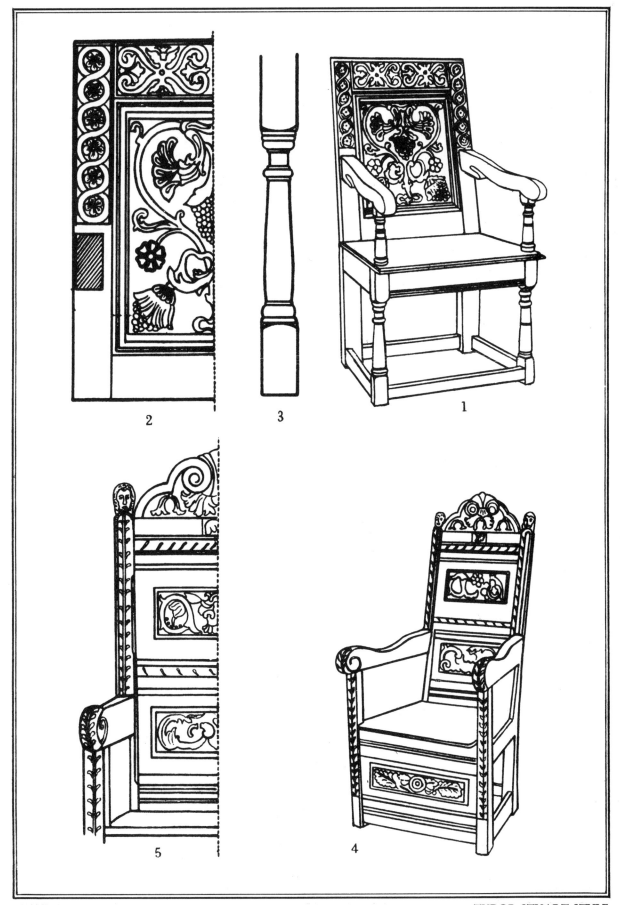

PLATE 27.   TUDOR-STUART STYLE.

1. Jacobean armchair.   2. Decoration on back.   3. Front leg.   4. Jacobean armchair.   5. Decorative detail of same.

Private collection.

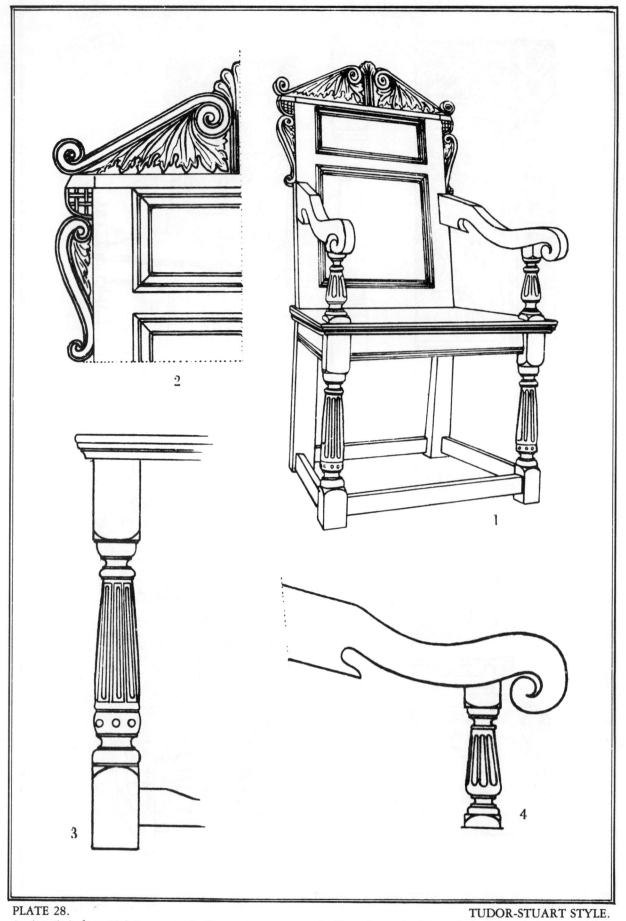

PLATE 28.
TUDOR-STUART STYLE.

1. Armchair from 17th century.   2. Decoration on crest.   3. Front leg.   4. Arm and support column.

Victoria and Albert Museum.

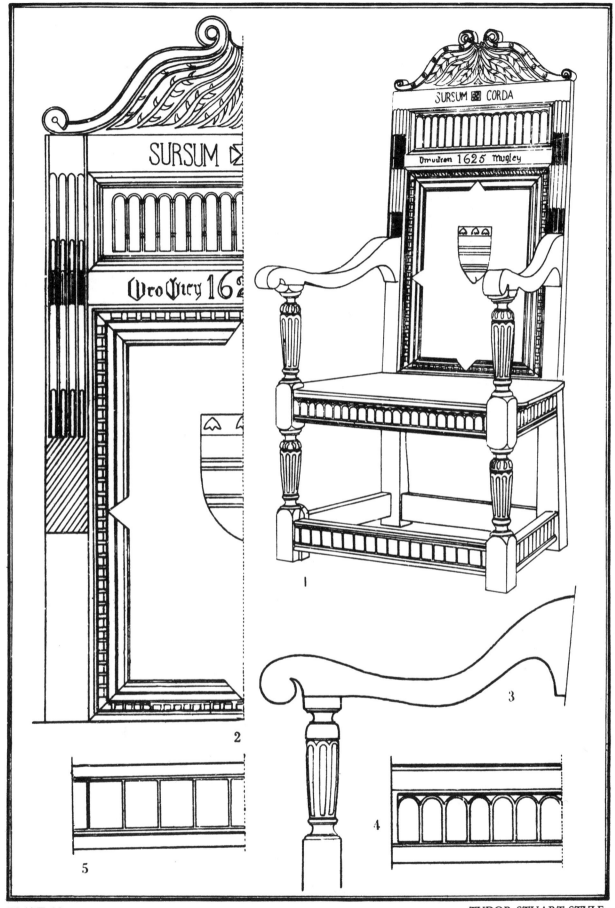

PLATE 29.   TUDOR-STUART STYLE.
1. Armchair from 17th century.   2. Decoration on back.   3. Arm and support column.   4. Detail of upper crosspiece.   5. Detail of lower crosspiece.

Victoria and Albert Museum.

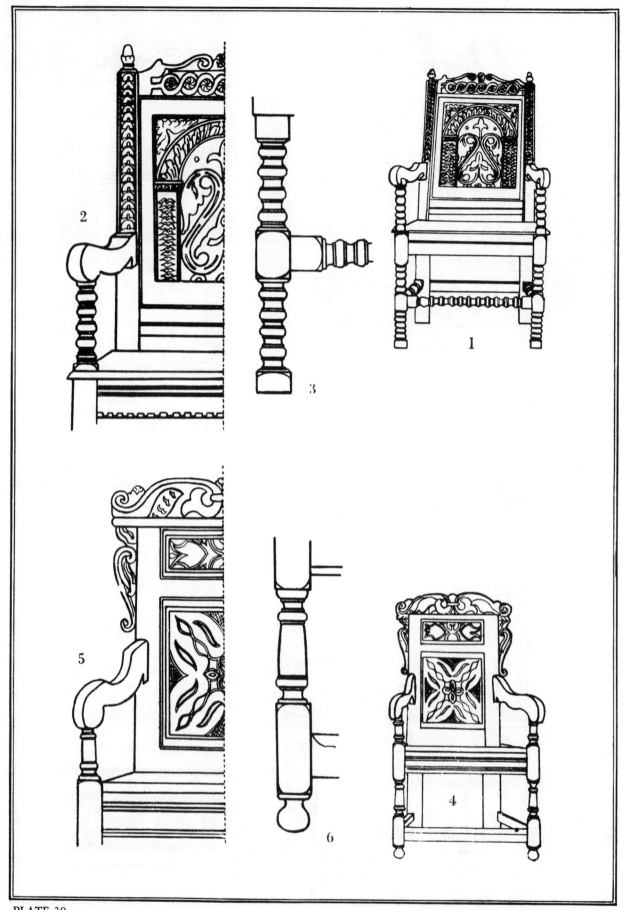

PLATE 30.   TUDOR-STUART STYLE.

1. Armchair from early 17th century. 2. Decoration on same. 3. Detail of turned legs and cross-pieces. 4. Armchair from early 17th century. 5. Detail of back. 6. Turned front legs.

Private collection.

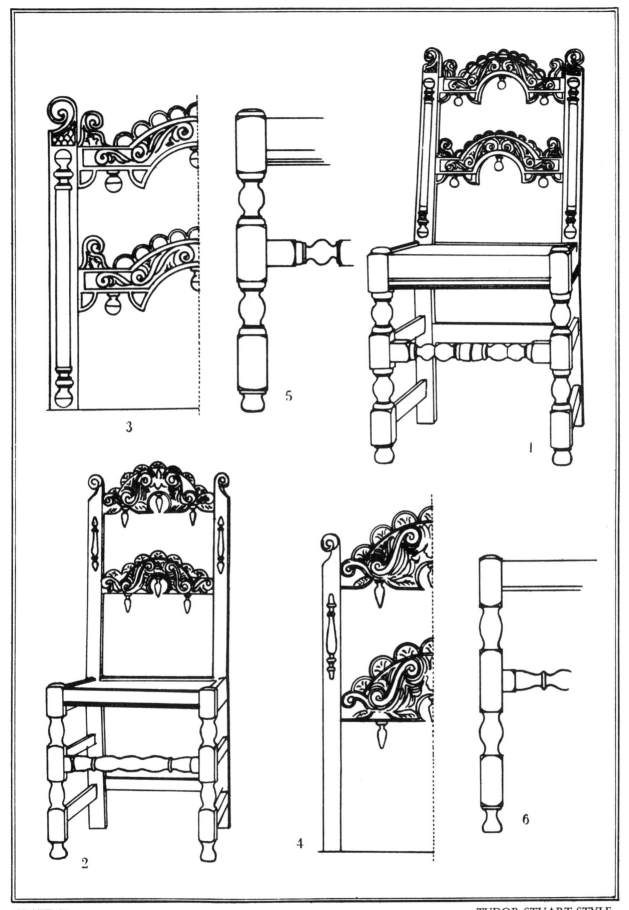

PLATE 31.   TUDOR-STUART STYLE.
1 and 2. Yorkshire and Derbyshire armchairs, 17th century.   3. Back detail of first armchair.   4. Detail of back of
second armchair.   5. Turned legs and crosspieces of first armchair.   6. Turned legs and crosspieces of second armchair.
Victoria and Albert Museum.

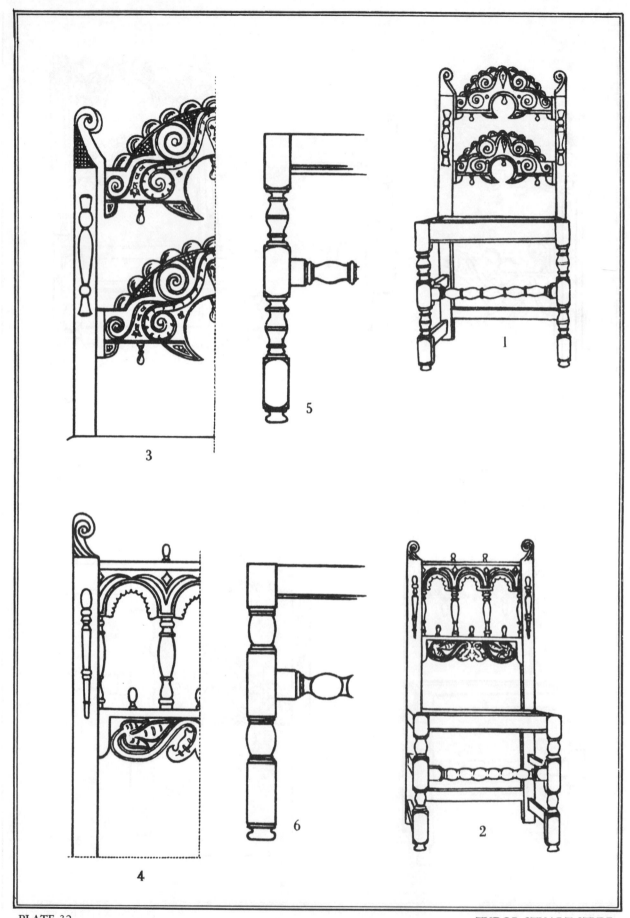

PLATE 32.

TUDOR-STUART STYLE.

1 and 2. Yorkshire and Derbyshire armchairs, 17th century.   3. Detail of back of first armchair.   4. Detail of back of second armchair.   5. Turned legs and crosspiece of first armchair.   6. Turned legs and crosspiece of second armchair.

Victoria and Albert Museum.

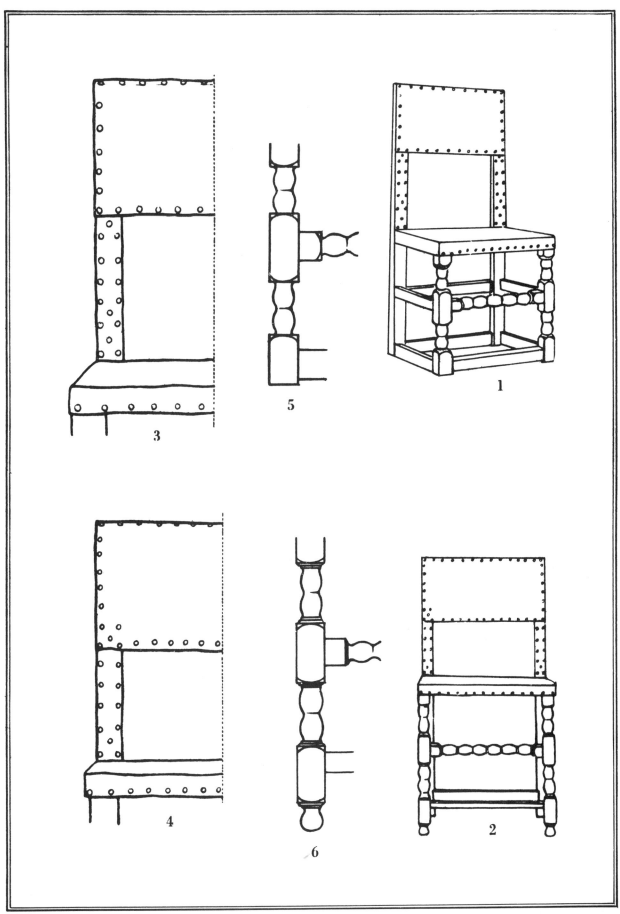

PLATE 33.   TUDOR-STUART STYLE.

1 and 2. Cromwell chairs.   3 and 4. Details of backs.   5 and 6. Turned legs and crosspieces.

Private collection.

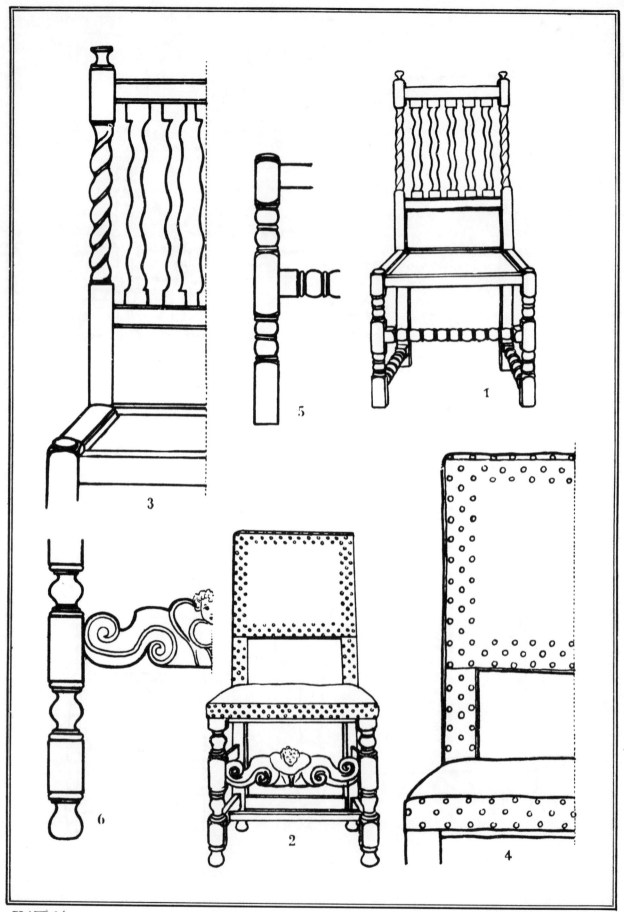

PLATE 34.   TUDOR-STUART STYLE.
1 and 2. Chairs from the end of the Cromwellian period, with decorative motifs from the next period.   3 and 4. Details of backs.   5. Turned legs and crosspiece of first chair.   6. Turned legs and crosspiece of second chair.

Private collection and Victoria and Albert Museum.

PLATE 35.   TUDOR-STUART STYLE.
1. Armchair from 17th century.   2. Back decoration.   3. Turned leg and decoration on back.   4. Armchair from
the 17th century.   5. Back decoration.   6. Upper crosspiece.   7. Lower crosspiece.   8. Turned leg.

Private collection.

39

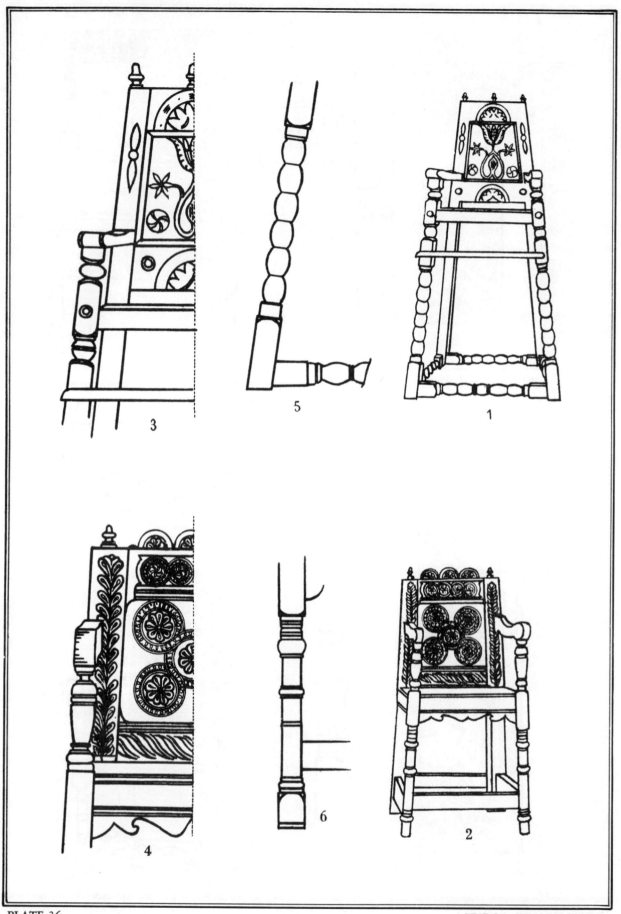

PLATE 36.   TUDOR-STUART STYLE.

1 and 2. Children's chairs; 17th century.   3 and 4. Decorations on back.   5 and 6. Turned legs and crosspieces.

Victoria and Albert Museum.

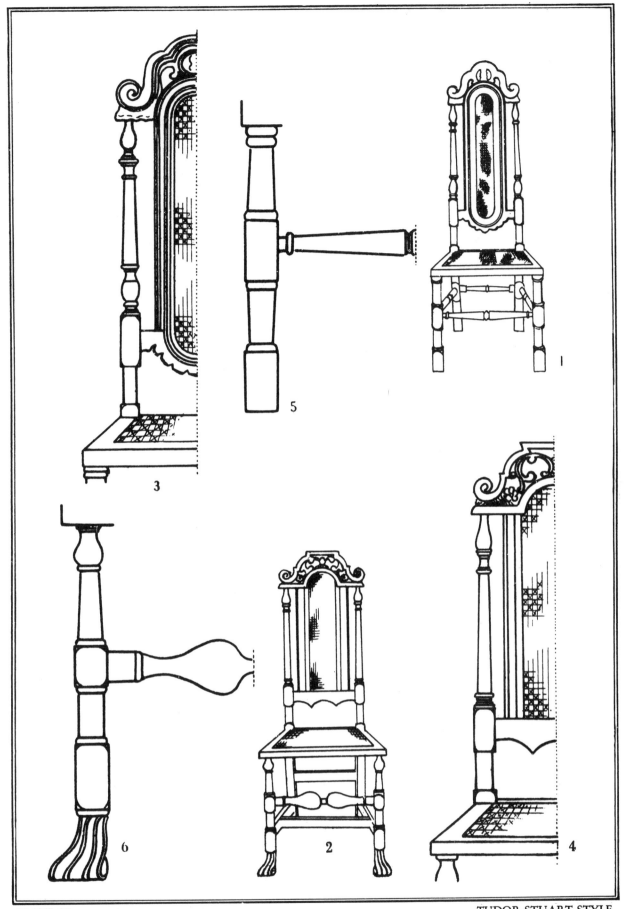

PLATE 37.   TUDOR-STUART STYLE.

1 and 2. Stuart chairs from the 17th century.   3 and 4. Turned uprights and crest on backs.   5 and 6. Turned legs and crosspieces.

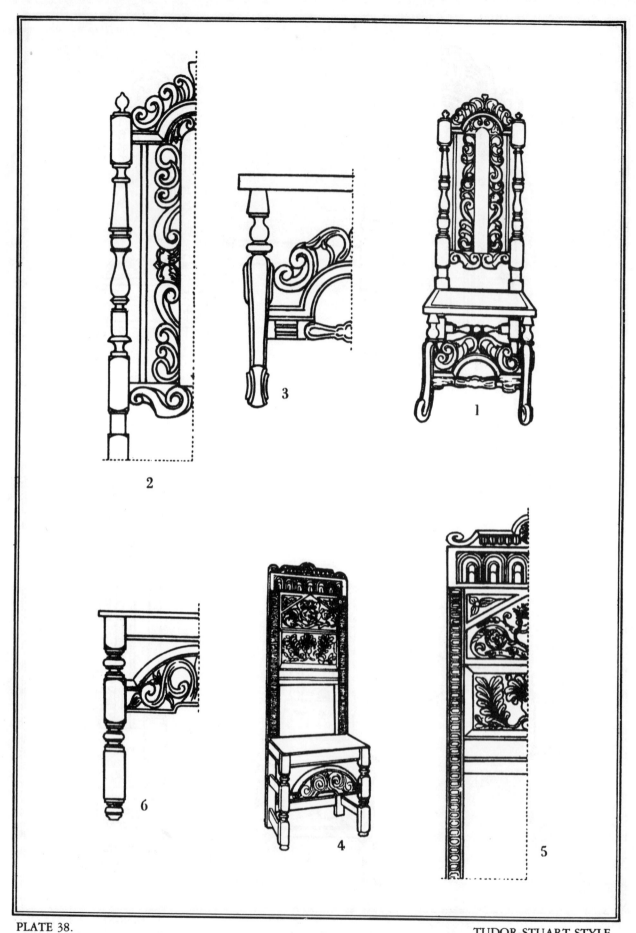

PLATE 38.   TUDOR-STUART STYLE.
1. Stuart chair.   2. Detail of turned upright and back decoration.   3. Detail of legs and front crosspiece.   4. Caroline
chair.   5. Back decoration.   6. Turned front legs and crosspiece.

Private collection and Victoria and Albert Museum

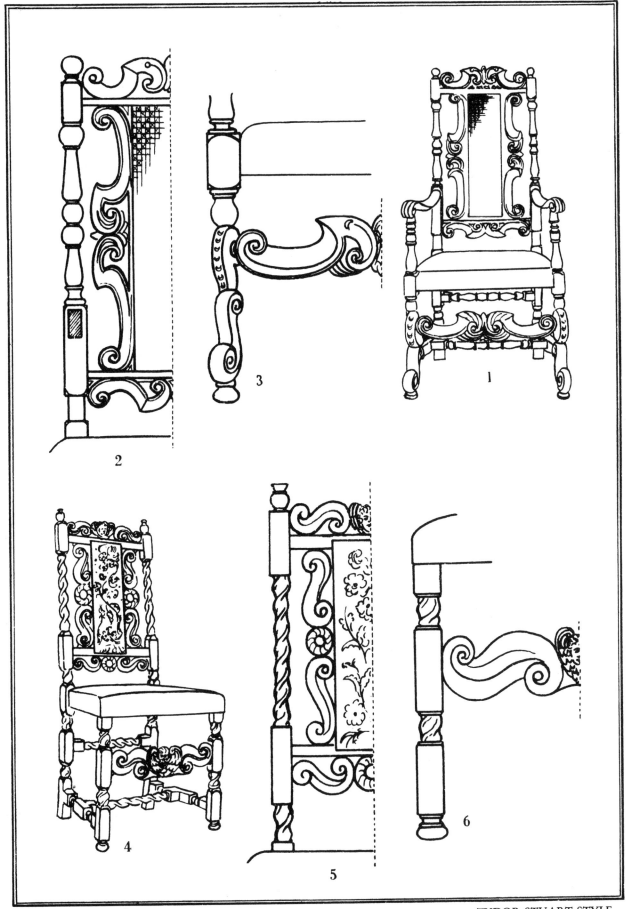

PLATE 39.   TUDOR-STUART STYLE.
1. Stuart armchair. 2. Detail of back. 3. Detail of leg and crosspiece. 4. Stuart chair. 5. Detail of
back. 6. Detail of leg and crosspiece.

Private collection.

PLATE 40.

1. Stuart armchair.   2. Detail of back.   3. Decoration on leg and crosspiece.

TUDOR-STUART STYLE.

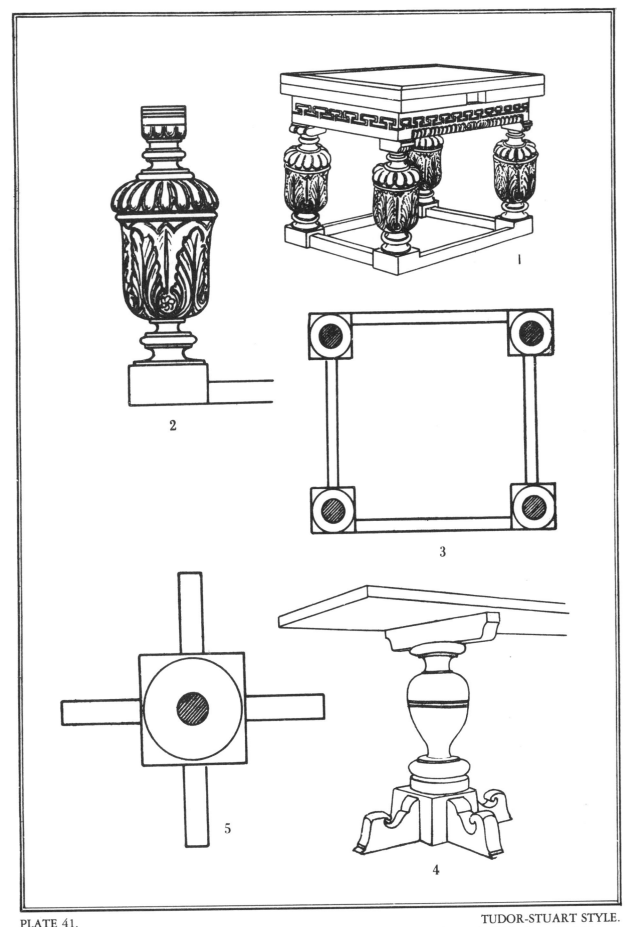

PLATE 41.   TUDOR-STUART STYLE.
1. Table from the Elizabethan period.   2. Decoration on leg.   3. Base of the table.   4. Table from the 16th century.   5. Base of same.

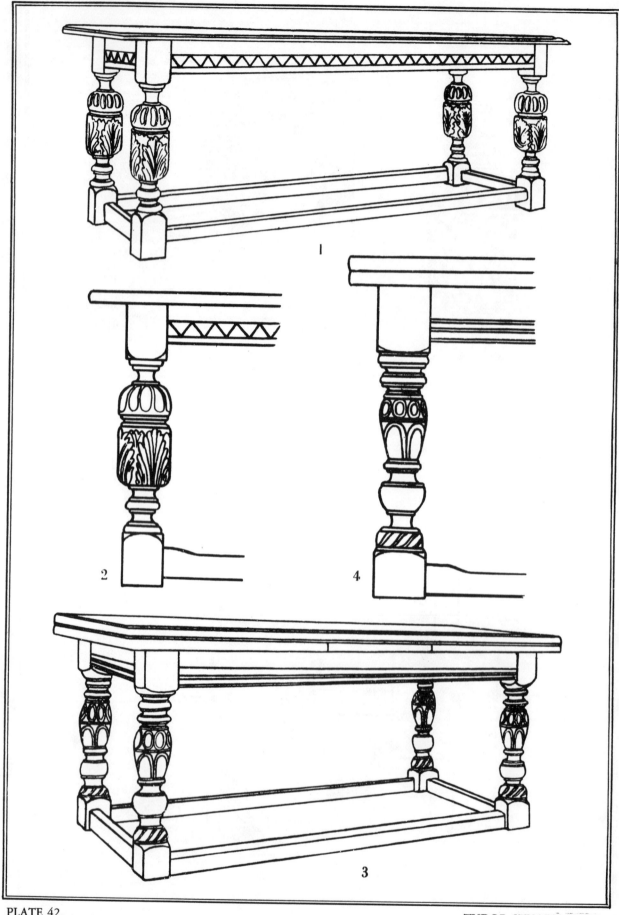

PLATE 42.

1. Table from end of 16th century.   2. Decoration.   3. Table from early 17th century.   4. Decoration.

TUDOR-STUART STYLE.

Private collection.

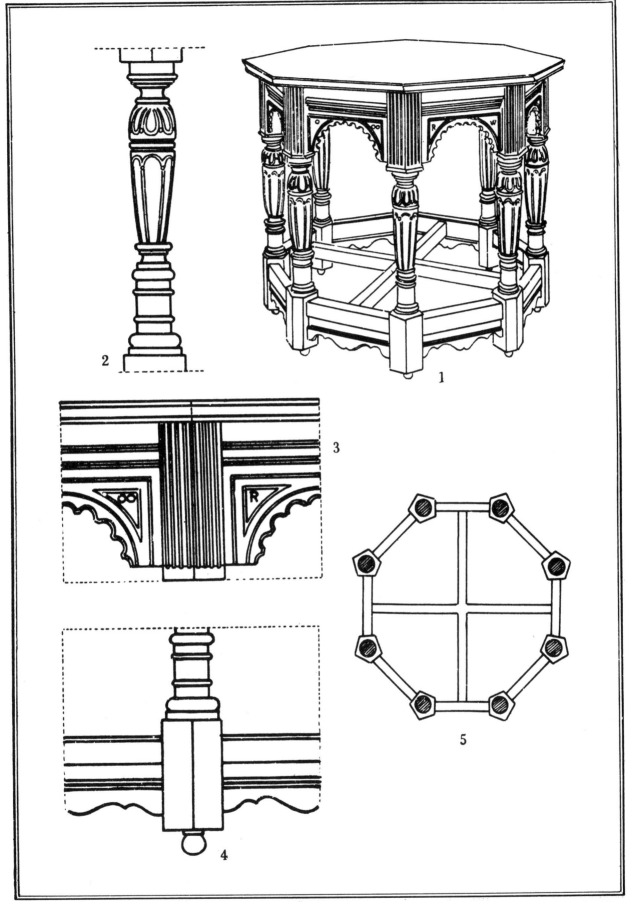

PLATE 43.   TUDOR-STUART STYLE.

1. Typical table from the end of the Elizabethan period, early 17th century. 2. Decoration on legs. 3 and
4. Decorations. 5. Base.

Private collection.

47

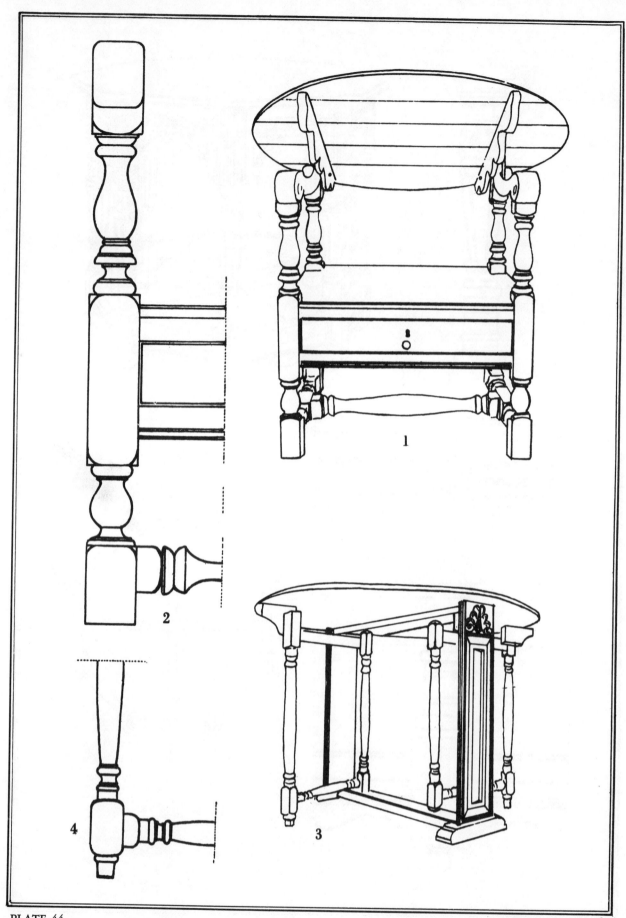

PLATE 44.   TUDOR-STUART STYLE.
1. Bench table from 17th century.   2. Details of legs and box seat.   3. Folding (gate-leg) table from the 17th century.   4. Turned legs and crosspiece.

Victoria and Albert Museum.

48

PLATE 45.

1, 2, 3 and 4. Folding (gate-leg) tables from the 17th century. 5, 6, 7 and 8. Turned legs of each table, respectively.

TUDOR-STUART STYLE.

Private collection and Guild Hall Museum, London (3).

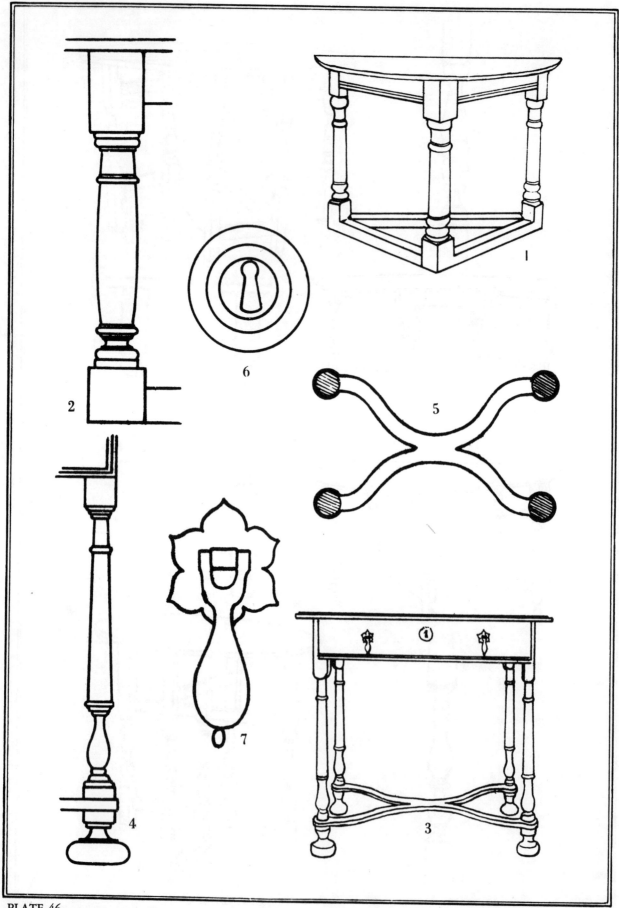

PLATE 46.   TUDOR-STUART STYLE.
1. Cromwell table. 2. Turned leg. 3. Stuart table. 4. Turned leg. 5. Base of crosspiece. 6. Escutcheon
plate. 7. Drawer pull.

Private collection.

PLATE 47.   TUDOR-STUART STYLE.
1. Cupboard, beginning of 16th century.   2. Decoration on side panels.   3 and 4. Decorations on middle panel.
5 and 6. Hinges.   7. Cupboard; 16th century.   8. Escutcheon plate.

Victoria and Albert Museum.

PLATE 48.
1. Cupboard, 17th century.   2. Detail.   3. Hinges.

TUDOR-STUART STYLE.

Victoria and Albert Museum.

PLATE 49.

1. Dresser from the 17th century.   2. Detail of side.   3. Decoration on upper portion.

TUDOR-STUART STYLE.

Victoria and Albert Museum.

PLATE 50.   TUDOR-STUART STYLE.

1. Elizabethan dresser, 17th century.   2. Decorations on legs and posts.   3. Middle panel on upper portion.   4. Decoration on side panels.

Metropolitan Museum of Art.

PLATE 51.   TUDOR-STUART STYLE.

1. Dresser from Elizabethan period, second half of 17th century.   2. Detail of upper side posts.   3. Detail of friezes.   4. Door panels.   5. Decoration on uprights.

Private collection.

PLATE 52.   TUDOR-STUART STYLE.

1. Dresser from 17th century with "guilloche" design on arches decorating doors.   2. Decoration on side panels.   3. Detail of upper and lower friezes and uprights.   4. Escutcheon plate.   5. Hinge.

Victoria and Albert Museum.

PLATE 53.   TUDOR-STUART STYLE.
1. Dresser from 17th century.   2. Details of uprights, panels and side friezes.   3. Lower middle panel.   4. Upper middle panel.   5. Hinge.

Private collection.

PLATE 54.   TUDOR-STUART STYLE.

1. Dresser from beginning of the Jacobean period, 17th century.   2. Details of posts and decorative panels.   3. Detail of side.   4. Hinge.

Private collection.

PLATE 55.   TUDOR-STUART STYLE.

1. Dresser on stand from 17th century.   2. Detail of mouldings and decorative panels.   3. Turned legs.   4. Escutcheon plate.   5. Drawer pull.

Private collection.

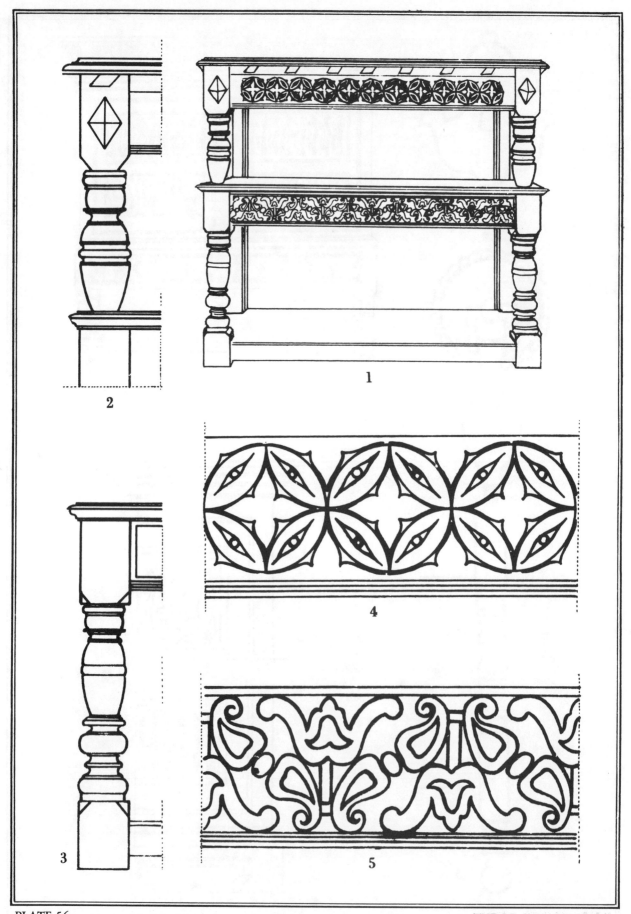

PLATE 56.   TUDOR-STUART STYLE.
1. Sideboard from middle of 17th century.   2. Turned posts.   3. Turned legs.   4. Upper frieze.   5. Central frieze.
Victoria and Albert Museum.

60

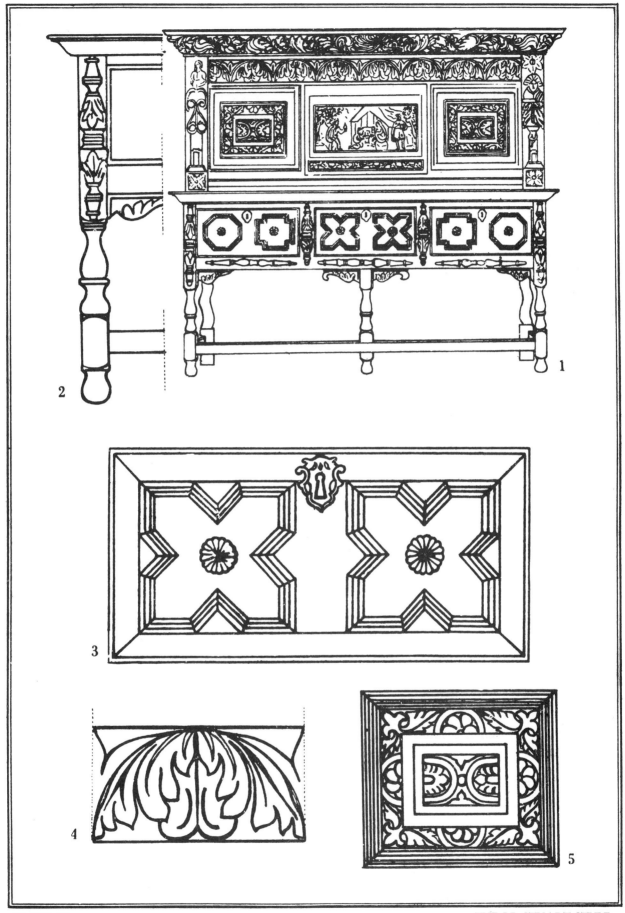

PLATE 57.   TUDOR-STUART STYLE.
1. Dresser from 17th century.   2. Detail of uprights.   3. Middle drawer panel.   4. Detail of upper frieze.   5. Upper side panel.

Victoria and Albert Museum.

PLATE 58.
1. Dresser, upper section has supports.   2. Detail.   3. Upper middle panel.

TUDOR-STUART STYLE.

Private collection.

PLATE 59.   TUDOR-STUART STYLE.
1. Cabinet with ornately carved crosspieces.   2. Detail of front legs.   3. Decoration on crosspiece.   4. Escutcheon plate.

J. S. Sykes collection.

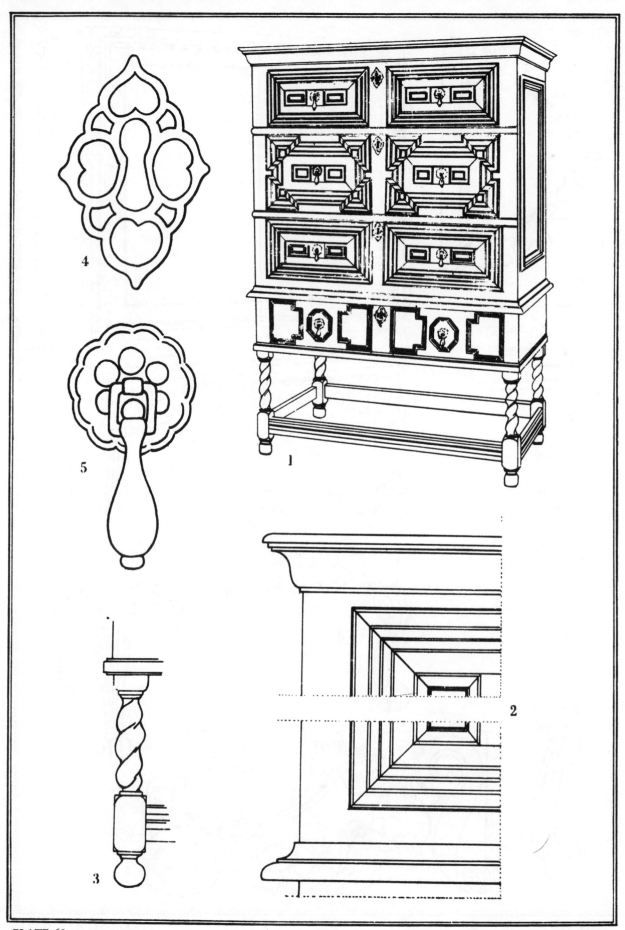

PLATE 60.   TUDOR-STUART STYLE.

1. Commode with turned legs, end of 17th century.   2. Detail of cornice and panels.   3. Turned legs.   4. Escutcheon plate.   5. Drawer pull.

Victoria and Albert Museum.

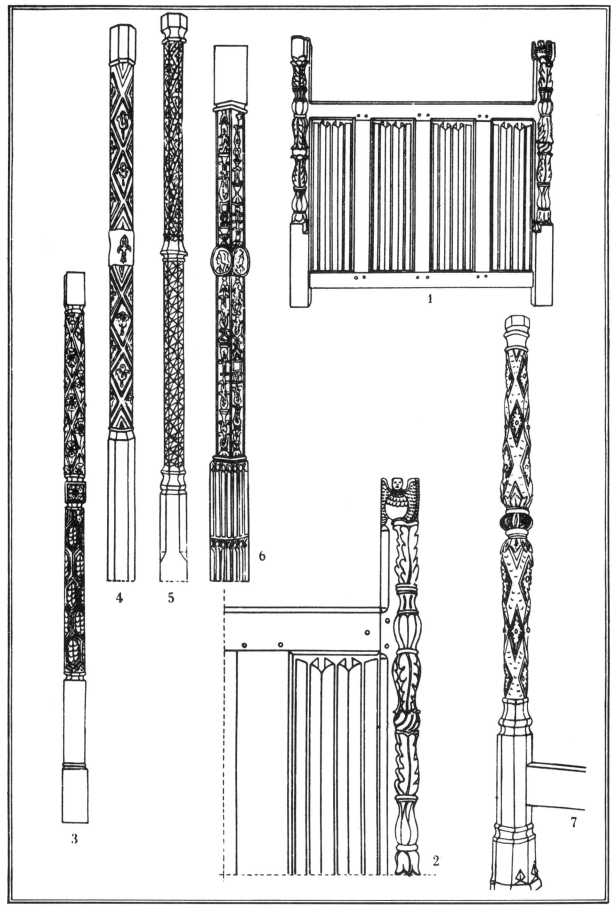

PLATE 61.   TUDOR-STUART STYLE.

1. Bed with panels imitating pleated cloth (Gothic influence), 16th century.   2. Details of post and decorative panels.

3, 4, 5, 6 and 7. Posts from other beds from the early 16th century.

Victoria and Albert Museum.

PLATE 62.

TUDOR-STUART STYLE.

1. Canopy bed with bulbous posts.   2. Detail of footboard panels.   3. Detail of posts.   4. Detail of canopy frieze.
Victoria and Albert Museum.

66

PLATE 63.   TUDOR-STUART STYLE.
1. Canopy bed, end of 16th century.   2. Headboard decoration.   3. Mouldings on pilasters at foot.   4. Decoration
on canopy mouldings.   5. Post.

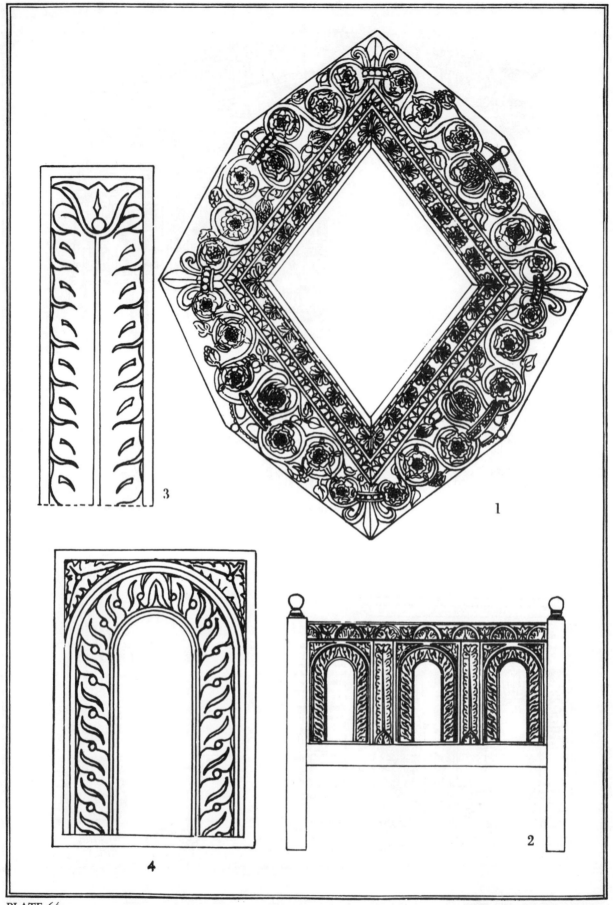

PLATE 64.   TUDOR-STUART STYLE.
1. Headboard section from 16th-century bed.   2. Bed with arches in "guilloche" design, 16th century.   3. Millet
decoration.   4. Panel decorations.

Victoria and Albert Museum.

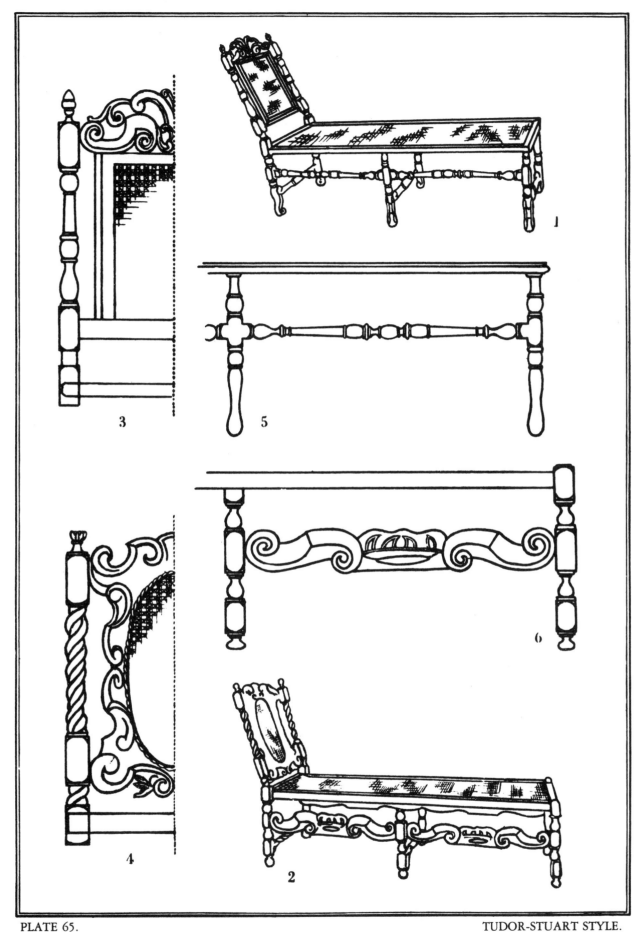

PLATE 65.   TUDOR-STUART STYLE.

1 and 2. Sofas from period of Charles II, 17th century.   3 and 4. Details of their respective headboards.   5 and 6. Details of legs and crosspieces.

Private collection.

PLATE 66.   TUDOR-STUART STYLE.

1 and 2. Cradles from the 17th century.   3 and 4. Details of their respective headboards.   5. Post at foot of second cradle.   6. Detail of upper post on second cradle.

Victoria and Albert Museum.

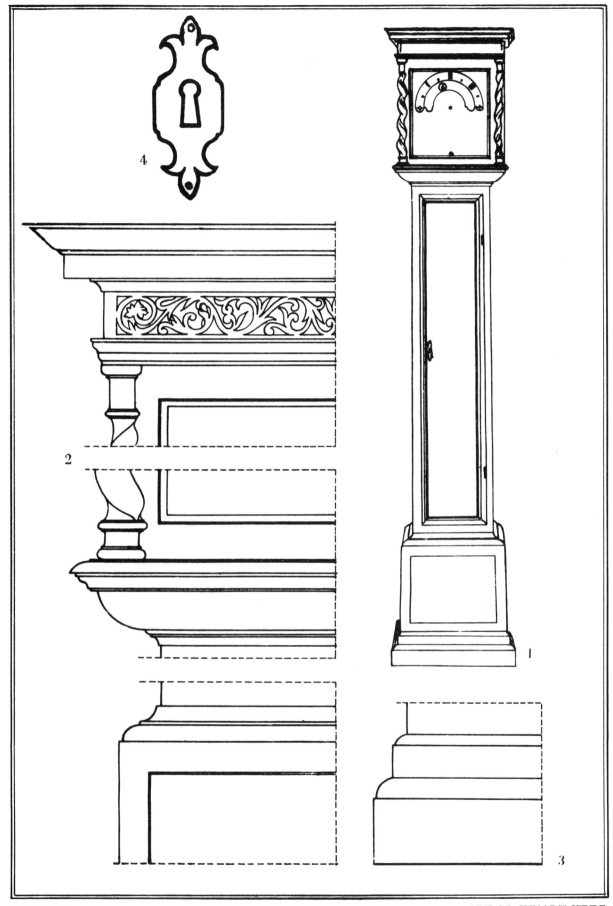

PLATE 67.
1. Clock case from period of Charles II.   2. Details of mouldings and upper frieze.   3. Detail of socle.   4. Escutcheon plate.

TUDOR-STUART STYLE.

J. S. Sykes collection.

71

PLATE 68.   TUDOR-STUART STYLE.
1. Clock case from period of Charles II.   2. Details of mouldings, finials and frieze.   3. Escutcheon plate.
Property of J. M. Botibol.

PLATE 69.

TUDOR-STUART STYLE.

1. Clock case from the period of Charles II.   2. Detail of mouldings, turned post and frieze.   3. Escutcheon plate.

Sir John Prestige Sr. collection.

PLATE 70.   TUDOR-STUART STYLE.
1. Clock case from the 17th century.   2. Twenty-four-hour clockface.   3. Detail of mouldings and crest.

S. E. Prestige collection.

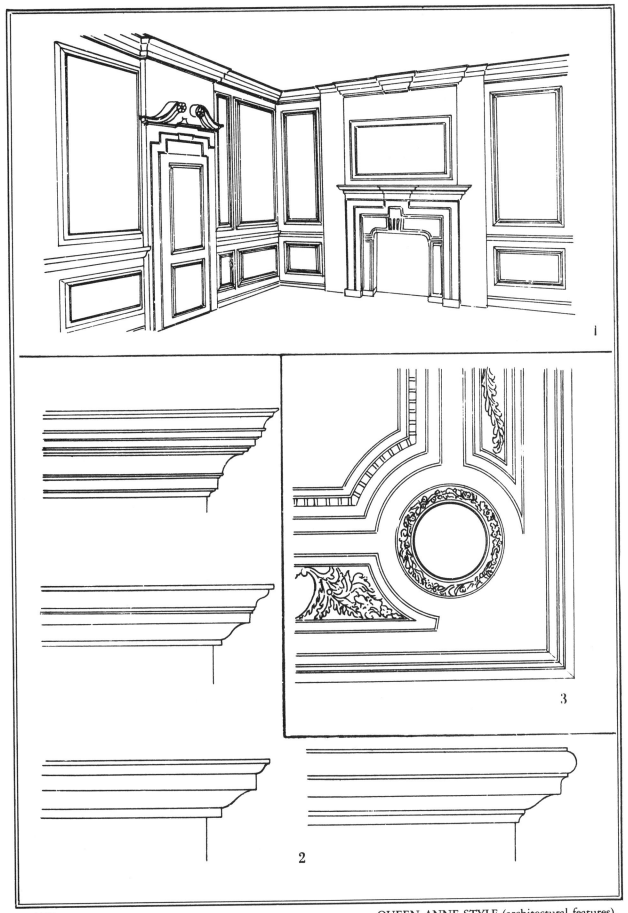

PLATE 71.   QUEEN ANNE STYLE (architectural features).
1. Room with oak wall panels, 1686–88. Clifford's Inn, London.   2. Several kinds of mouldings used during Queen
Anne's reign.   3. Ceiling section, 1689. Dining room of the Belton House, Grantham, Lincoln County.

PLATE 72.   QUEEN ANNE STYLE (architectural features).

1. Section of carved pine stairway, end of 17th century. Castlenau house, Chortlake.   2. Door. Clifford's Inn, London.   3. Georgian windows. The first is from Swan House, Chichester; the second from Raynham Hall, Norfolk.   4. Fireplace by Grinling Gibbon, Hampton Court.

PLATE 73.

QUEEN ANNE STYLE (William and Mary period).

1. Chair from William and Mary period. 2. Back detail. 3. Front leg. 4. William and Mary chair. 5. Back detail. 6. Turned leg.

Metropolitan Museum of Art and Kunstgewerbe Museum, Budapest.

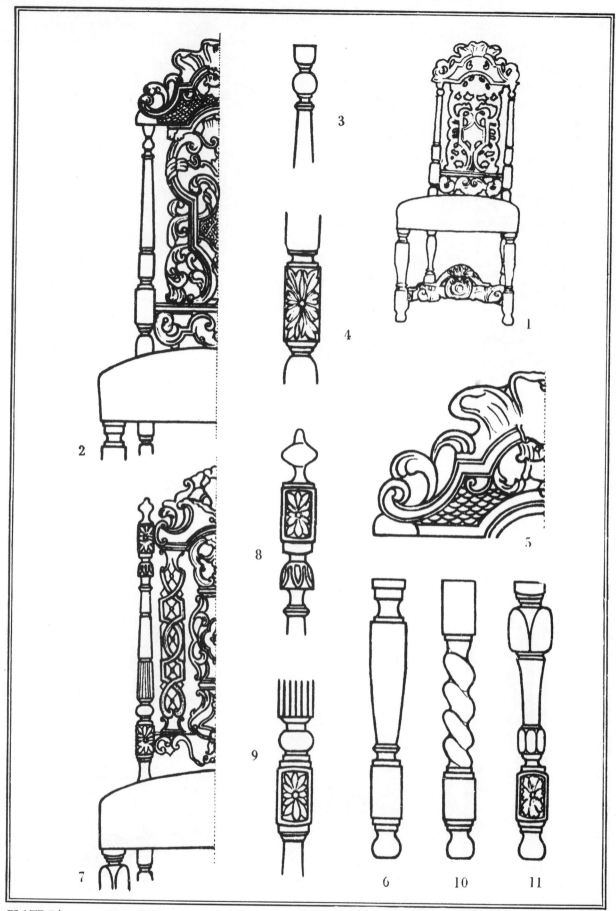

PLATE 74.   QUEEN ANNE STYLE (William and Mary period).
1. Chair from William and Mary period.   2. Back detail.   3 and 4. Detail of turned section and back-post decoration.   5. Decoration on crest.   6. Turned leg.   7. Back detail of another William and Mary chair.   8 and 9. Detail of turned section and decorations on posts at sides of back.   10 and 11. Turned legs in this style.

From the old Richmond Palace.

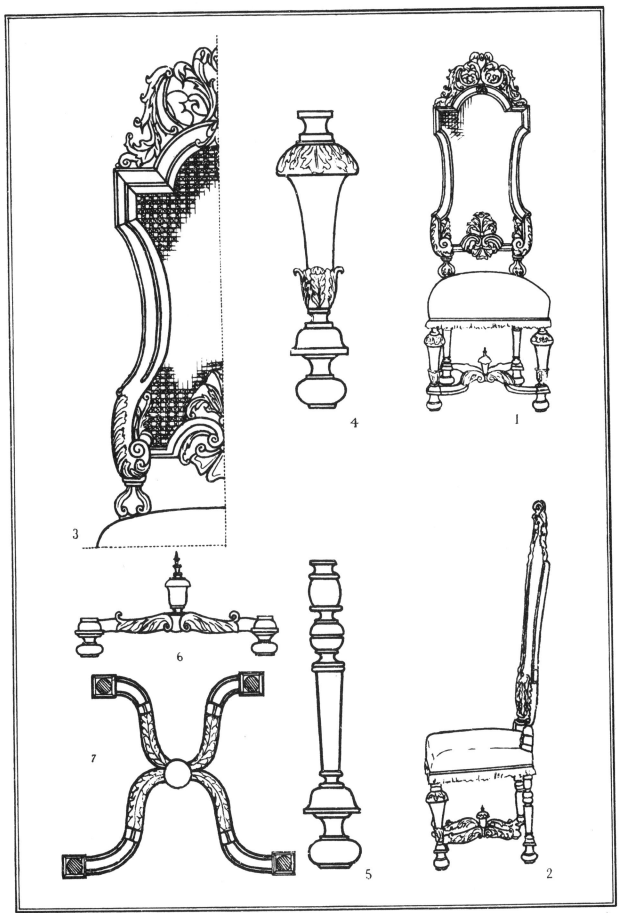

PLATE 75.

QUEEN ANNE STYLE (William and Mary period).

1 and 2. William and Mary chair with cane back.   3. Back detail.   4. Front leg.   5. Back leg.   6 and 7. Decoration on x-shaped crosspieces.

Metropolitan Museum of Art.

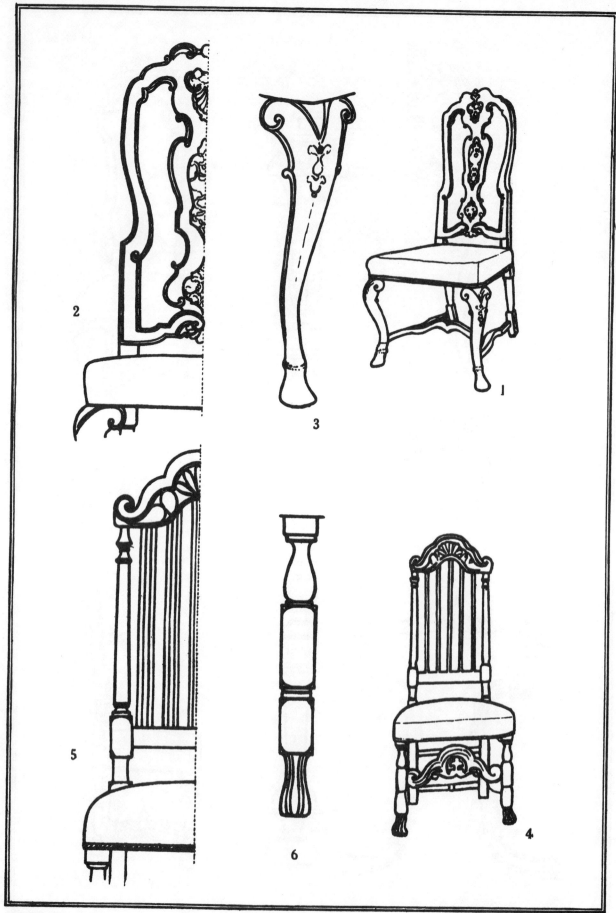

PLATE 76.   QUEEN ANNE STYLE (William and Mary period).
1. William and Mary chair. 2. Detail of back. 3. Front leg. 4. William and Mary chair. 5. Back detail. 6. Front leg.

PLATE 77.   QUEEN ANNE STYLE (William and Mary period).

1. William and Mary sofa. 2. Detail of front leg. 3. William and Mary stool. 4. Bottom of the cross-pieces. 5. Detail of leg.

Private collection.

PLATE 78.   QUEEN ANNE STYLE (William and Mary period).

1 and 2. William and Mary tables with turned legs.   3 and 4. Turned legs of first and second tables, respectively.   5. Drawer pull of first table.   6 and 7. Marquetry decorations on drawer front of second table.   8. Drawer pull of second table.

Private collection.

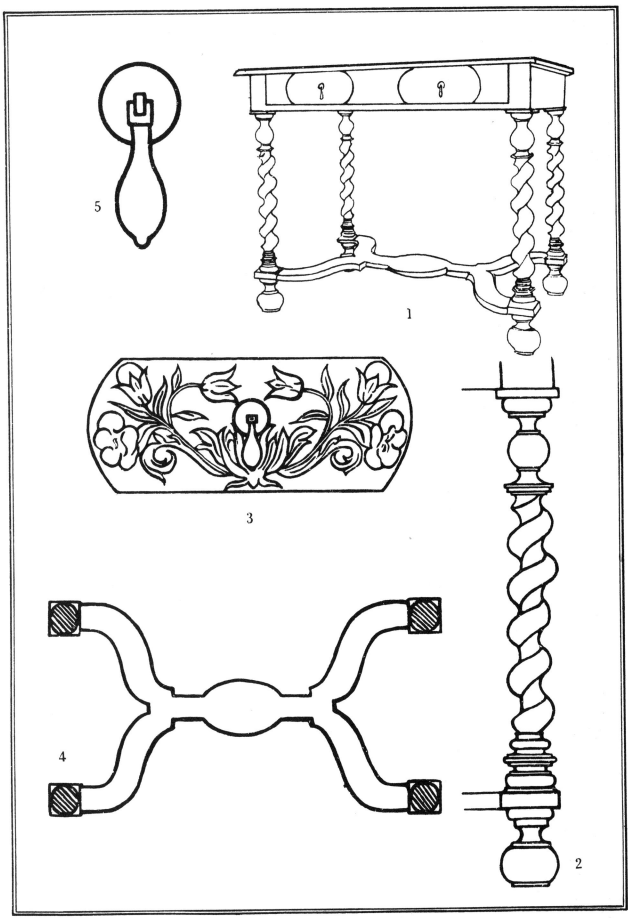

PLATE 79.

1. William and Mary table with marquetry decorations.   2. Turned leg.   3. Drawer front panel decorated with marquetry.   4. Base of crosspiece.   5. Drawer pull.

Victoria and Albert Museum.

PLATE 80.   QUEEN ANNE STYLE (William and Mary period).
1. William and Mary desk, beginning of 18th century.   2. Decoration on drawer panel.   3. Detail of upright and foot.   4. Drawer pull.

Private collection.

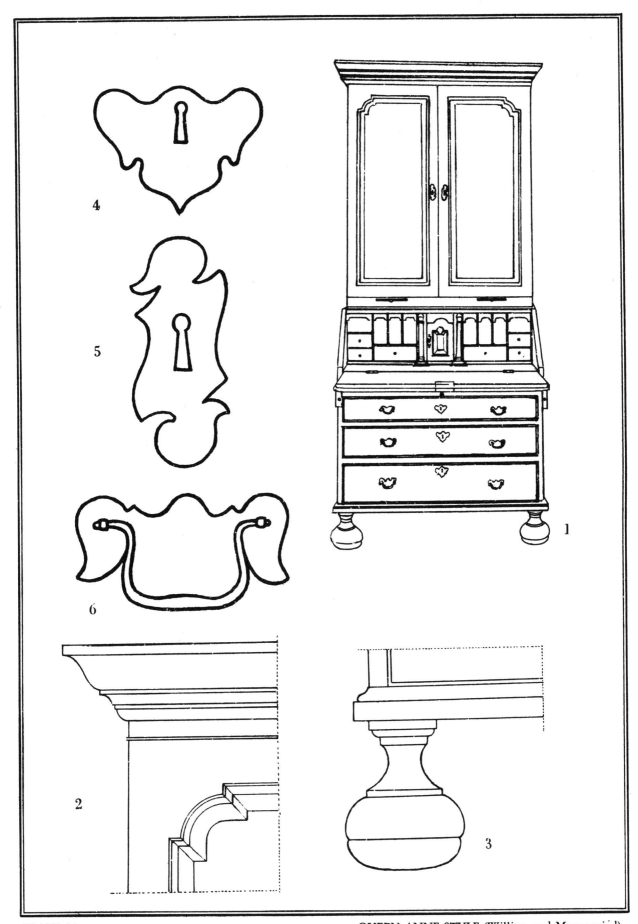

PLATE 81.   QUEEN ANNE STYLE (William and Mary period).
1. William and Mary desk, beginning of 18th century.   2. Detail of moulding and upper section.   3. Socle and
foot.   4 and 5. Escutcheon plates.   6. Drawer pull.

Private collection.

PLATE 82.

1. Richly adorned commode from period of William and Mary.
drawer panels.   4. Drawer pull.   5. Escutcheon plate.

QUEEN ANNE STYLE (William and Mary period).
2. Upper moulding, socle and foot.   3. Decorative

Private collection.

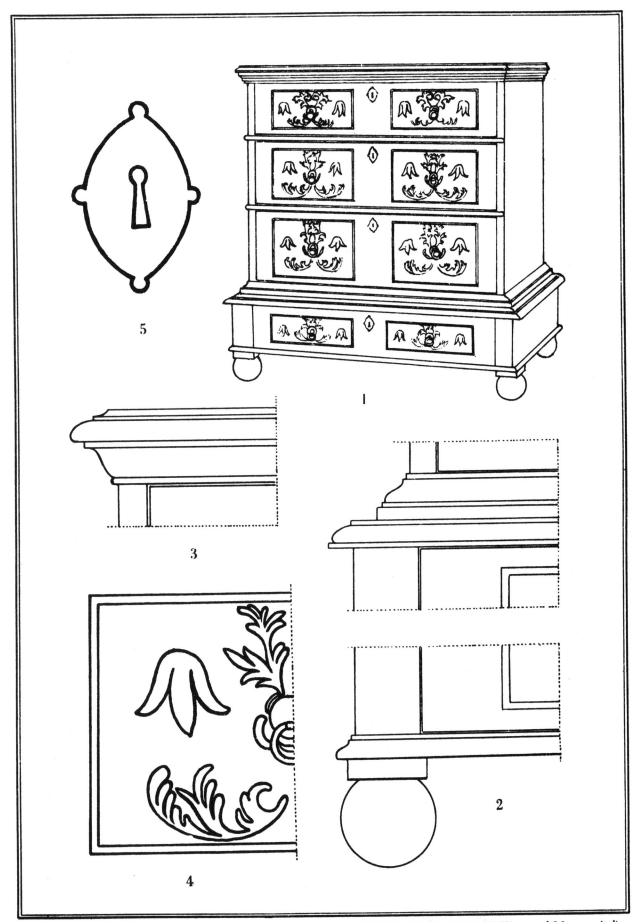

PLATE 83.   QUEEN ANNE STYLE (William and Mary period).

1. William and Mary commode with marquetry decoration.   2. Moulding of socle and foot.   3. Upper cornice.   4. Drawer panels with marquetry decoration.   5. Escutcheon plate.

Private collection.

PLATE 84.
QUEEN ANNE STYLE (William and Mary period).
1. William and Mary commode.   2. Moulding on cornice, socles and foot.   3. Escutcheon plate.   4. Drawer pull.
Victoria and Albert Museum.

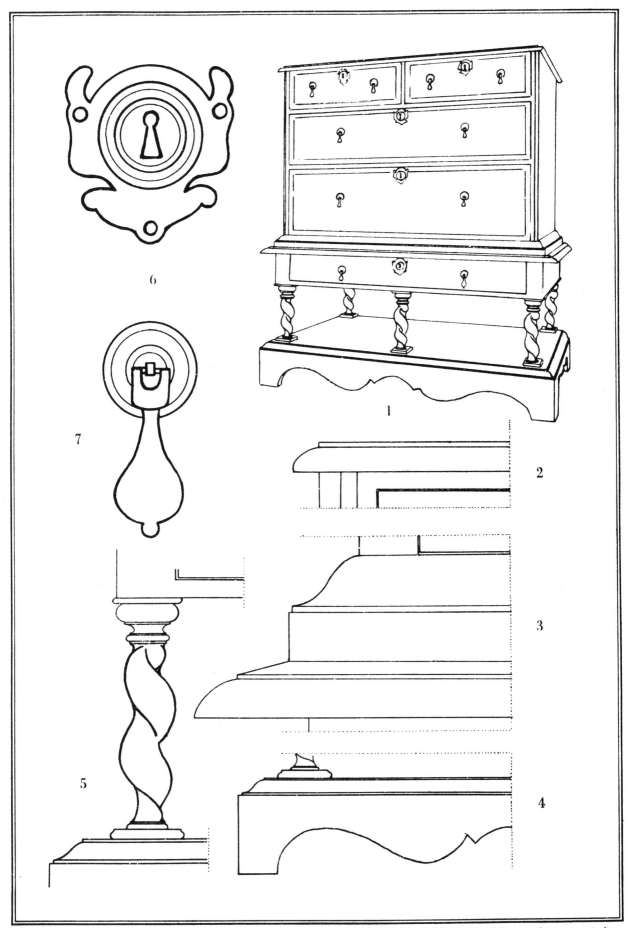

PLATE 85.   QUEEN ANNE STYLE (William and Mary period).
1. Commode on turned legs from the period of William and Mary.   2. Cornice.   3. Socle.   4. Foot.   5. Turned
leg.   6. Escutcheon plate.   7. Drawer pull.

Victoria and Albert Museum.

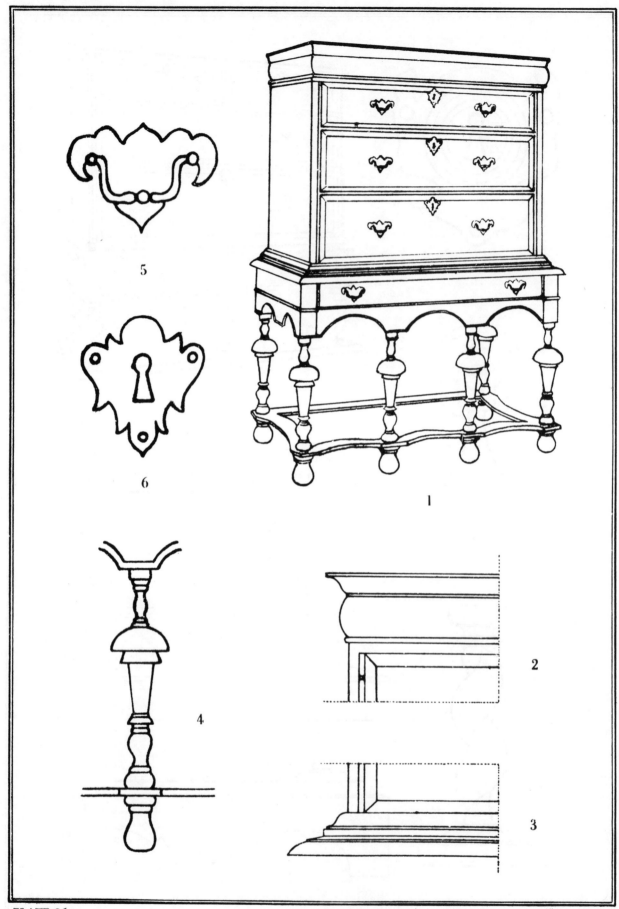

PLATE 86.   QUEEN ANNE STYLE (William and Mary period).
1. Commode on stand from period of William and Mary.   2. Cornice mouldings.   3. Moulding on socle.
4. Leg.   5. Drawer pull.   6. Escutcheon plate.

Private collection.

PLATE 87. QUEEN ANNE STYLE (William and Mary period).

1. William and Mary commode on stand. 2. Cornice. 3. Socle of upper section. 4. Leg. 5. Escutcheon plate. 6. Drawer pull.

Private collection.

PLATE 88.   QUEEN ANNE STYLE (William and Mary period).
1. William and Mary wardrobe, end of 17th century. 2. Cornice. 3. Socle of upper section. 4. Foot.
5. Escutcheon plate.   6. Drawer pull.

Private collection.

PLATE 89.   QUEEN ANNE STYLE (William and Mary period).
1. William and Mary display cabinet.   2. Cornice.   3. Top of base.   4. Leg.   5. Escutcheon plate.

Property of M. M. Story et Triggs, Ltd., London.

93

PLATE 90.   QUEEN ANNE STYLE (William and Mary period).
1. Display cabinet from end of 17th century. 2. Details of upper section. 3. Details of lower section. 4. Escutcheon plate.

PLATE 91.   QUEEN ANNE STYLE (William and Mary period).
1. Clock from 17th century.   2 and 3. Details.   4. Handle.   5. Hands.

Victoria and Albert Museum.

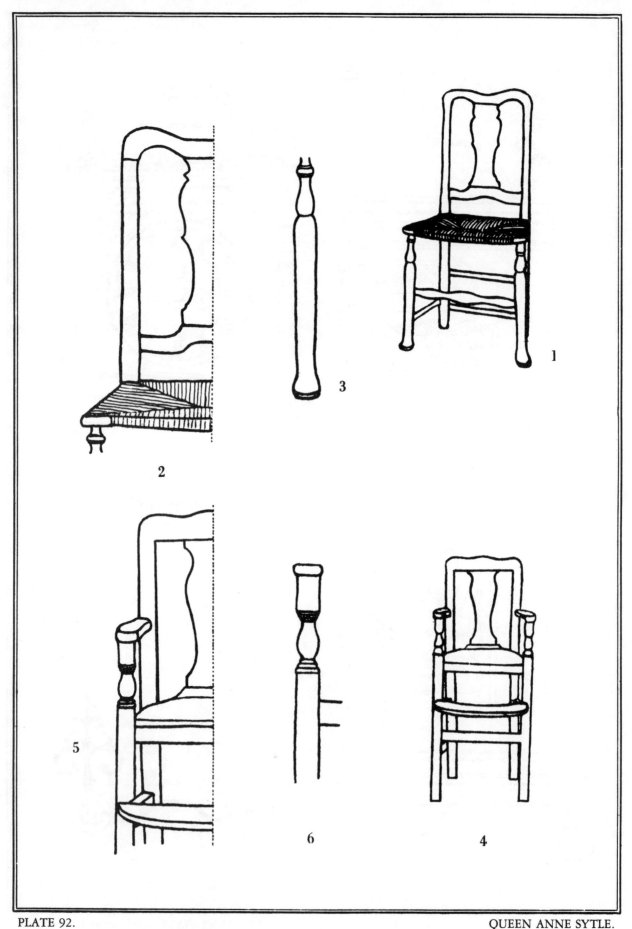

PLATE 92.   QUEEN ANNE SYTLE.
1. Country chair from Queen Anne period.   2. Back detail.   3. Turned front leg.   4. Country child's chair of the
same period.   5. Detail.   6. Turned post.

Private collection.

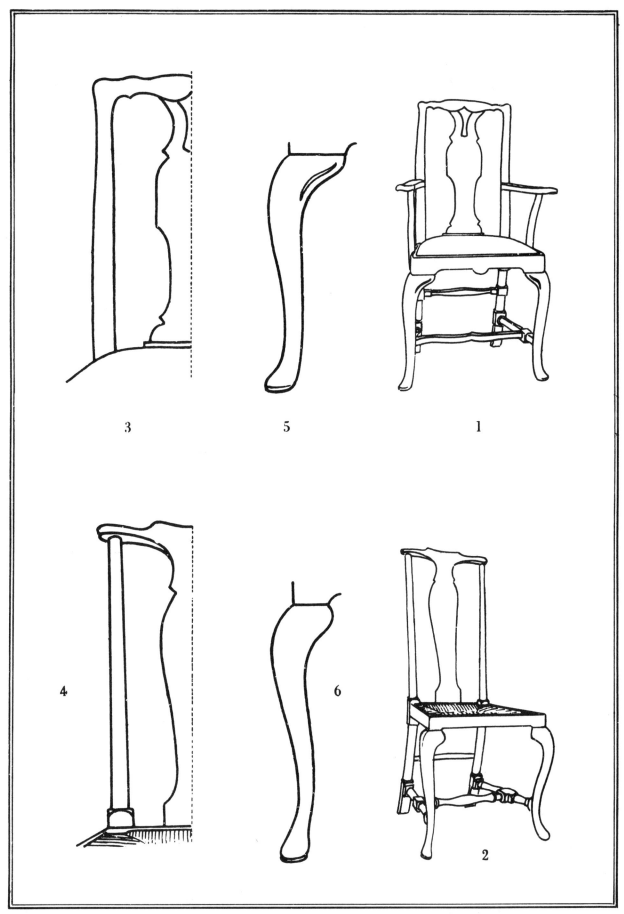

PLATE 93.   QUEEN ANNE STYLE.

1 and 2. Armchair and chair with connected legs from the Queen Anne period.   3 and 4. Details of backs.   5 and
6. Legs of armchair and chair, respectively.

Private collection.

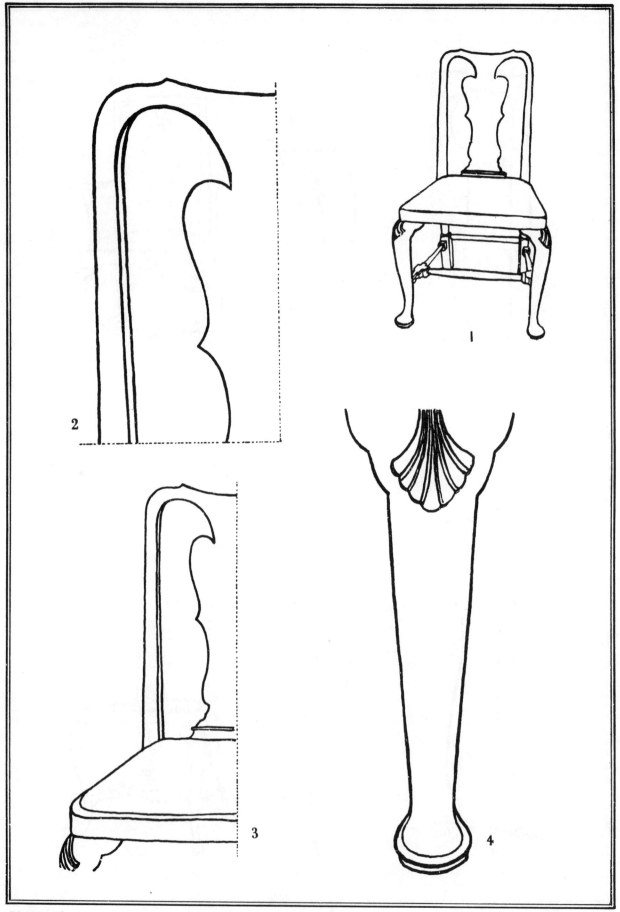

PLATE 94.
1. Simple but reinforced Queen Anne chair.   2 and 3. Details.   4. Front leg.

QUEEN ANNE STYLE.

Private collection.

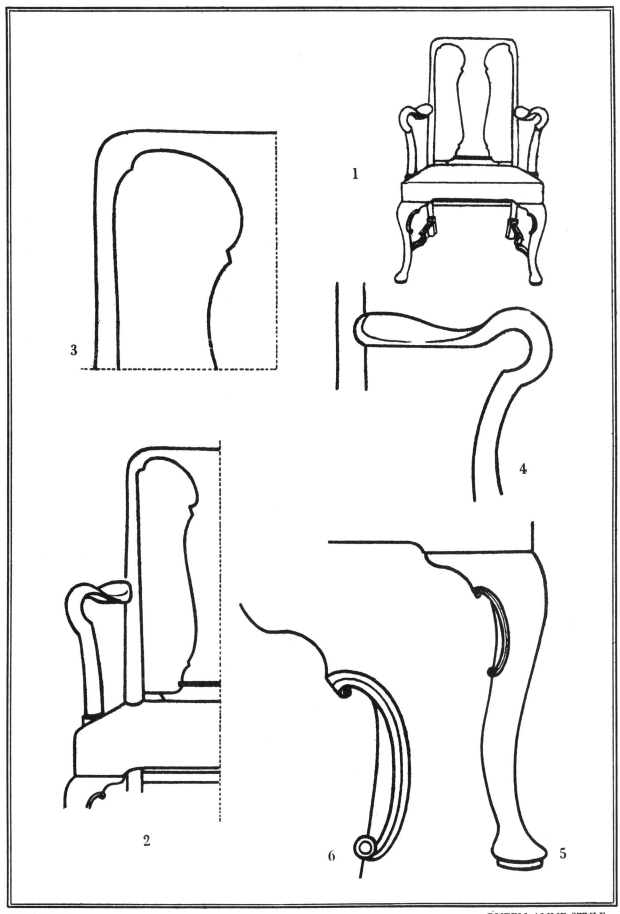

PLATE 95.   QUEEN ANNE STYLE.
1. Queen Anne armchair.   2. Detail.   3. Upper corner of back.   4. Detail of arm.   5. Front leg.   6. Leg decoration.

Victoria and Albert Museum.

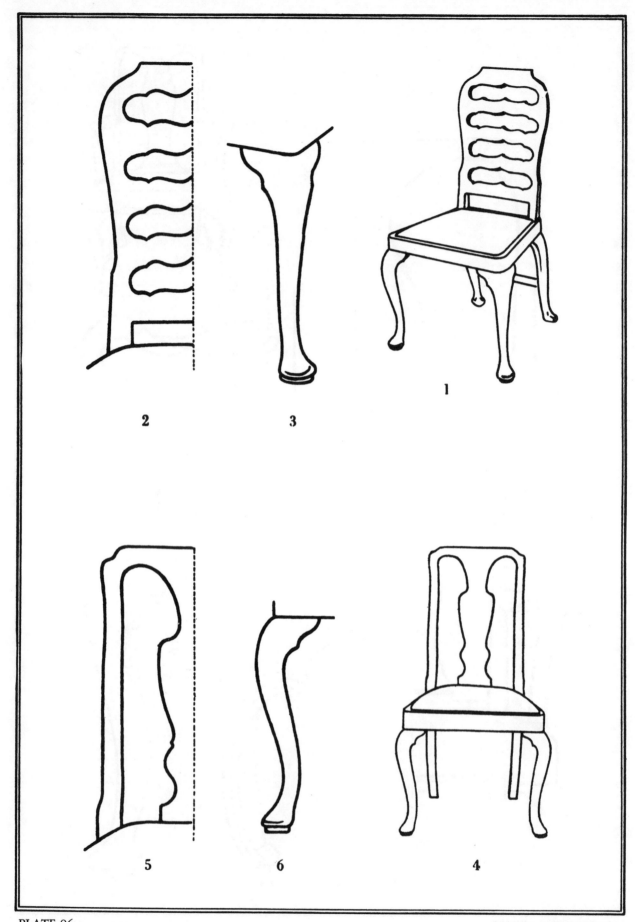

PLATE 96.   QUEEN ANNE STYLE.
1. Delicate chair from end of Queen Anne period.   2. Detail of back.   3. Front leg.   4. Delicate chair from same
period.   5. Detail of back.   6. Front leg.

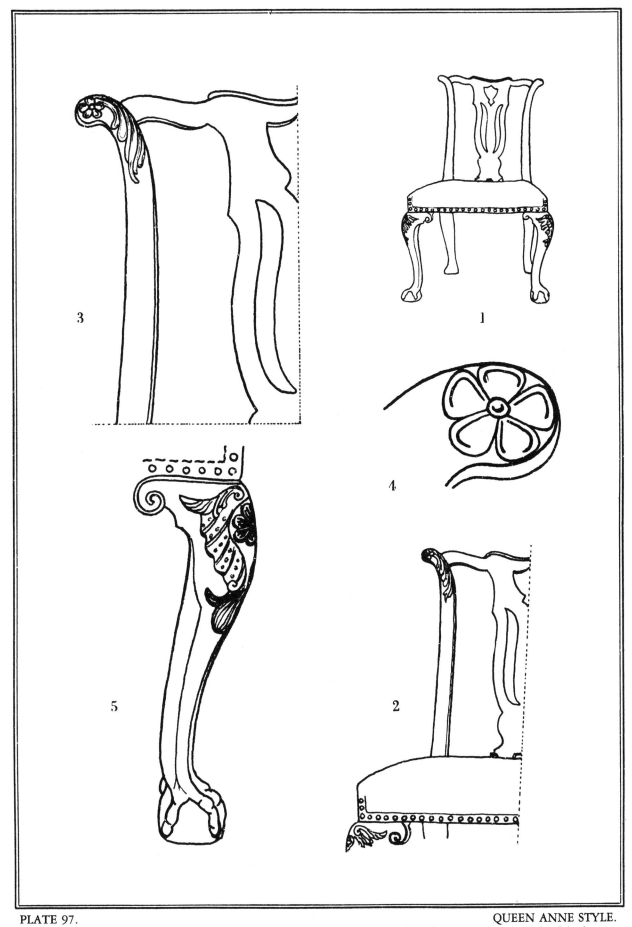

PLATE 97. QUEEN ANNE STYLE.

1. Ornate chair from end of Queen Anne period. 2. Detail. 3. Back. 4. Decoration on end of back support. 5. Decoration on front leg.

Victoria and Albert Museum.

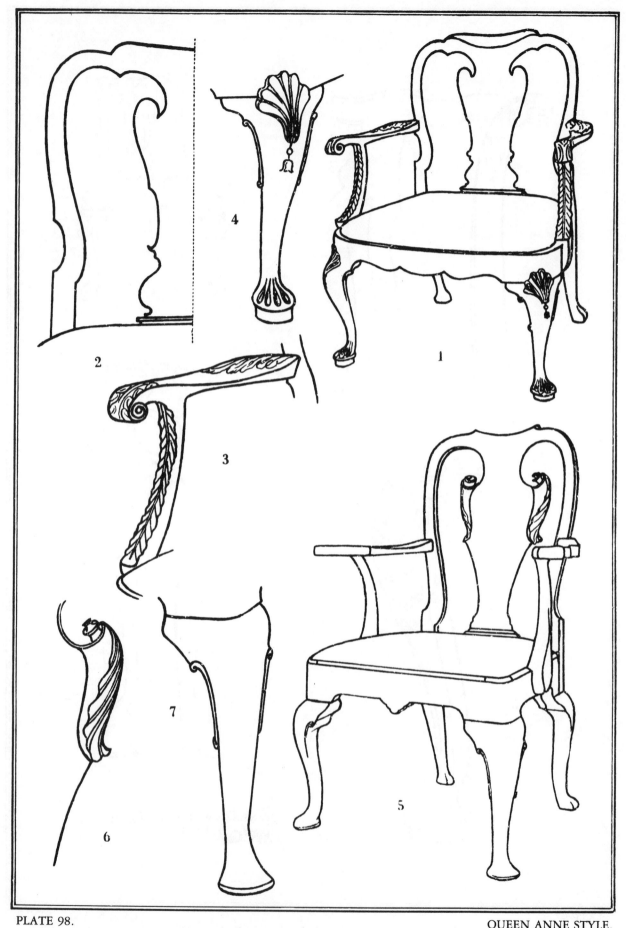

PLATE 98.   QUEEN ANNE STYLE.
1. Queen Anne armchair.   2, 3 and 4. Decorations: back, arms and front leg.   5. Armchair from same period.
6 and 7. Decorations: carving on back and front leg.

Metropolitan Museum of Art and private collection.

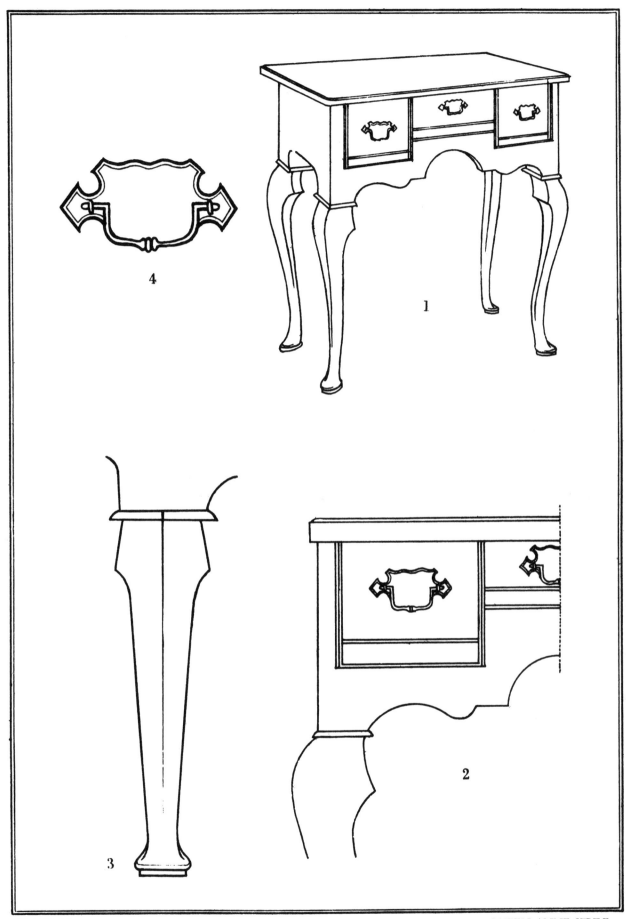

PLATE 99.

QUEEN ANNE STYLE.

1. Cabriole table.   2. Detail.   3. Leg.   4. Drawer pull.

Private collection.

103

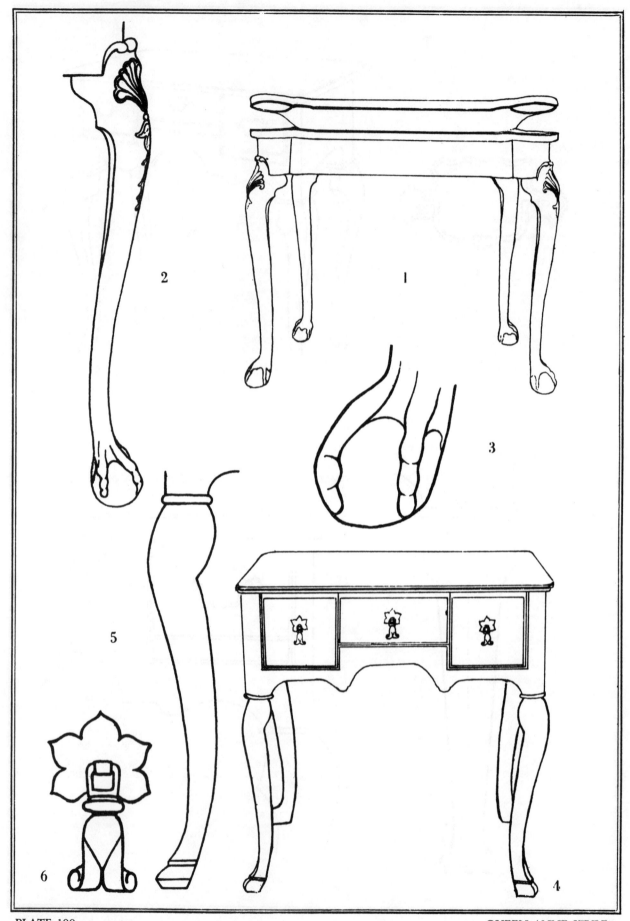

PLATE 100.   QUEEN ANNE STYLE.
1. Queen Anne table.   2. Leg.   3. Base of leg.   4. Table from same period.   5. Leg.   6. Drawer pull.
Victoria and Albert Museum and private collection.

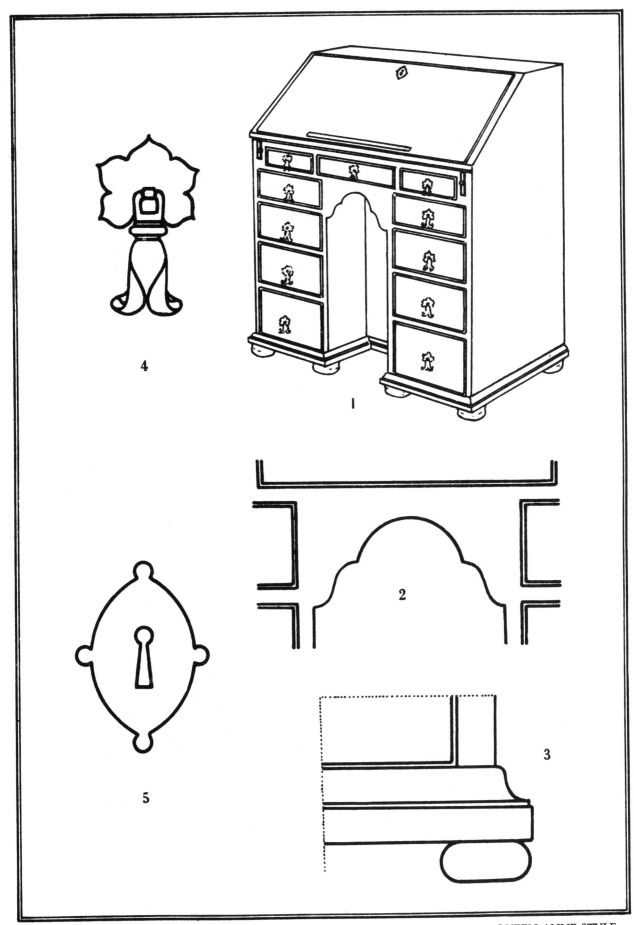

PLATE 101.   QUEEN ANNE STYLE.

1. Queen Anne desk.   2. Central detail.   3. Socle and foot.   4. Drawer pull.   5. Escutcheon plate.

Private collection.

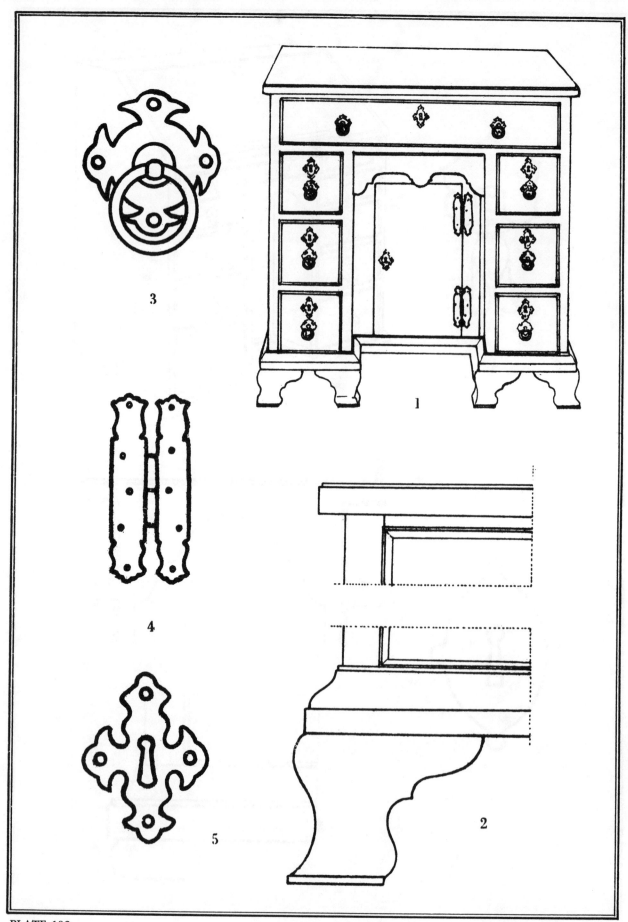

PLATE 102.

QUEEN ANNE STYLE.

1. Queen Anne desk.   2. Mouldings, socle and leg.   3. Drawer pull.   4. Hinge.   5. Escutcheon plate.

Private collection.

PLATE 103.

QUEEN ANNE STYLE.

1. Opened chest-on-chest from Queen Anne period. 2. Same chest-on-chest, closed. 3. Upper cornice. 4. Socle of upper chest. 5. Socle and foot of lower chest. 6. Escutcheon plate and drawer pull.

Private collection.

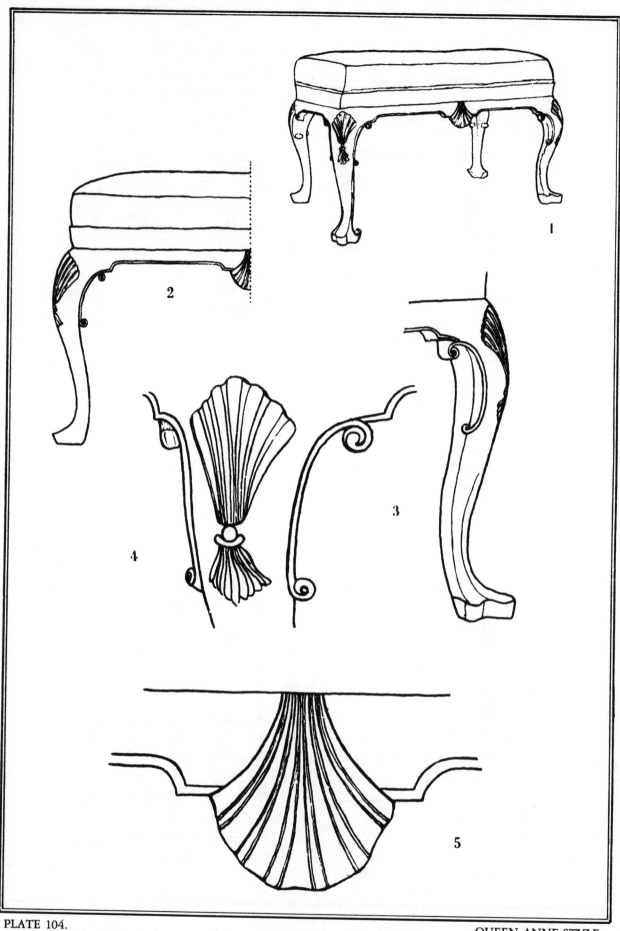

PLATE 104.

1. Queen Anne stool.   2. Detail.   3. Leg.   4. Decoration on angle of leg.   5. Central decoration on crosspiece.

QUEEN ANNE STYLE.

Victoria and Albert Museum.

PLATE 105.   QUEEN ANNE STYLE.

1. Elegant clock case from beginning of 18th century. 2. Details of crest and moulding. 3. Detail of socle. 4. Hardware. 5. Hands.

S. E. Prestige collection.

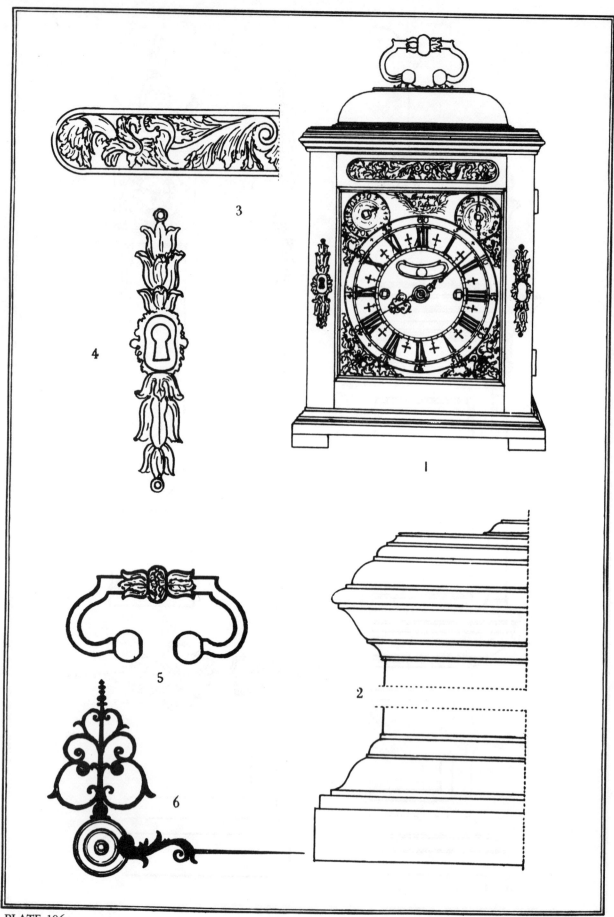

PLATE 106.

QUEEN ANNE STYLE.

1. Queen Anne desk clock.   2. Detail of moulding.   3. Frieze.   4. Escutcheon plate.   5. Handle.   6. Hands.

S. E. Prestige collection.

PLATE 107.   QUEEN ANNE STYLE.
1. Queen Anne clock case (by Thomas Tompion).   2. Detail of crest.   3. Decoration on lower part and foot.   4. Hands.
                                                               Private collection.

PLATE 108.
1. Clock case from early 18th century. 2. Details.

QUEEN ANNE STYLE.

Victoria and Albert Museum.

PLATE 109.

1. Clock case from early 18th century.   2. Detail of moulding.

QUEEN ANNE STYLE.

Victoria and Albert Museum.

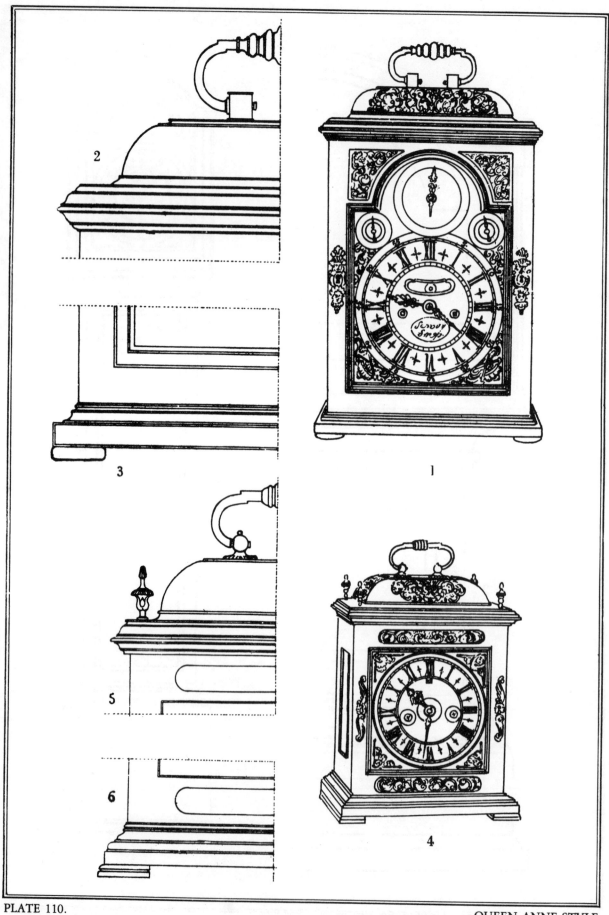

PLATE 110.
1. Desk clock from early 18th century.   2 and 3. Details.   4. Desk clock from end of 17th century.   5 and 6. Details.

QUEEN ANNE STYLE.

S. E. Prestige and J. S. Sykes collections.

PLATE 111.   QUEEN ANNE STYLE.

1. Wall clock by Anthony Marsh (between 1720 and 1730).   2. Detail of cornice and upper moulding.   3. Detail of bottom of clock.   4. Face.

Private collection.

PLATE 112.   QUEEN ANNE STYLE.
1. Clock case decorated with marquetry, late 17th century.   2. Details of moulding.   3. Decoration on central
panel.   4. Decoration on socle panel.

Victoria and Albert Museum.

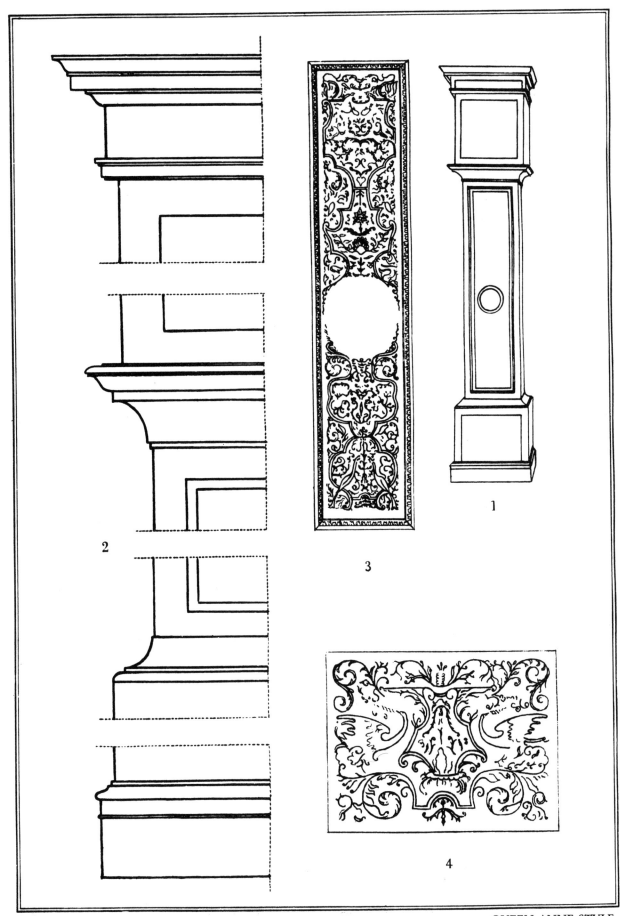

PLATE 113.   QUEEN ANNE STYLE.

1. Clock decorated with marquetry, early 18th century.   2. Details of moulding.   3. Central panel.   4. Panel on socle.

Victoria and Albert Museum.

PLATE 114.
QUEEN ANNE STYLE.
1. Clock case decorated with marquetry, early 18th century. 2. Details of crest and moulding. 3. Central panel. 4. Lower panel.

Victoria and Albert Museum.

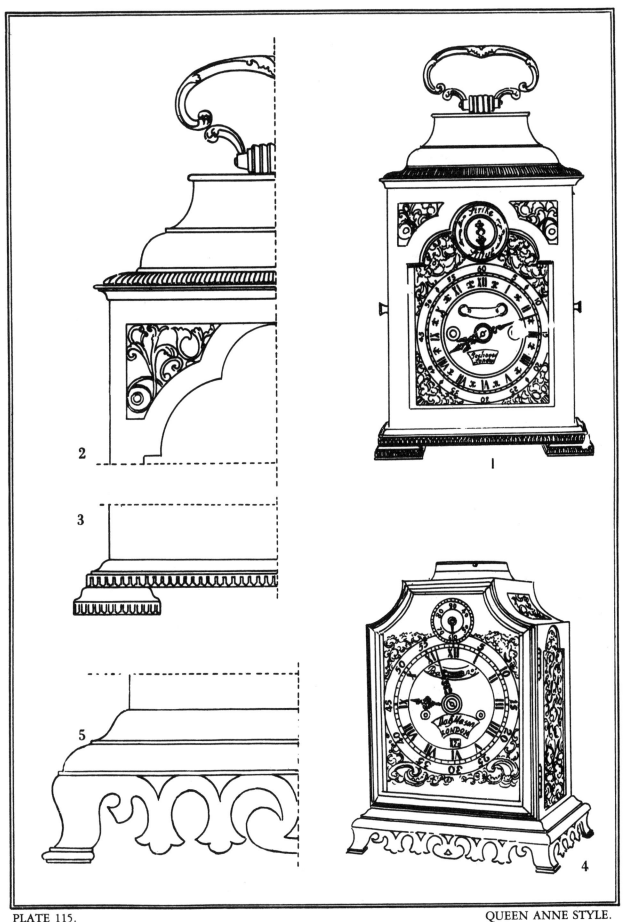

PLATE 115.   QUEEN ANNE STYLE.

1. Desk clock from mid-18th century.   2 and 3. Details.   4. Desk clock from mid-18th century.   5. Decoration on foot.

S. E. Prestige and Malcolm Webster collections.

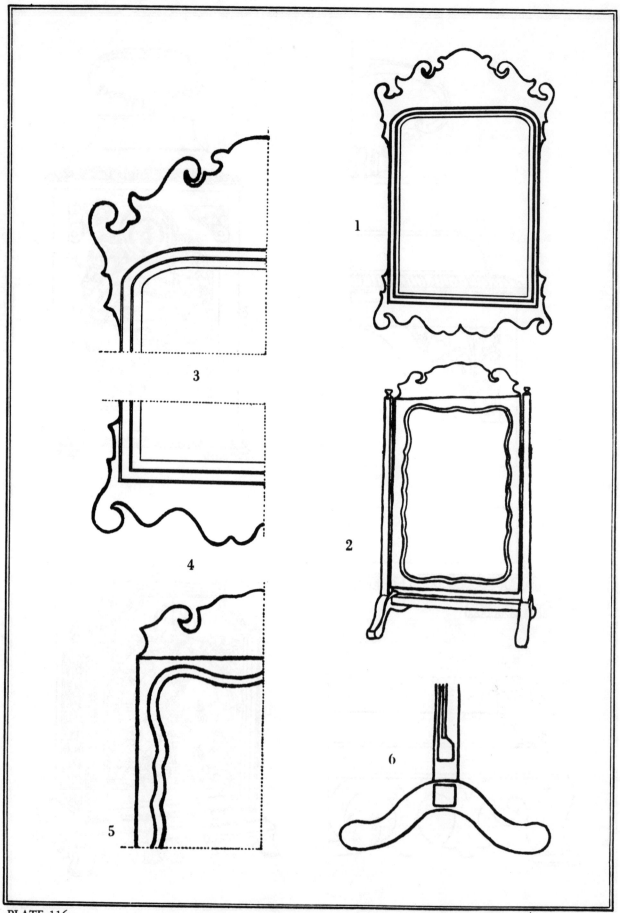

PLATE 116.   QUEEN ANNE STYLE.
1 and 2. Simple Queen Anne mirrors.   3, 4 and 5. Decorations on same.   6. Foot of second mirror.

Private collection.

PLATE 117.   QUEEN ANNE STYLE.

1. Queen Anne mirror.   2. Detail of moulding.   3. Profile of moulding.   4. Queen Anne mirror.   5. Detail of
moulding and upper frame.   6. Detail of lower frame.   7. Profile of moulding.

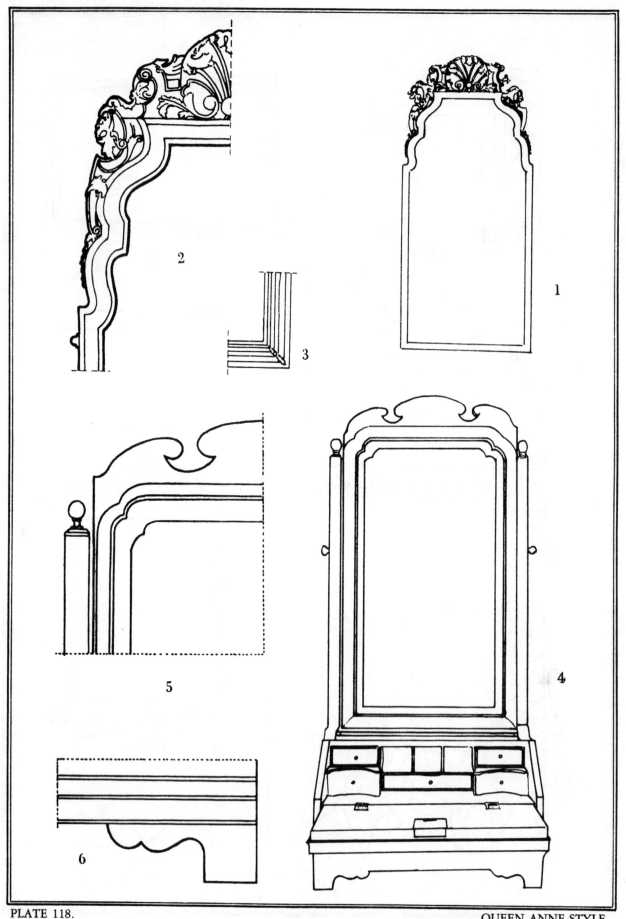

PLATE 118.

1. Queen Anne mirror. 2. Frame decoration. 3. Detail of moulding. 4. Dressing-table mirror. 5. Detail of frame and support. 6. Detail of foot.

Property of H. M. Lee & Sons and Victoria and Albert Museum

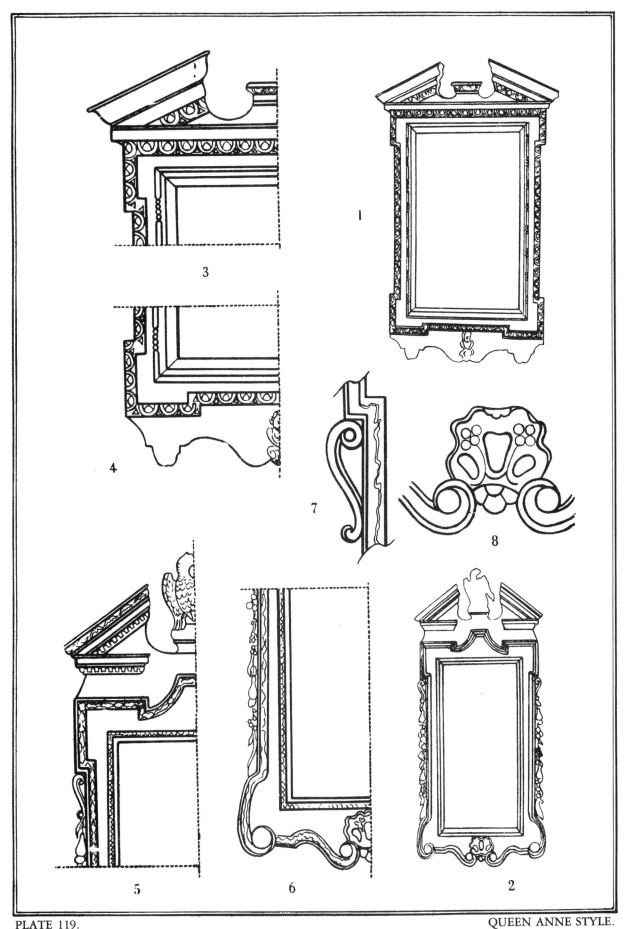

PLATE 119.   QUEEN ANNE STYLE.

1 and 2. Mirrors with architectonic elements.   3 and 4. Details of mouldings and top and bottom of frame of first mirror.   5 and 6. Details of top and bottom of second frame.   7 and 8. Decorations on second frame.

Private collection.

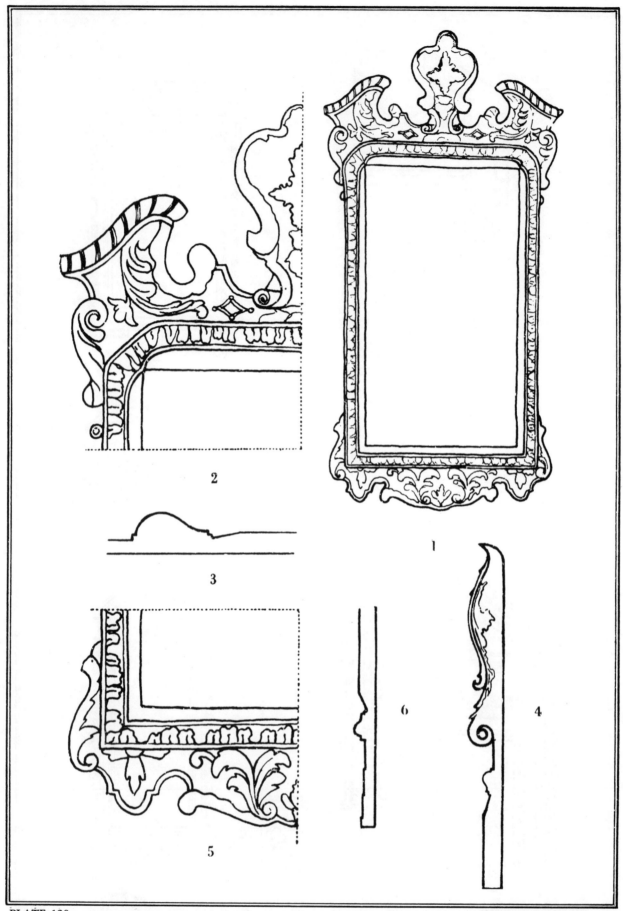

PLATE 120.   QUEEN ANNE STYLE.

1. Ornate Queen Anne mirror.   2. Detail of top of frame.   3. Profile of side moulding.   4. Profile of central part of frame and upper moulding.   5. Detail of bottom of frame.   6. Profile of moulding and bottom of frame.

Victoria and Albert Museum.

124

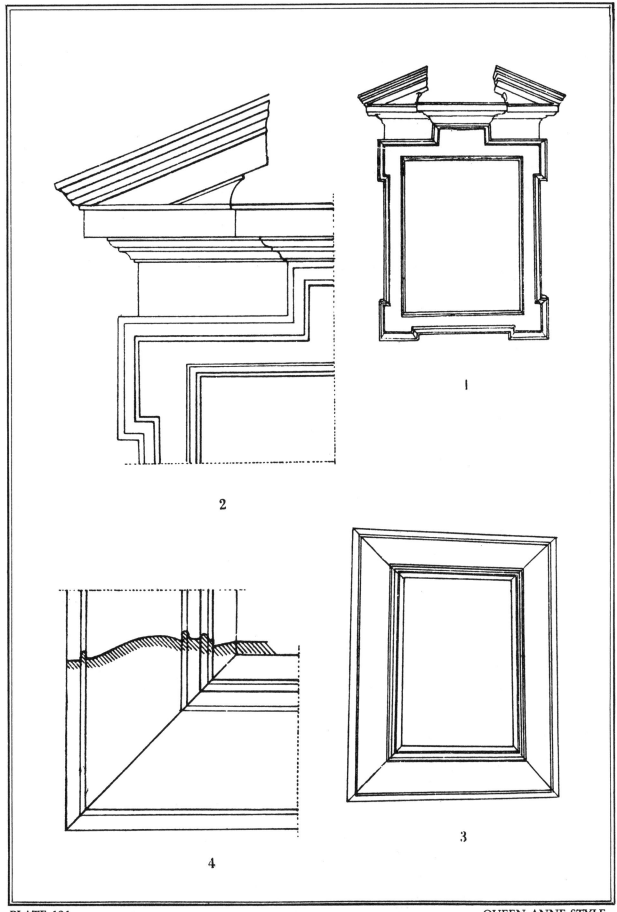

PLATE 121.   QUEEN ANNE STYLE.

1. Mirror from early 18th century.   2. Details of mouldings and upper frame.   3. Mirror from early 18th century.   4. Detail of corner showing profile of moulding.

Private collection.

PLATE 122.

1. Ornately decorated Queen Anne mirror.   2. Detail of upper frame.   3. Detail of lower frame.

QUEEN ANNE STYLE.

Collection of Lord Plender G.B.E.

126

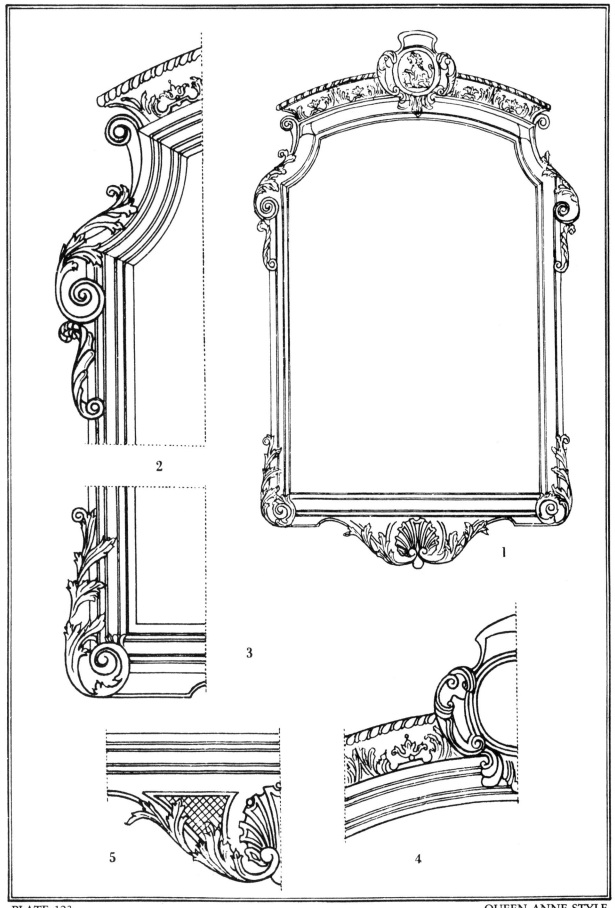

PLATE 123.   QUEEN ANNE STYLE.
1. Queen Anne mirror.   2 and 3. Details of frame side.   4. Detail of upper frame.   5. Detail of lower frame.

Private collection.

PLATE 124.

1 and 2. Queen Anne mirrors.   3. Detail of top of frame of first mirror.   4 and 5. Detail of top and bottom of second frame.

QUEEN ANNE STYLE.

J. S. Sykes collection.

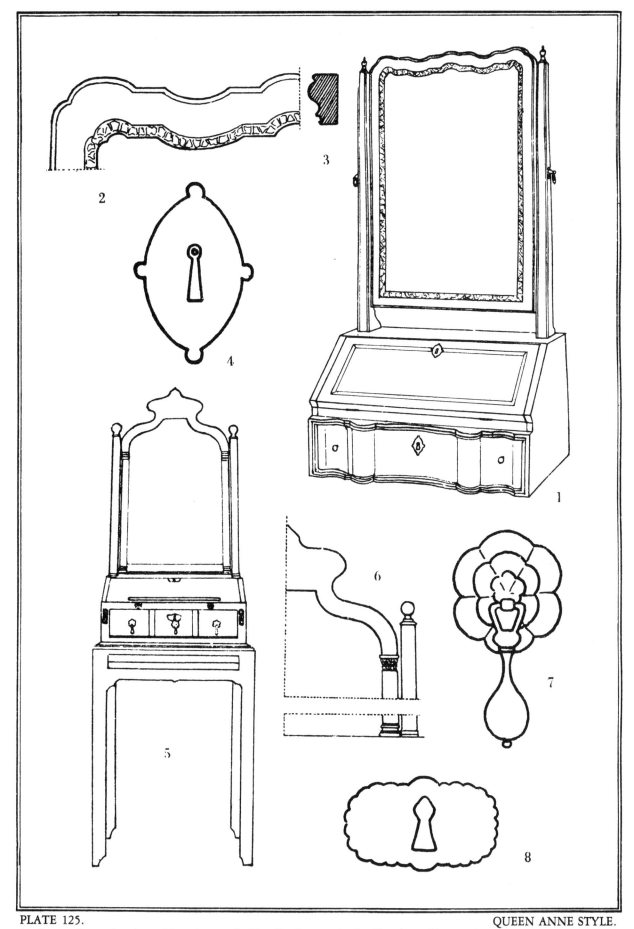

PLATE 125.   QUEEN ANNE STYLE.

1. Queen Anne dressing-table mirror.   2. Detail of top.   3. Profile of moulding.   4. Escutcheon plate. Private collection.   5. Queen Anne dressing-table mirror.   6. Details of frame top, uprights and supports.   7. Drawer pull. 8. Escutcheon plate.

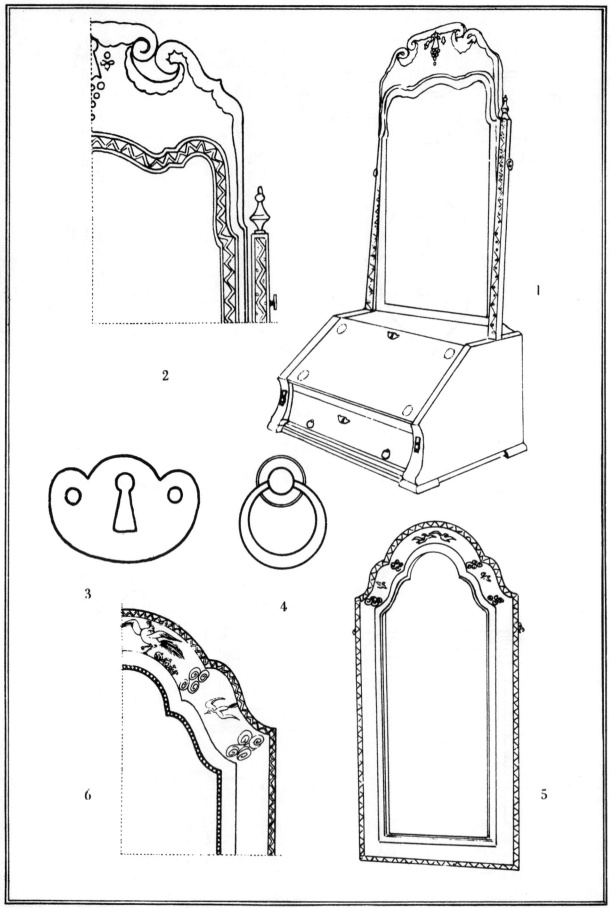

PLATE 126.   QUEEN ANNE STYLE.
1. Dressing-table mirror.   2. Detail of top of frame and support.   3. Escutcheon plate.   4. Drawer pull.   5. Mirror
showing Dutch influence.   6. Detail of frame.

Victoria and Albert Museum.

PLATE 127.   QUEEN ANNE STYLE.
1. Cabinet from early 18th century.   2. Detail of corner of upper section.   3. Leg.   4. Escutcheon plate.
Geoffrey Hart collection.

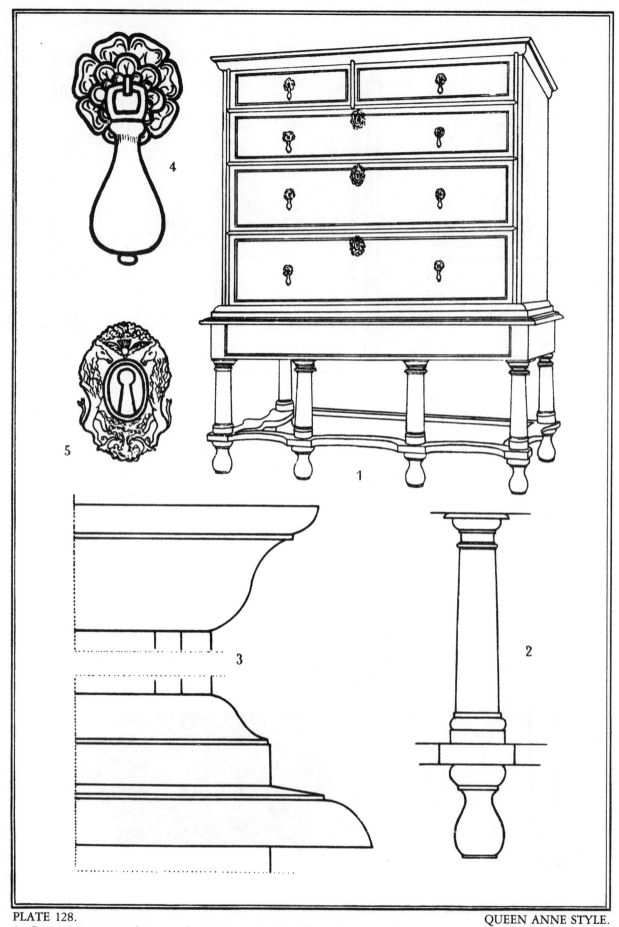

PLATE 128.   QUEEN ANNE STYLE.

1. Queen Anne commode on stand.   2. Leg.   3. Mouldings of cornice and socle.   4. Drawer pull.   5. Escutcheon plate.

Victoria and Albert Museum.

PLATE 129.   QUEEN ANNE STYLE.

1. Type of commode called a Tallboy, from the middle of the Queen Anne period.   2. Detail of mouldings and beveled upright.   3. Leg.   4. Escutcheon plate.   5. Drawer pull.

Private collection.

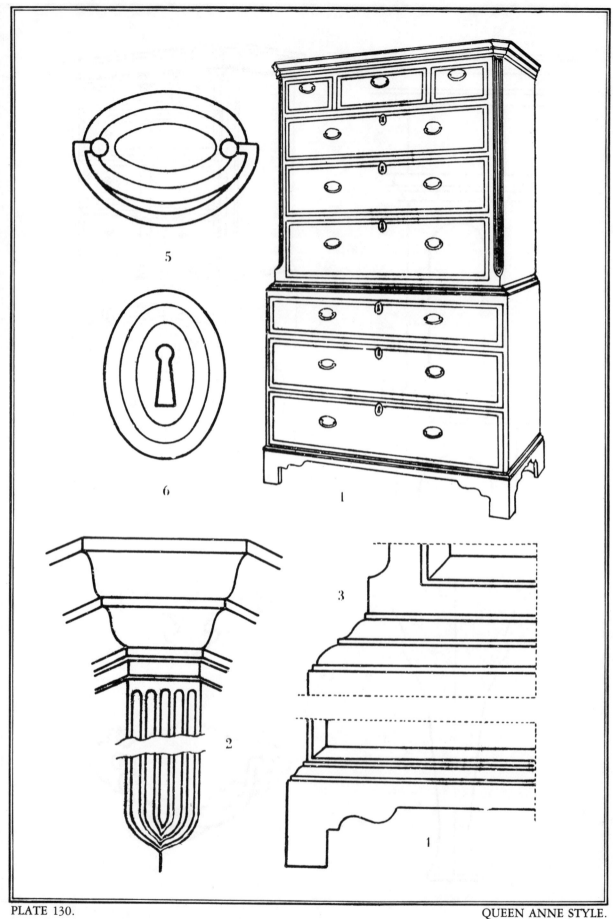

PLATE 130.   QUEEN ANNE STYLE.

1. Tallboy from the end of the Queen Anne period.   2. Cornice and carving on upright.   3. Socle of upper section.   4. Foot.   5. Drawer pull.   6. Escutcheon plate.

Private collection.

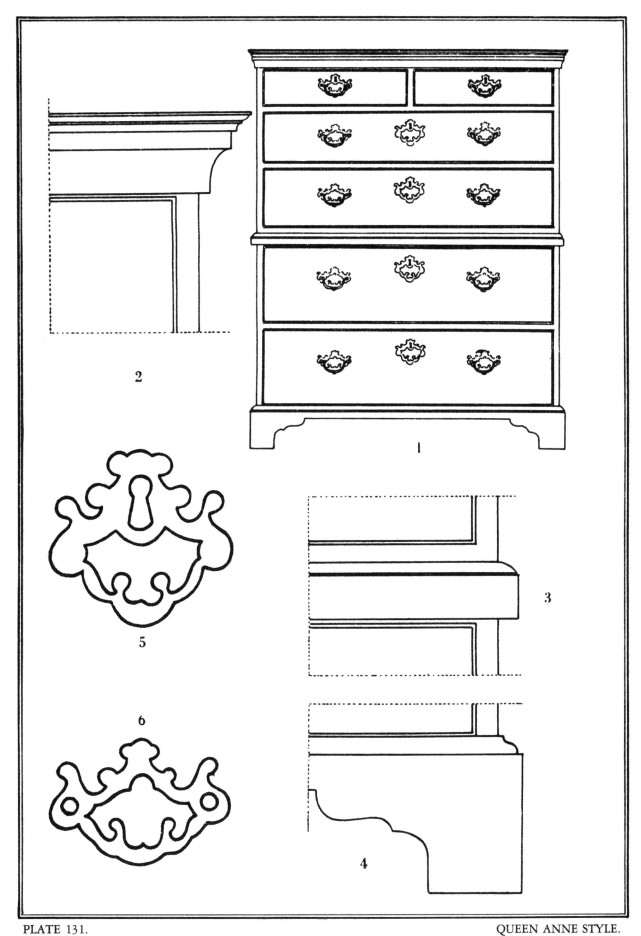

PLATE 131.   QUEEN ANNE STYLE.
1. Tallboy from early 18th century.   2. Upper corner.   3. Socle of upper section.   4. Foot.   5. Escutcheon
plate.   6. Drawer pull.

Property of M.J.H. Springett, Rochester.

135

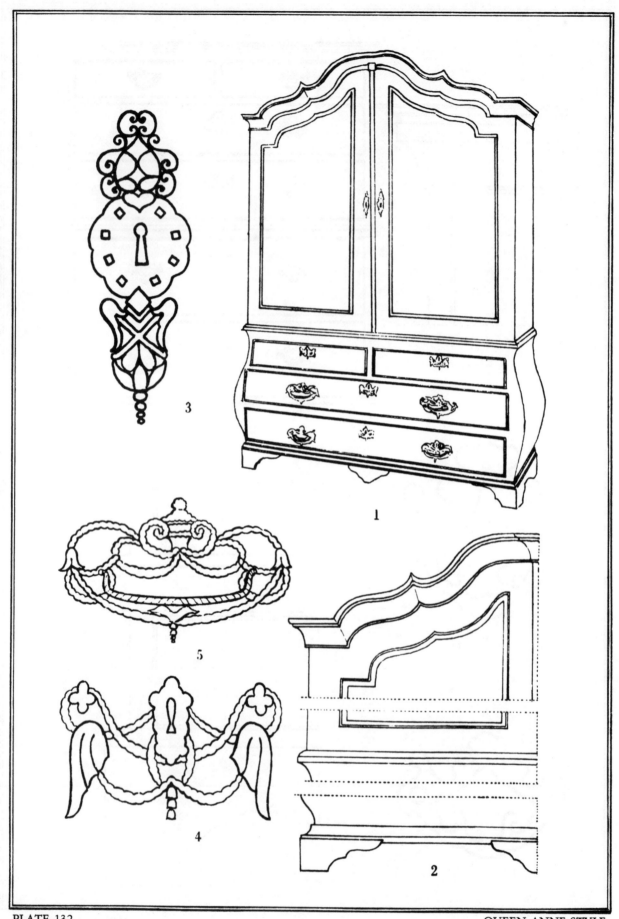

PLATE 132.   QUEEN ANNE STYLE.
1. Wardrobe showing Dutch influence. 2. Detail of cornice, mouldings and foot. 3 and 4. Escutcheon plates. 5. Drawer pull.

Private collection.

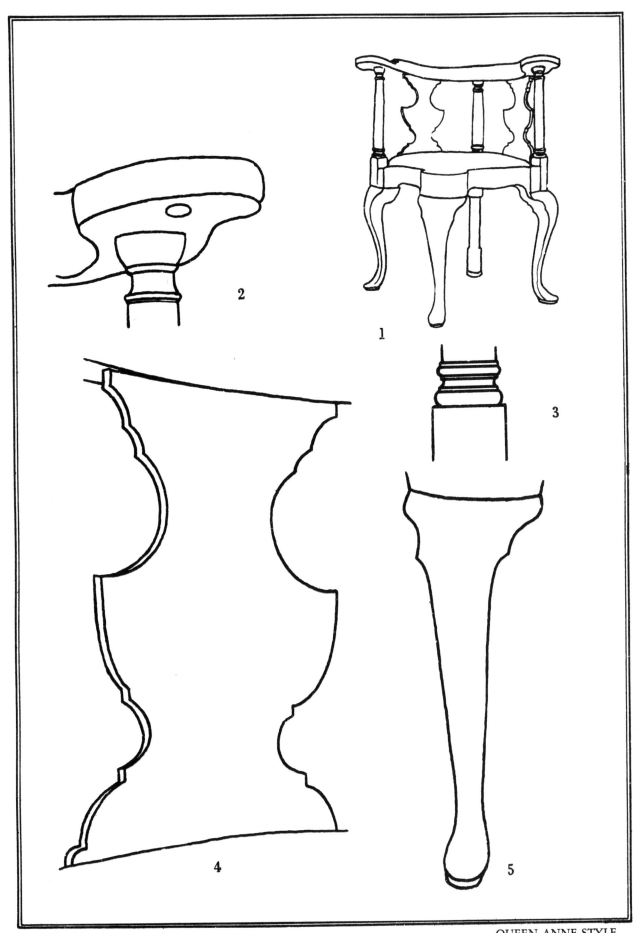

PLATE 133.   QUEEN ANNE STYLE.

1. Corner armchair from end of Queen Anne period.   2. Detail of arm support.   3. Base of support.   4. Detail of
back.   5. Leg.

Victoria and Albert Museum.

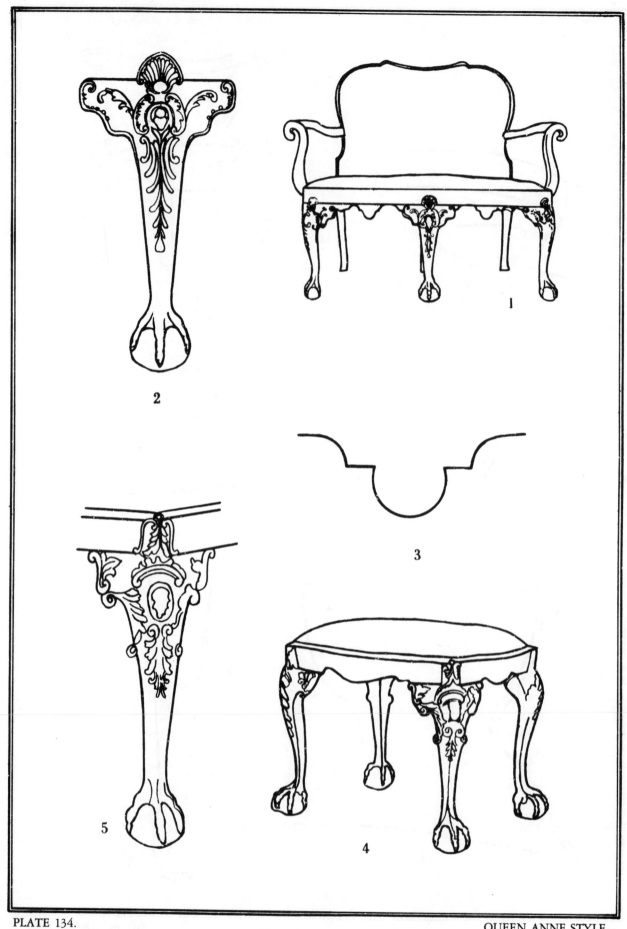

PLATE 134.   QUEEN ANNE STYLE.
1. Sofa from end of Queen Anne period.   2. Front leg.   3. Festoon on crosspiece.   4. Stool from end of Queen Anne
period.   5. Leg.

Private collections.

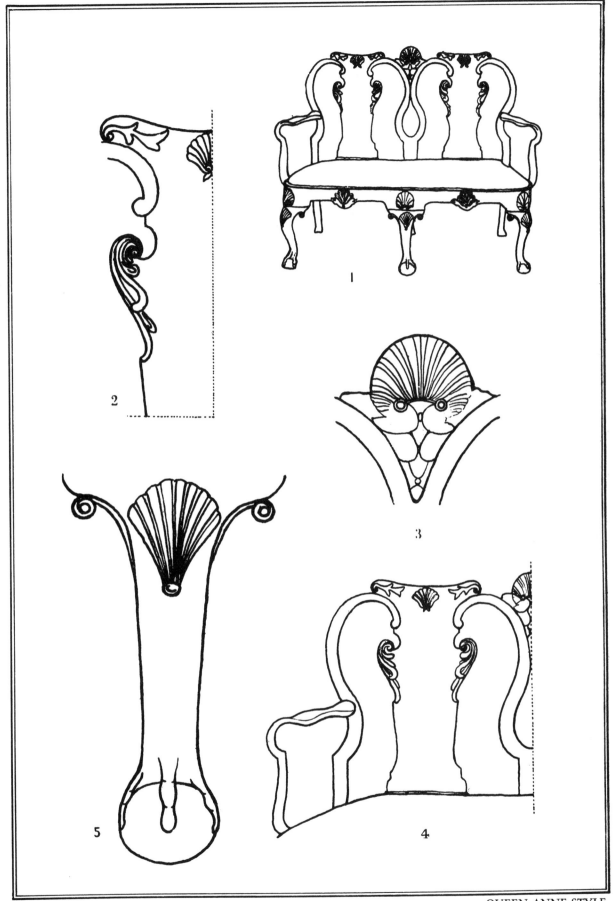

PLATE 135.

QUEEN ANNE STYLE.

1. Sofa from end of Queen Anne period.   2, 3 and 4. Details of back.   5. Leg.

Victoria and Albert Museum.

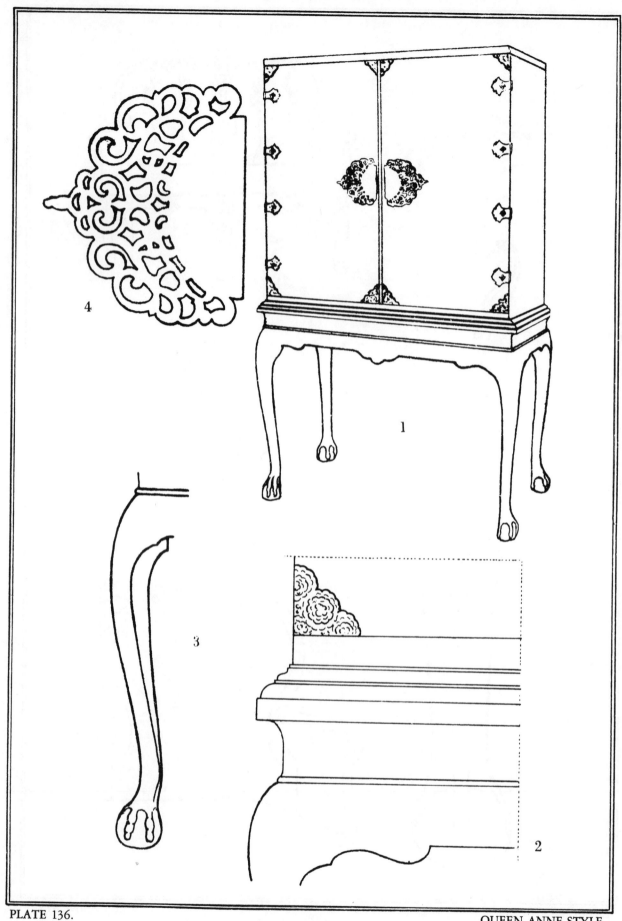

PLATE 136.

1. Queen Anne cabinet.   2. Corner and socle of upper section and spring of leg arch.   3. Leg.   4. Escutcheon plate.

Private collection.

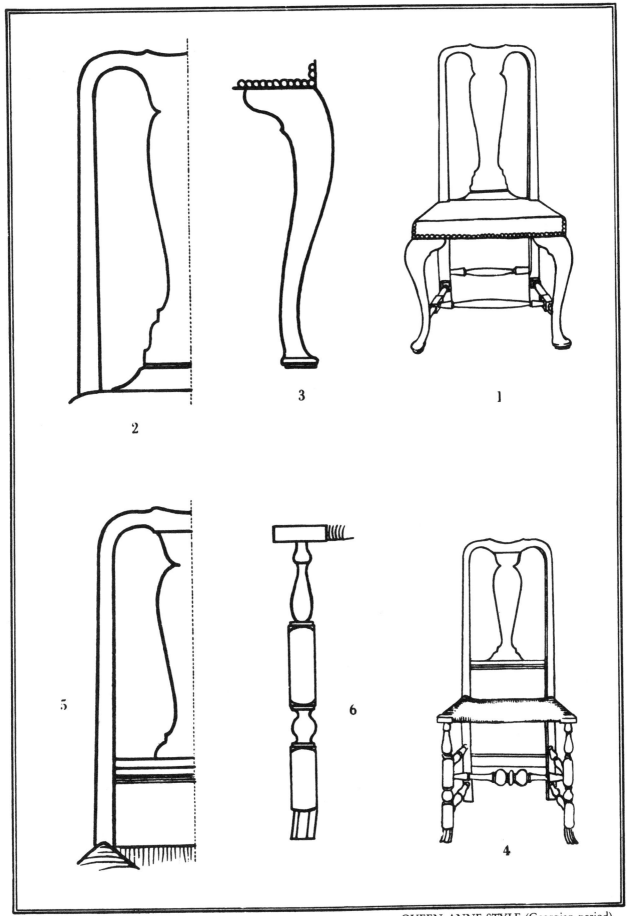

PLATE 137.   QUEEN ANNE STYLE (Georgian period).
1. Simple Georgian chair. 2. Detail of back. 3. Front leg. 4. Simple Georgian chair. 5. Detail of back. 6. Turned leg.

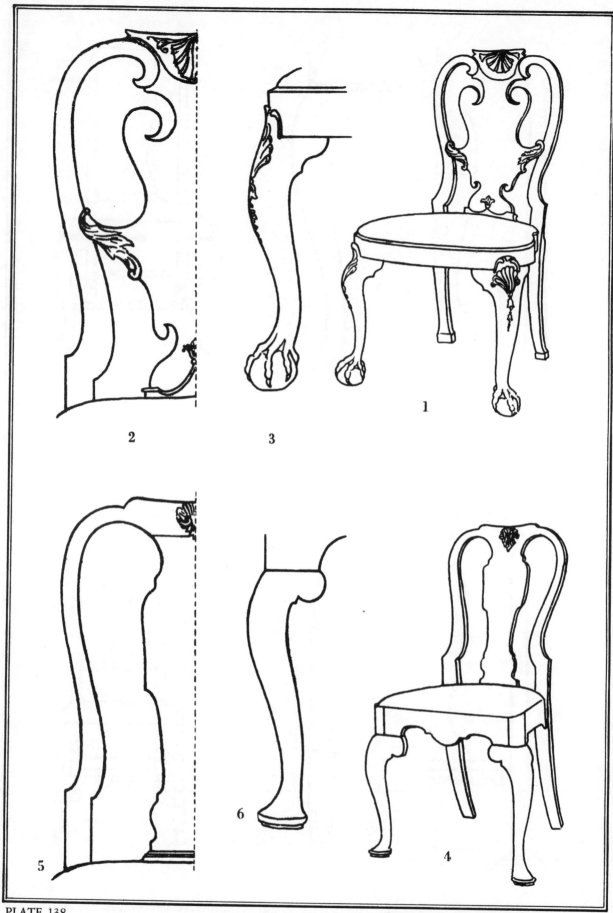

PLATE 138.

QUEEN ANNE STYLE (Georgian period).

1. Chair from period of George I.   2. Detail of back.   3. Front leg.   4. Chair from period of George I.   5. Back detail.   6. Front leg.

Geoffrey Hart and Lord Plender collections.

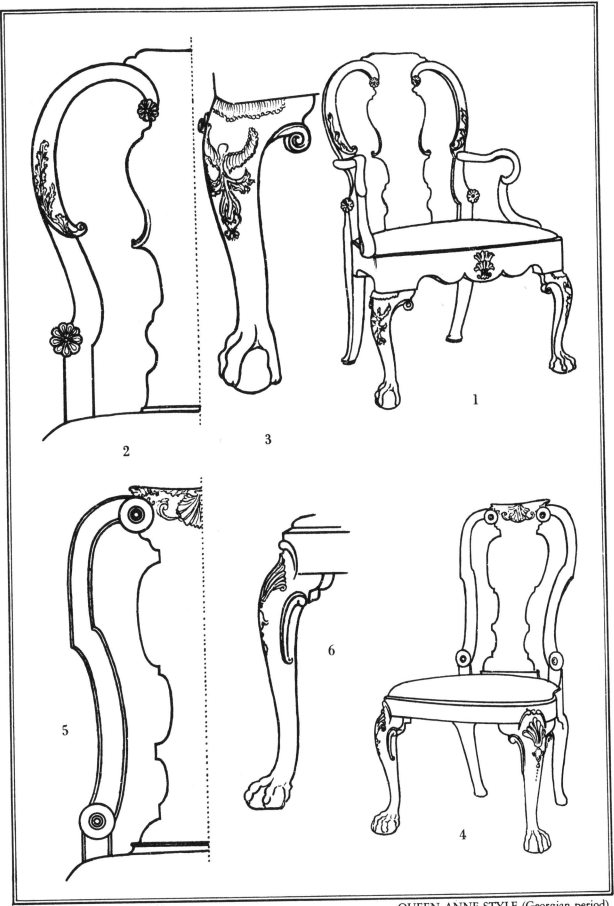

PLATE 139.

QUEEN ANNE STYLE (Georgian period).

1. Armchair from period of George I.   2. Back detail.   3. Front leg.   4. Chair from George I period.   5. Back detail.   6. Front leg.

J. S. Sykes and Guy N. Charrington collections.

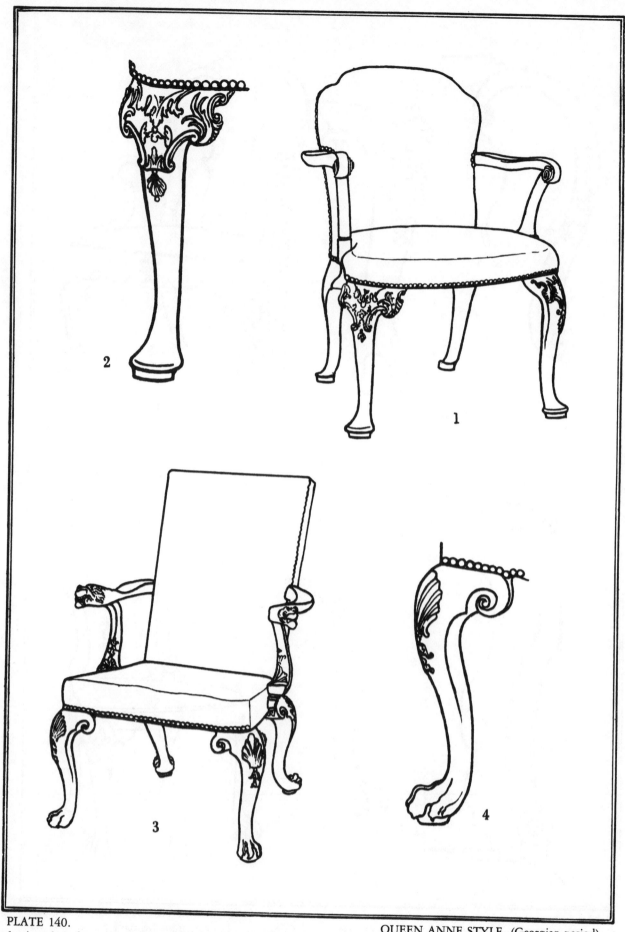

PLATE 140.

1. Armchair from reign of George I.   2. Detail of front leg.   3. Armchair from reign of George II.   4. Front leg.

QUEEN ANNE STYLE. (Georgian period).

J. S. Sykes collection.

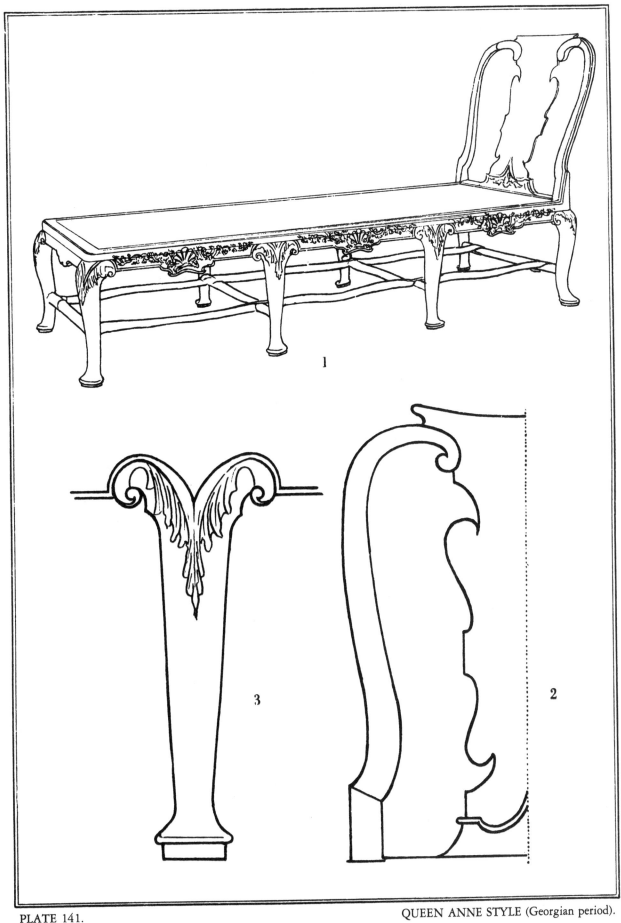

PLATE 141.
1. Sofa from reign of George I.   2. Detail of back.   3. Leg.

QUEEN ANNE STYLE (Georgian period).

Private collection.

145

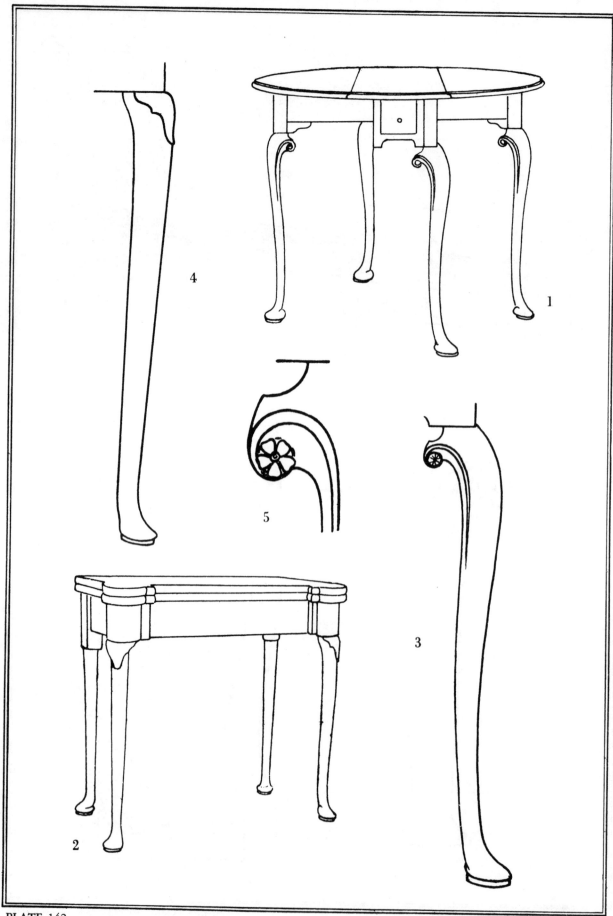

PLATE 142.
1 and 2. Graceful Georgian tables.   3 and 4. Legs.   5. Decoration on first table.

QUEEN ANNE STYLE (Georgian period).

Private collections.

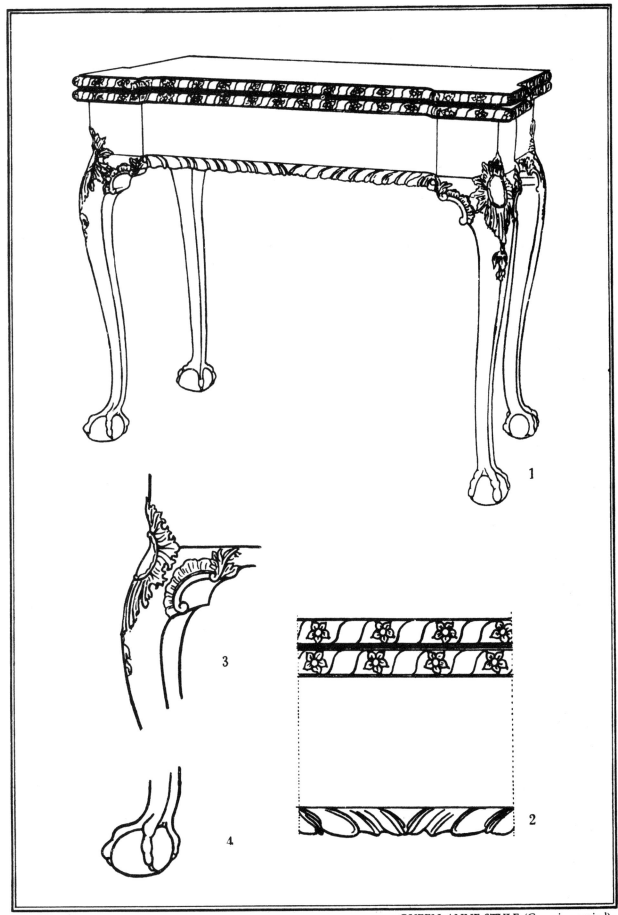

PLATE 143.   QUEEN ANNE STYLE (Georgian period).

1. Mahogany table from the mid-18th century.   2. Detail of friezes.   3 and 4. Decorations on legs.

J. S. Sykes Collection.

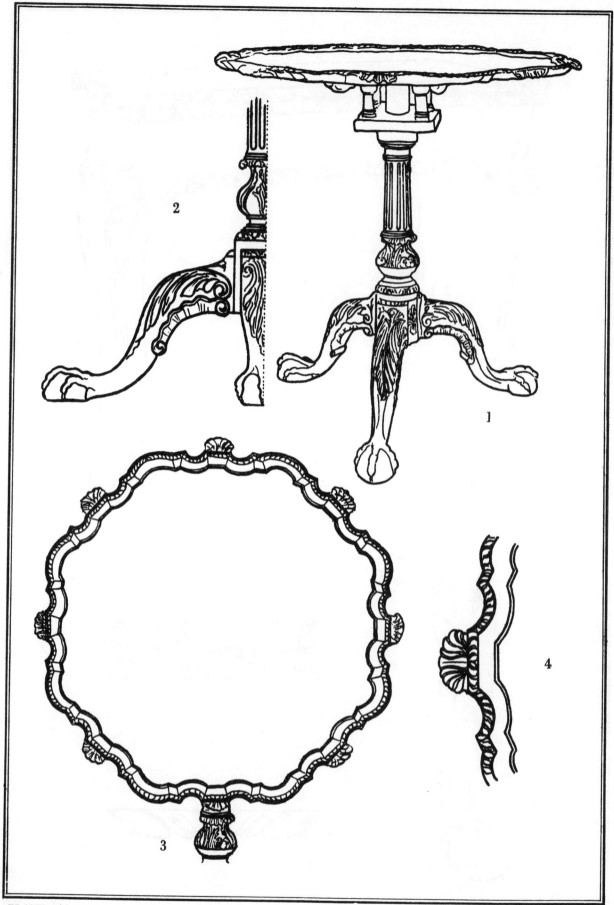

PLATE 144.

QUEEN ANNE STYLE (Georgian period).

1. Mahogany table from the mid-18th century. 2. Decoration on legs. 3. Tabletop. 4. Detail of moulding and frieze on tabletop.

Collection of Lord Plendar G.B.E.

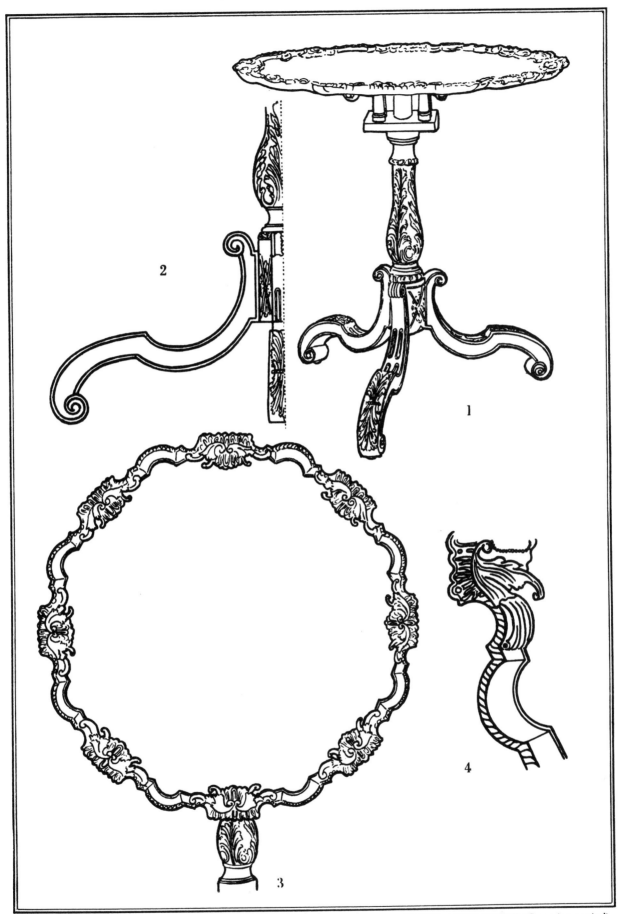

PLATE 145.

QUEEN ANNE STYLE (Georgian period).

1. Mahogany table from the mid-18th century.　2. Decoration on legs.　3. Tabletop.　4. Details of mouldings and frieze on tabletops.

J. S. Sykes collection.

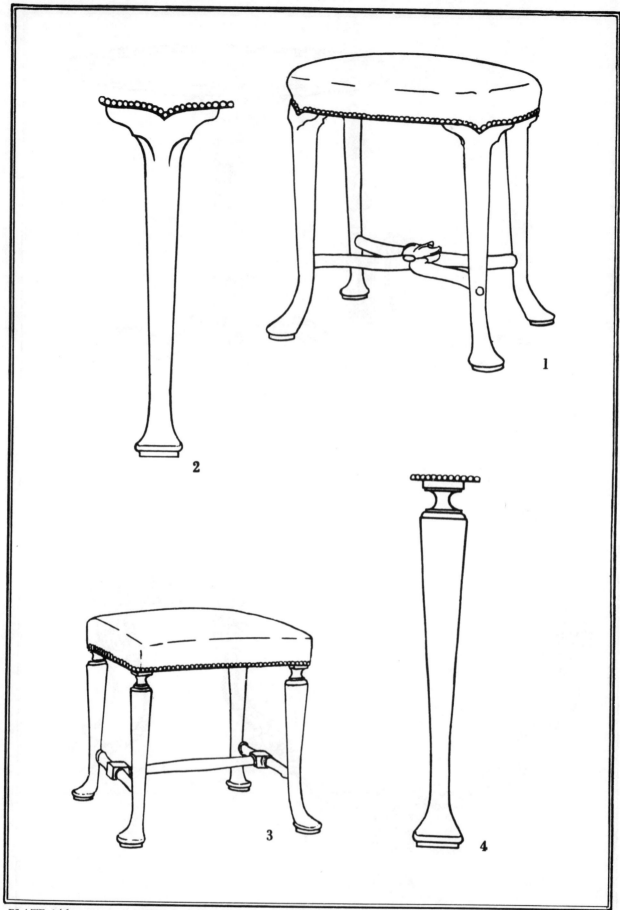

PLATE 146.

QUEEN ANNE STYLE (Georgian period).

1. Stool from period of George I.   2. Leg.   3. Stool from period of George I.   4. Leg.

Private and J. S. Sykes collections.

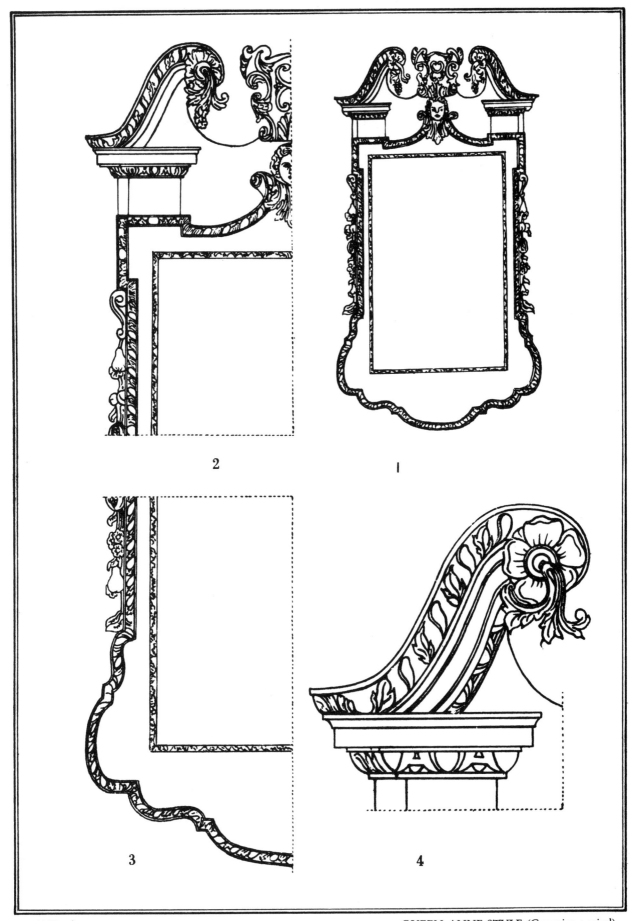

PLATE 147.   QUEEN ANNE STYLE (Georgian period).

1. Mirror from reign of George I.   2. Detail of top of frame.   3. Detail of frame bottom.   4. Decoration.

Collection of Lord Plender G. B. E.

151

PLATE 148.   QUEEN ANNE STYLE (Georgian period).
1. Mirror from reign of George II.   2. Decoration on frame.   3. Mirror from reign of George II.   4. Frame decoration.

Private and J. S. Sykes collections.

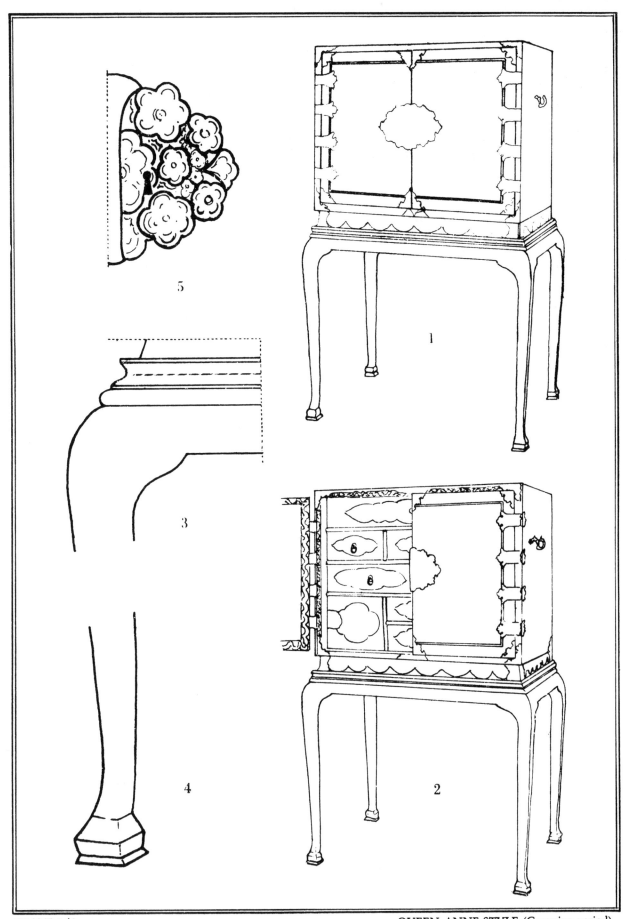

PLATE 149.   QUEEN ANNE STYLE (Georgian period).
1. Cabinet from reign of George II, closed.   2. Same, opened.   3. Mouldings and spring of leg arch.   4. Base of leg.   5. Escutcheon plate.

Private collection.

PLATE 150.   CHIPPENDALE STYLE (architectural features).
1. Room with pine wall panels, 1730.   2. Windows from Georgian homes; the second one with sash was more common than the first.   3. Type of moulding used during Chippendale period. 4. Doorway of room.

Hatton Garden, London.

154

PLATE 151.   CHIPPENDALE STYLE (architectural features).
1. Fireplace designed by Gibbs.   2. Fireplace screen designed by Chippendale.   3. Iron fireplace basket designed by Chippendale.   4. Drawer pull designed by Chippendale.

The Gentleman and Cabinet Maker's Director, T. Chippendale.

155

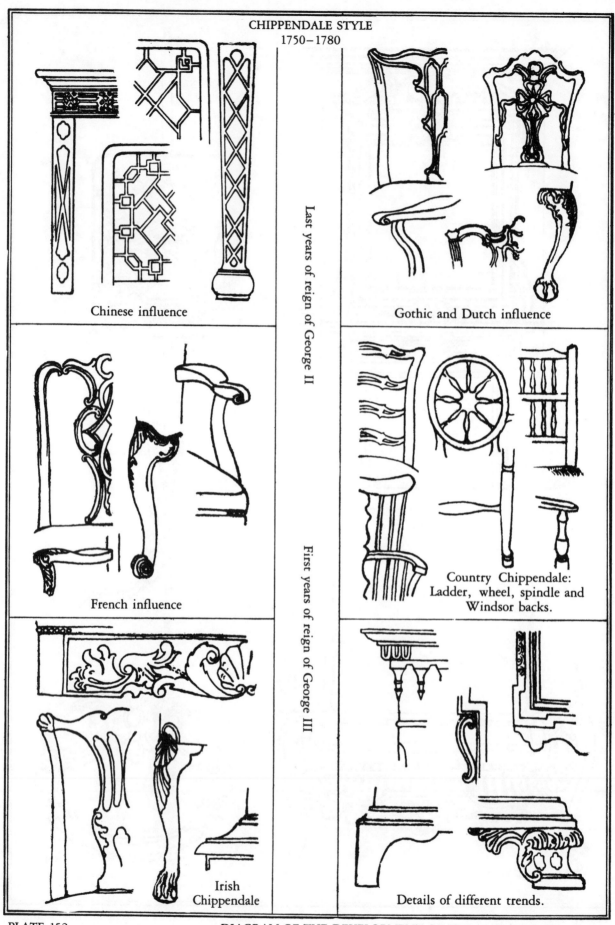

Chinese influence

Gothic and Dutch influence

Last years of reign of George II

French influence

Country Chippendale:
Ladder, wheel, spindle and
Windsor backs.

First years of reign of George III

Irish
Chippendale

Details of different trends.

PLATE 152. DIAGRAM OF THE DEVELOPMENT OF THE CHIPPENDALE STYLE.

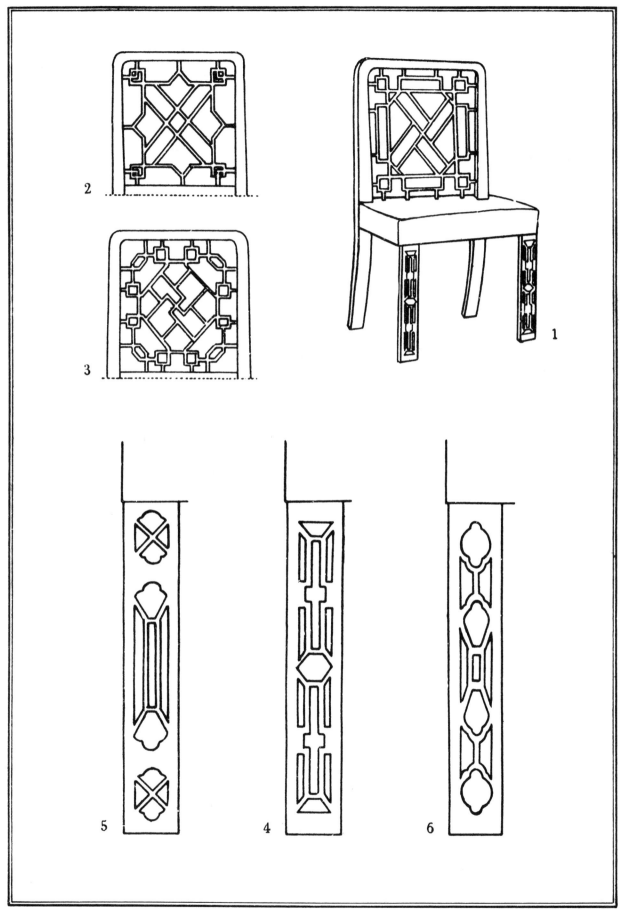

PLATE 153.   CHIPPENDALE STYLE.

1. Chippendale chair in the style called "Chinese."   2 and 3. Backs of other chairs in the same style.   4. Leg of first chair.   5 and 6. Legs in same style.

The Gentleman and Cabinet Maker's Director. T. Chippendale.

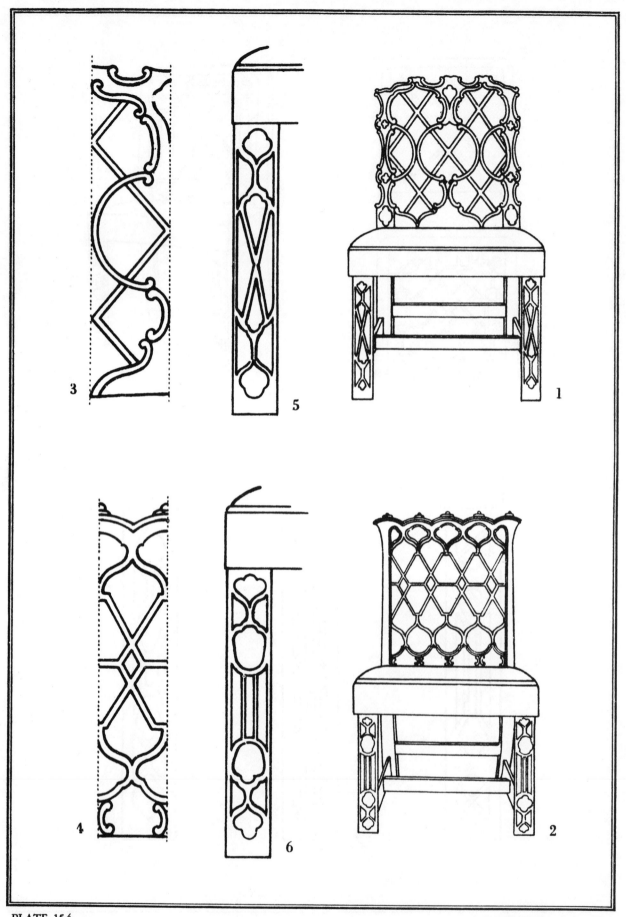

PLATE 154.

1 and 2. Chippendale chairs showing Gothic influence.   3 and 4. Details of backs.   5 and 6. Legs of first and second chair, respectively.

The Gentleman and Cabinet Maker's Director. T. Chippendale.

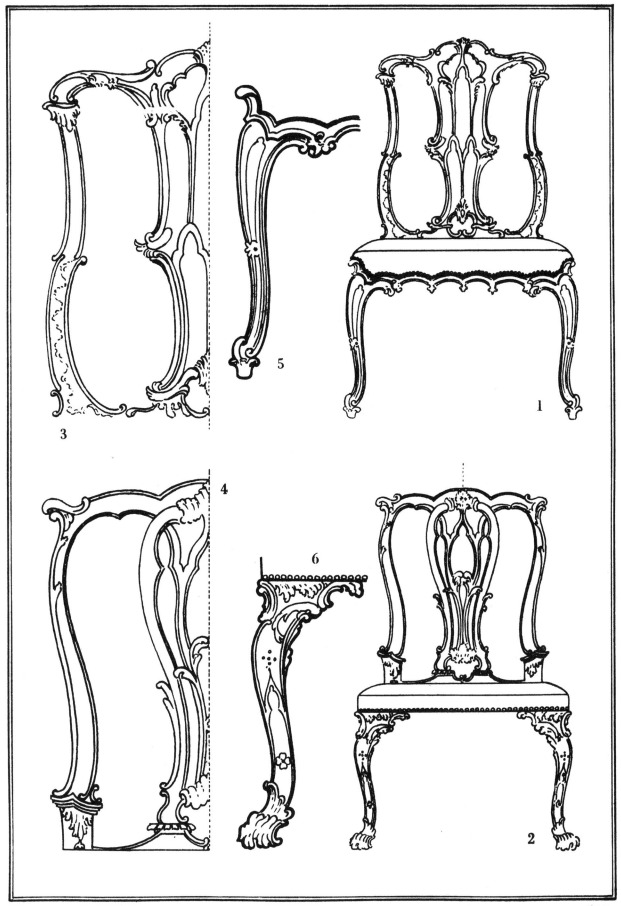

PLATE 155.   CHIPPENDALE STYLE.
1 and 2. Gothic Chippendale chairs.   3 and 4. Details of backs.   5 and 6. Legs.

The Gentleman and Cabinet Maker's Director. T. Chippendale.

PLATE 156.   CHIPPENDALE STYLE.
1 and 2. Chippendale chairs with Gothic backs.   3 and 4. Detail of backs.
                          The Gentleman and Cabinet Maker's Director. T. Chippendale.

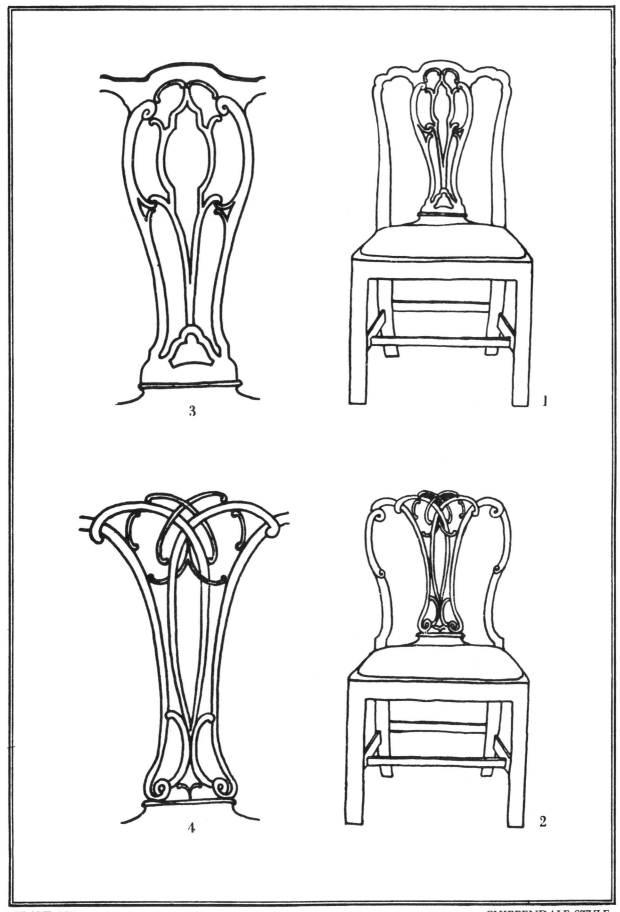

PLATE 157.   CHIPPENDALE STYLE.
1 and 2. Chippendale chairs with Gothic backs.   3 and 4. Details of backs.
The Gentleman and Cabinet Maker's Director. T. Chippendale.

PLATE 158.   CHIPPENDALE STYLE.
1 and 2. Chippendale chairs with Gothic backs.   3 and 4. Detail of backs.

The Gentleman and Cabinet Maker's Director. T. Chippendale.

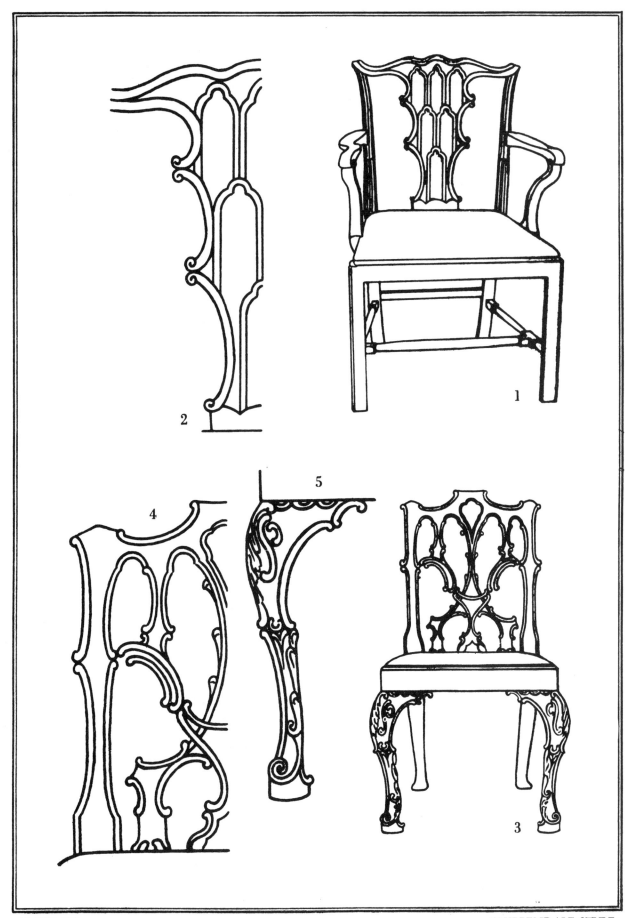

PLATE 159.   CHIPPENDALE STYLE.
1. Armchair with Gothic back.   2. Detail of back.   3. Gothic Chippendale chair.   4. Back detail.   5. Leg.
The Gentleman and Cabinet Maker's Director. T. Chippendale.

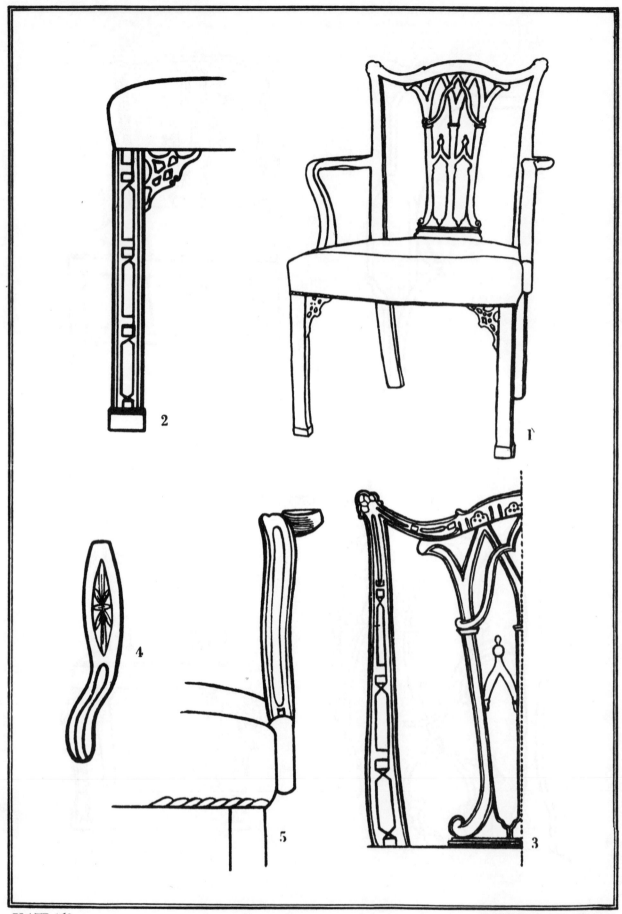

PLATE 160.   CHIPPENDALE STYLE.
1. Gothic armchair.   2. Detail of leg.   3. Detail of back.   4. Decoration on arm.   5. Arm.

Metropolitan Museum of Art.

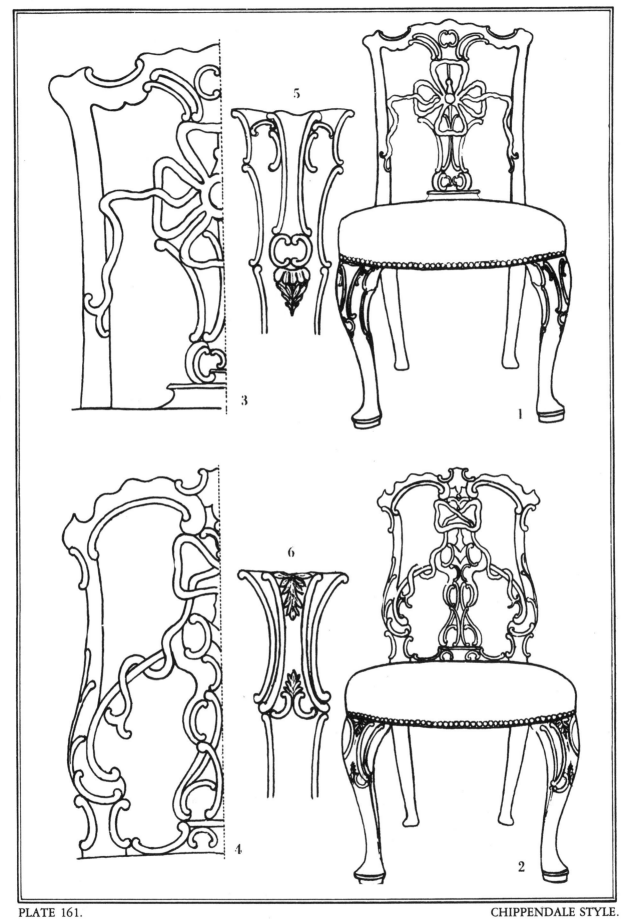

PLATE 161.   CHIPPENDALE STYLE.

1 and 2. Chippendale chairs with backs of intertwining ribbons.   3 and 4. Detail of respective backs.   5 and 6. Decoration
on legs.

The Gentleman and Cabinet Maker's Director. T. Chippendale.

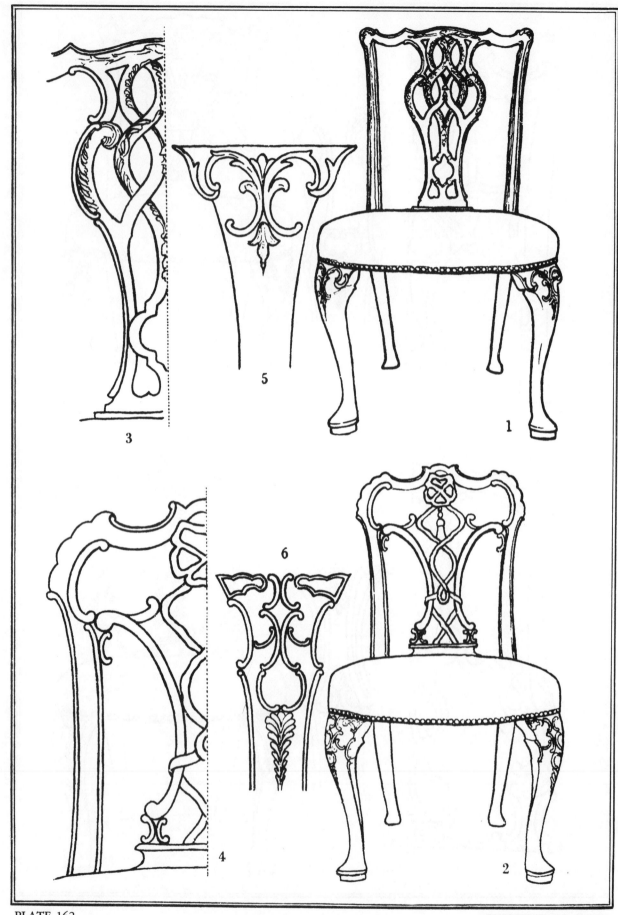

PLATE 162.   CHIPPENDALE STYLE.
1 and 2. Chippendale chairs with backs of intertwining ribbons.   3 and 4. Details of backs.   5 and 6. Decoration
on legs.

Private collection.

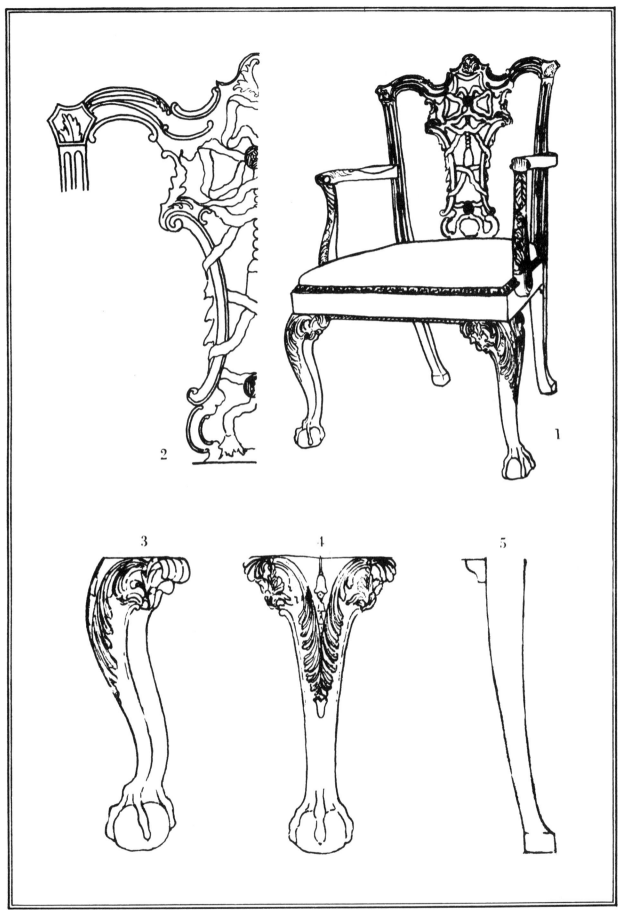

PLATE 163.   CHIPPENDALE STYLE.

1. Chippendale armchair with intertwining ribbon back of French influence and Dutch style legs.   2. Detail of back.

3 and 4. Details of decorations on front legs.   5. Back leg.

Victoria and Albert Museum.

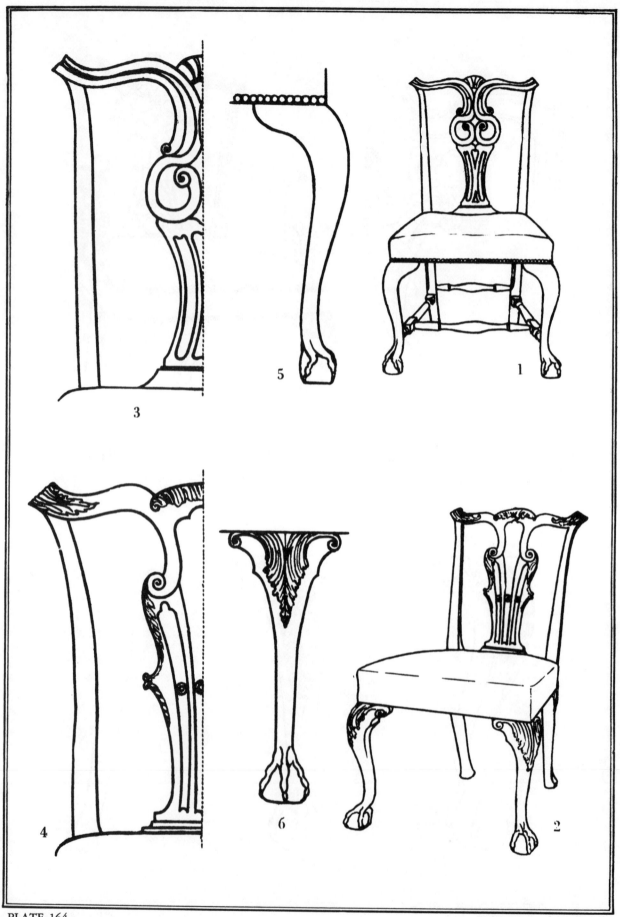

PLATE 164.
1 and 2. Elegant straight-backed Chippendale chairs.   3 and 4. Detail of backs.   5 and 6. Legs.

CHIPPENDALE STYLE.

Private collection.

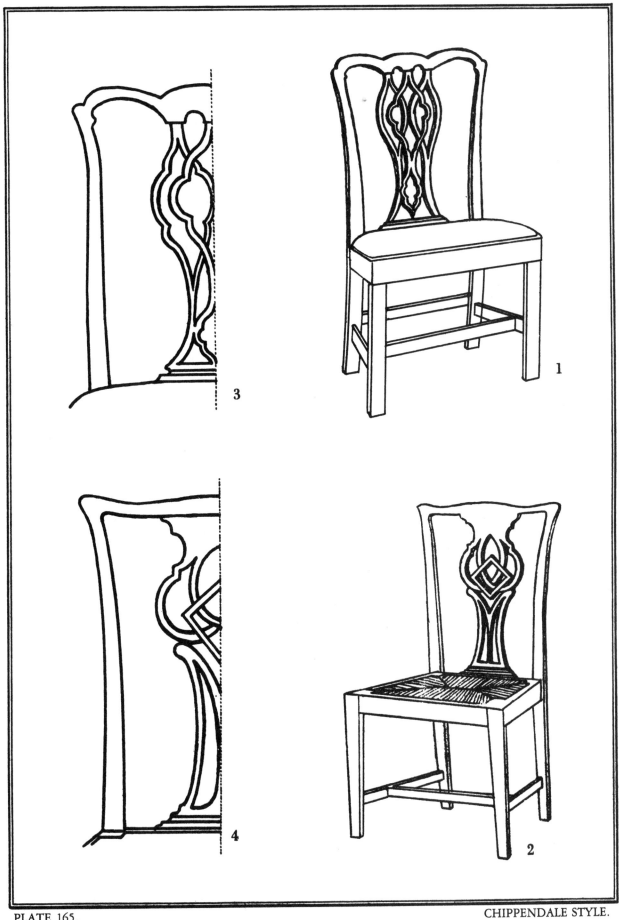

PLATE 165.

1 and 2. Simple straight-backed Chippendale chairs. 3 and 4. Detail of backs.

Sketches of photographs in "Revista Oro" and "The Studio," respectively.

CHIPPENDALE STYLE.

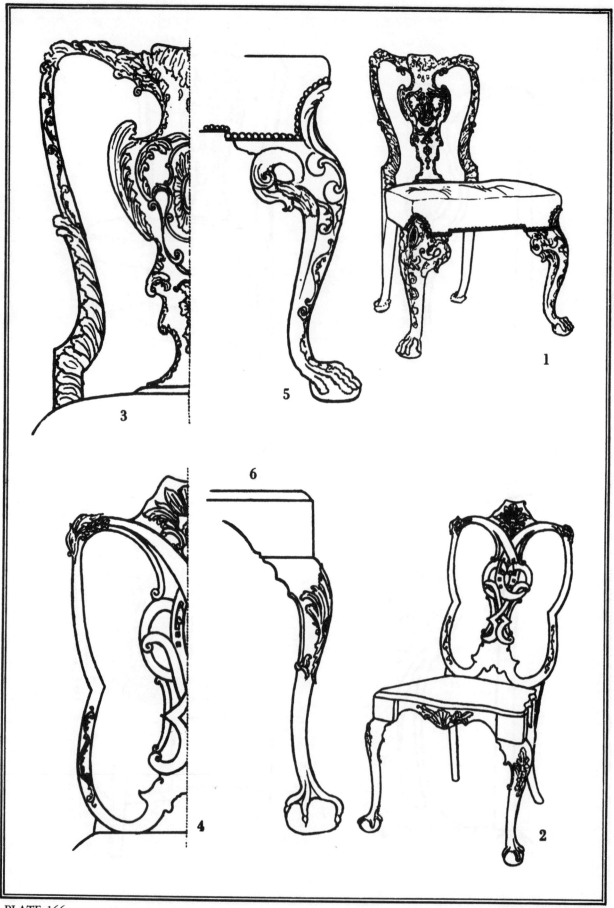

PLATE 166.

1 and 2. Extremely ornate Chippendale chairs.   3 and 4. Detail of backs.   5 and 6. Detail of legs.

Private collections.

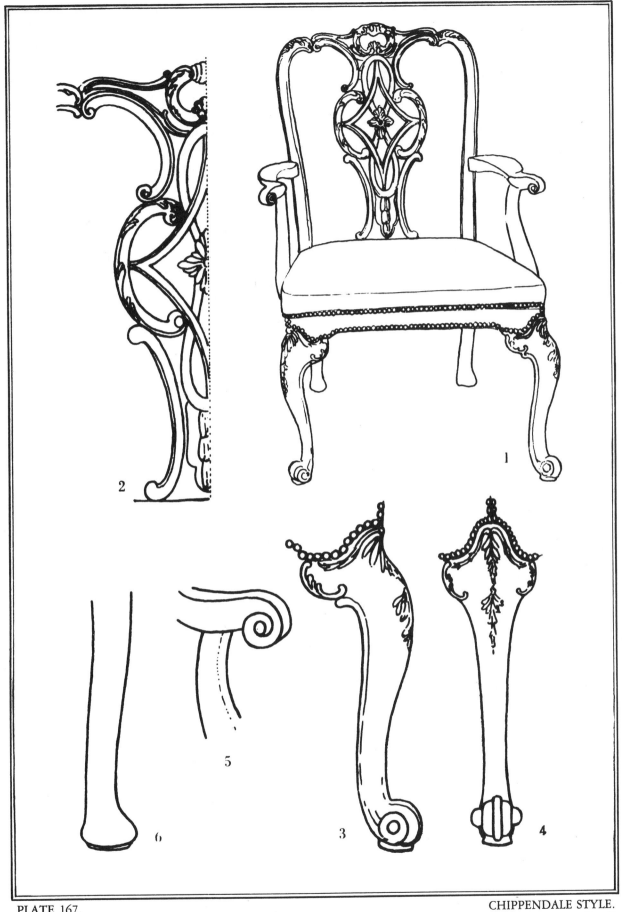

PLATE 167.   CHIPPENDALE STYLE.

1. Chippendale armchair showing French influence.   2. Detail of back.   3 and 4. Decoration on front legs.   5. Detail of arm end.   6. Back leg.

Saint Pierre Hospital, Bristol.

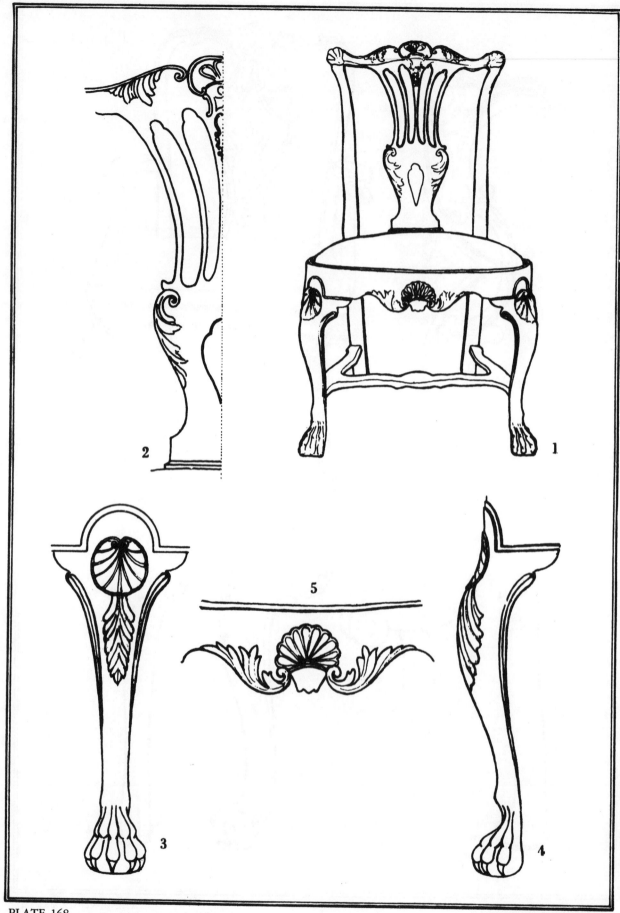

PLATE 168.
1. Irish Chippendale chair.   2. Detail of back.   3 and 4. Decoration on front legs.   5. Decoration on front edge of seat.

CHIPPENDALE STYLE.

Private collection.

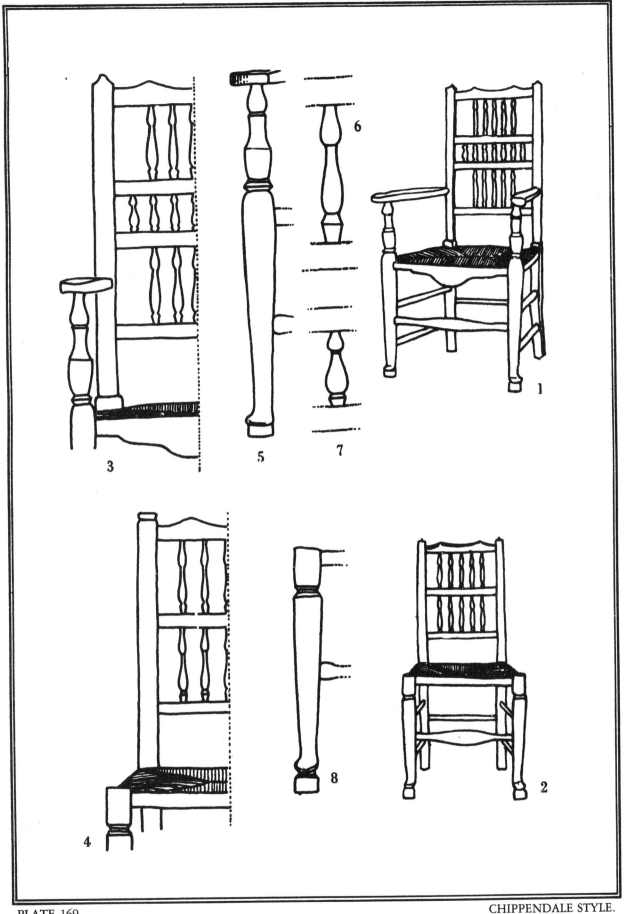

PLATE 169.
1 and 2. Chippendale armchair and chair with spindle backs.   3 and 4. Details of backs.   5. Front leg of armchair.   6
and 7. Details of back spindles.   8. Front leg of chair.

CHIPPENDALE STYLE.

Private collection.

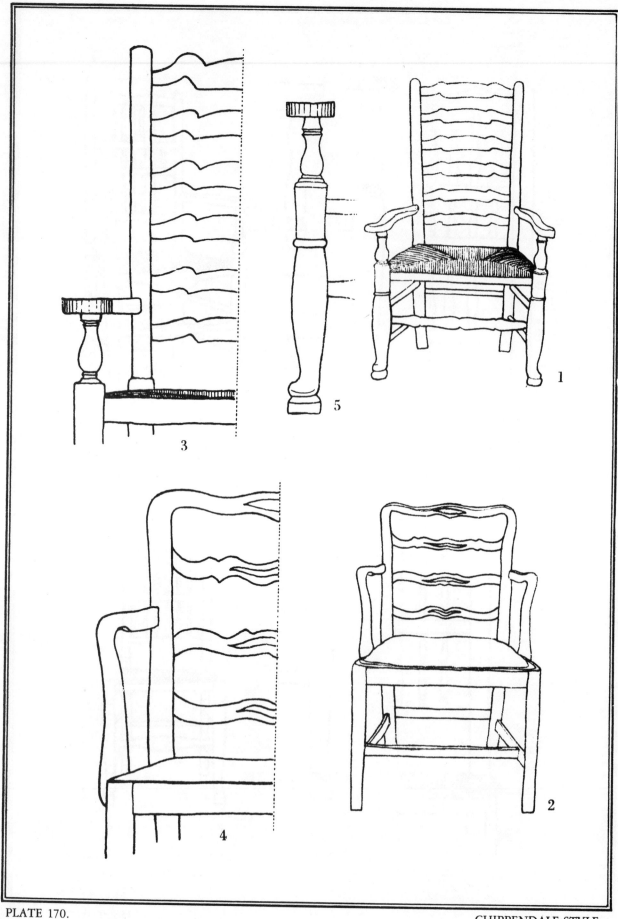

PLATE 170.

CHIPPENDALE STYLE.

1 and 2. Chippendale armchairs with ladder backs.   3 and 4. Detail of backs.   5. Front leg of first armchair.

Private collection.

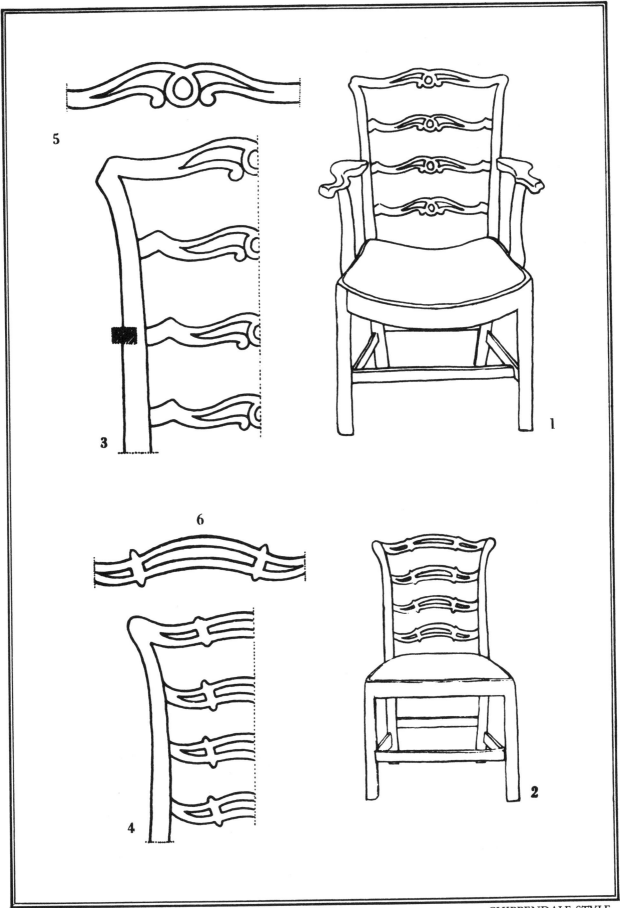

PLATE 171.

CHIPPENDALE STYLE.

1 and 2. Chippendale armchair and chair with ladder backs.   3 and 4. Detail of backs.   5 and 6. Detail of back crosspieces.

Private collection.

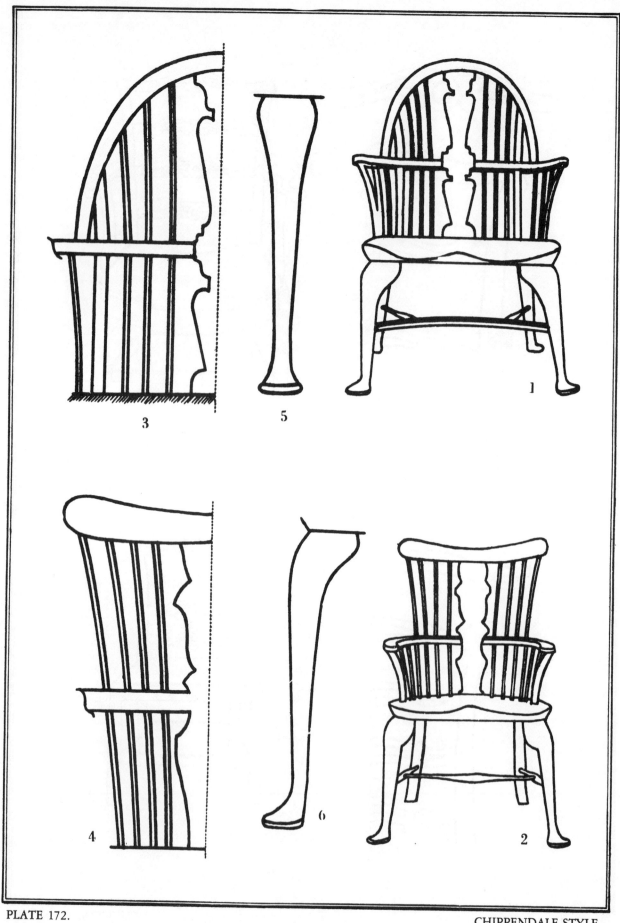

PLATE 172.
1 and 2. Windsor chairs.   3 and 4. Detail of backs.   5 and 6. Legs.

CHIPPENDALE STYLE.

Private collection.

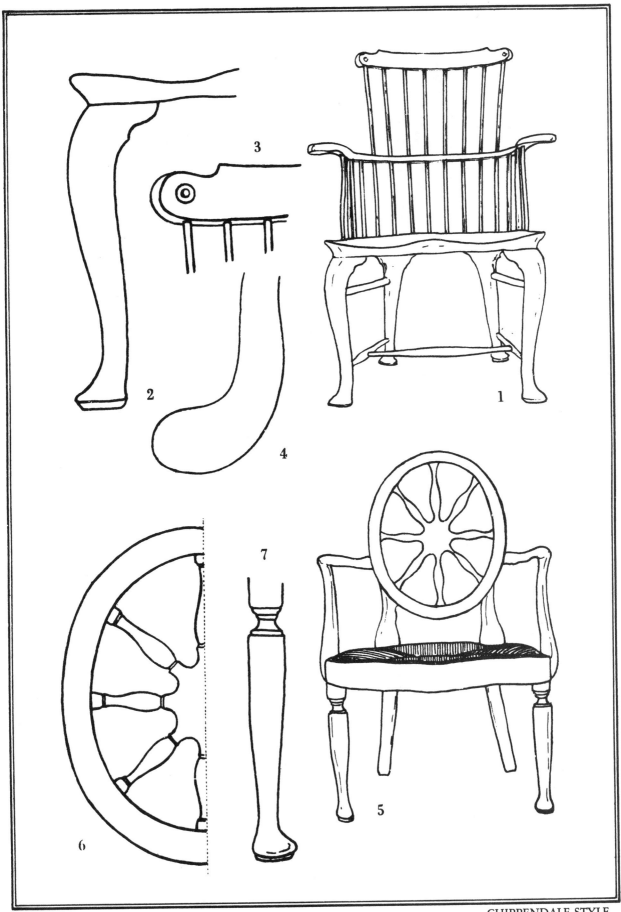

PLATE 173.   CHIPPENDALE STYLE.
1. Windsor armchair.   2. Front leg.   3. Detail of top of back.   4. Blade of arm.   5. Armchair with wheel
back.   6. Detail of back.   7. Leg.

Private collection.

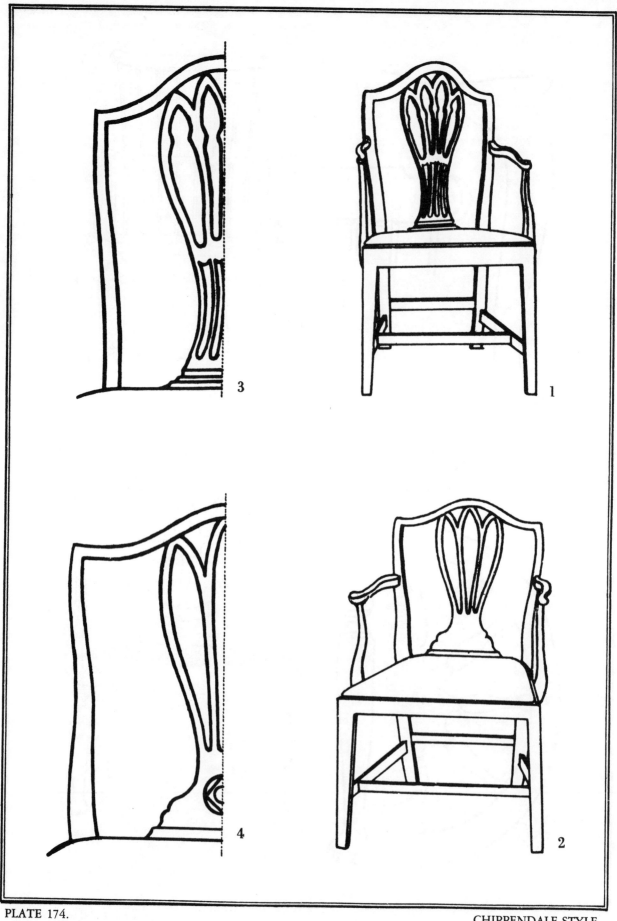

PLATE 174.
1 and 2. Straight-backed Chippendale armchairs with Hepplewhite frame (almost Colonial style).   3 and 4. Detail of backs.

CHIPPENDALE STYLE.

Private collection.

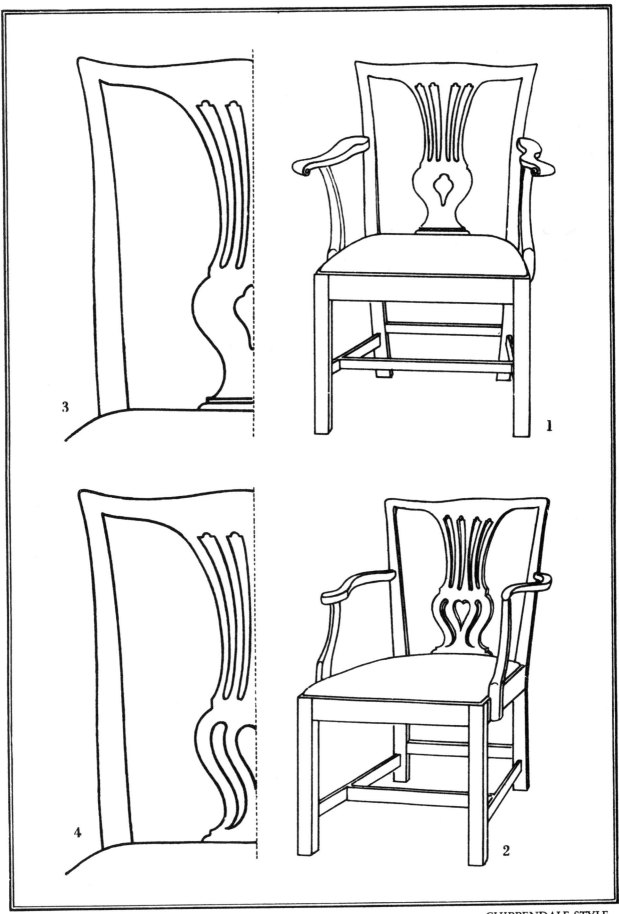

PLATE 175.
1 and 2. Straight-backed Chippendale armchairs.   3 and 4. Detail of backs.

CHIPPENDALE STYLE.

Private collection.

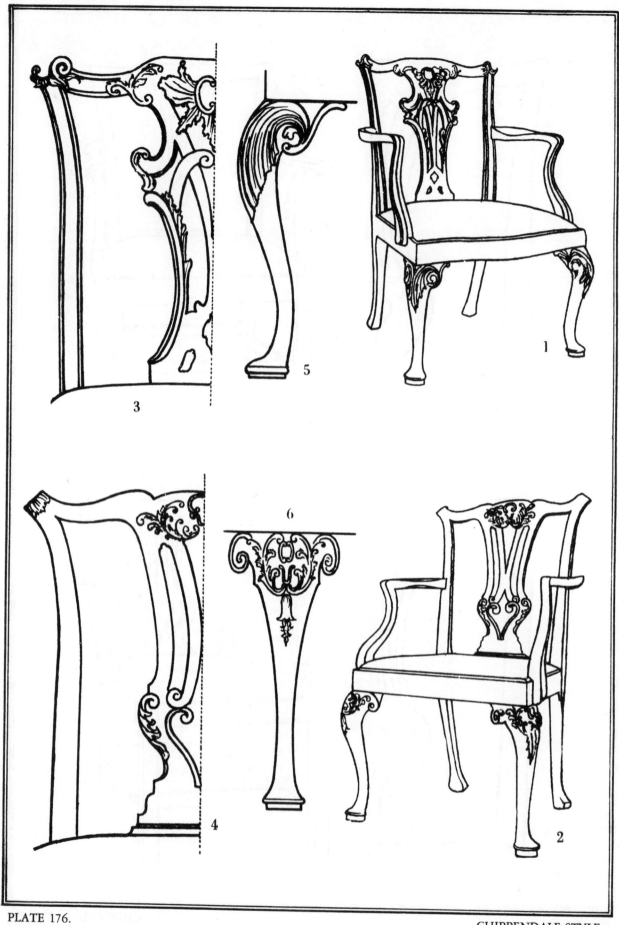

PLATE 176.

1 and 2. Elegant straight-backed Chippendale armchairs.   3 and 4. Detail of backs.   5 and 6. Details of front legs.

CHIPPENDALE STYLE.

Private collection.

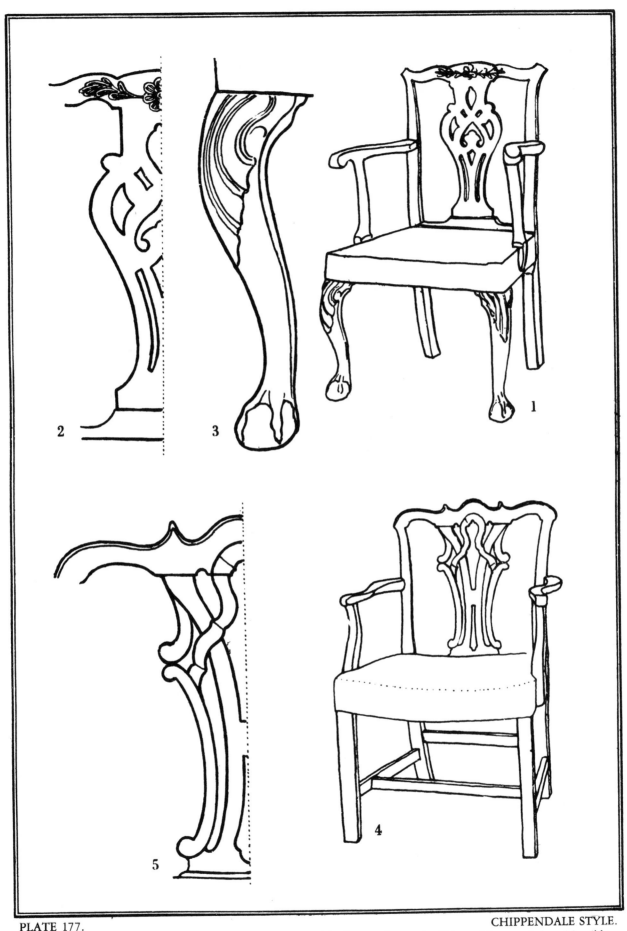

PLATE 177.   CHIPPENDALE STYLE.

1. Straight-backed Chippendale armchair. 2. Detail of back. 3. Leg. 4. Chippendale armchair with ribbon back. 5. Detail of back.

Private collection.

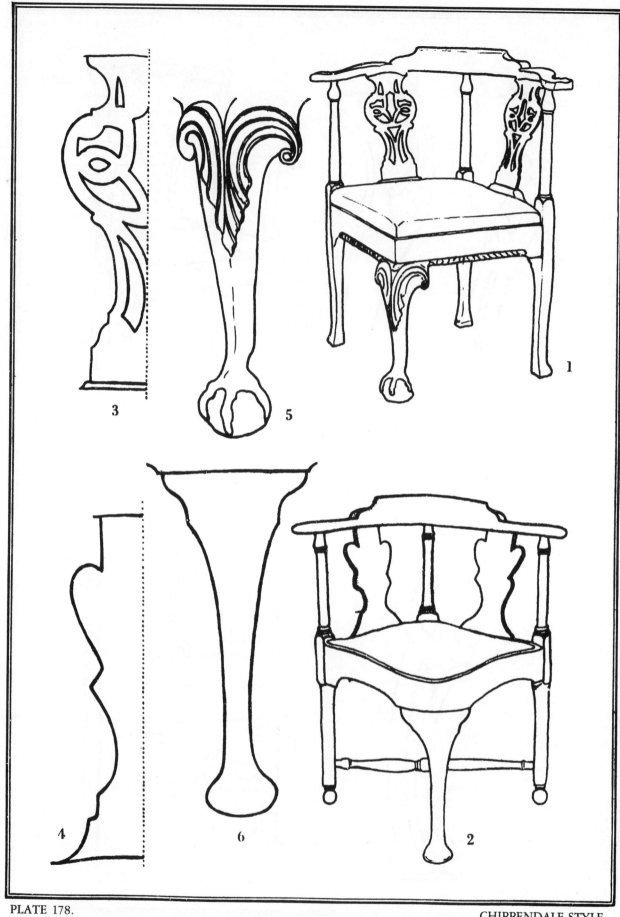

PLATE 178.
1 and 2. Chippendale corner armchairs.   3 and 4. Detail of backs.   5 and 6. Legs.

CHIPPENDALE STYLE.

Private collection.

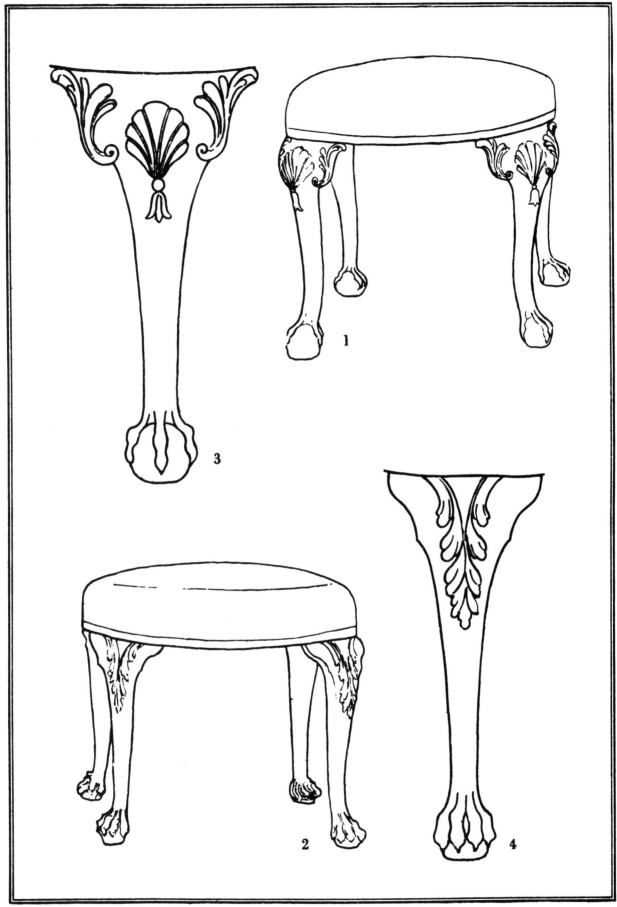

PLATE 179.   CHIPPENDALE STYLE.
1 and 2. Chippendale stools with elegant legs.   3 and 4. Decorations on legs.

Victoria and Albert Museum and private collection.

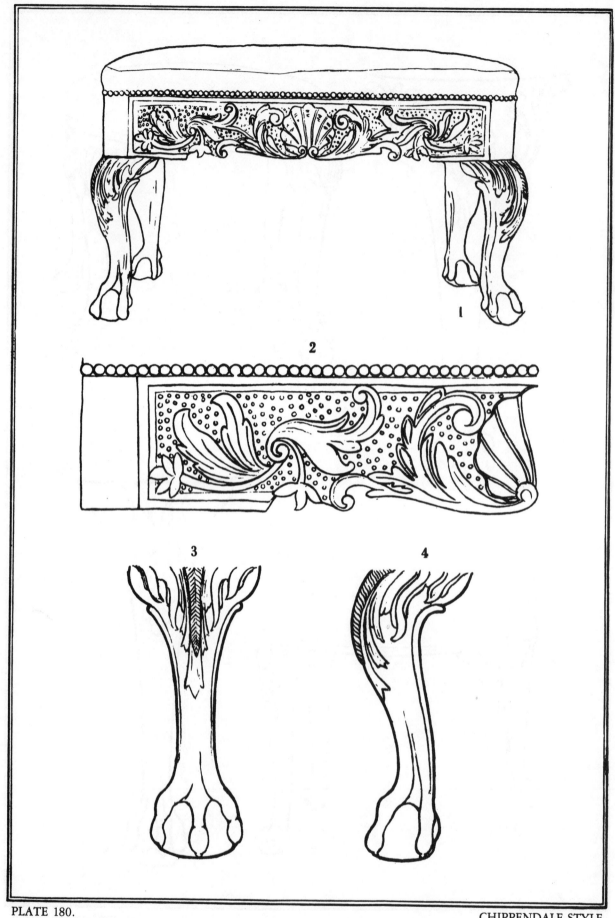

PLATE 180.

CHIPPENDALE STYLE.

1. Irish Chippendale stool.   2. Decoration on edge of seat.   3 and 4. Decorations on legs.

Private collection.

PLATE 181.   CHIPPENDALE STYLE.
1. Sofa from the first Chippendale period.   2. Detail of back.   3. Leg.   4. Simple Chippendale sofa.   5. Detail of
back.

Private collection.

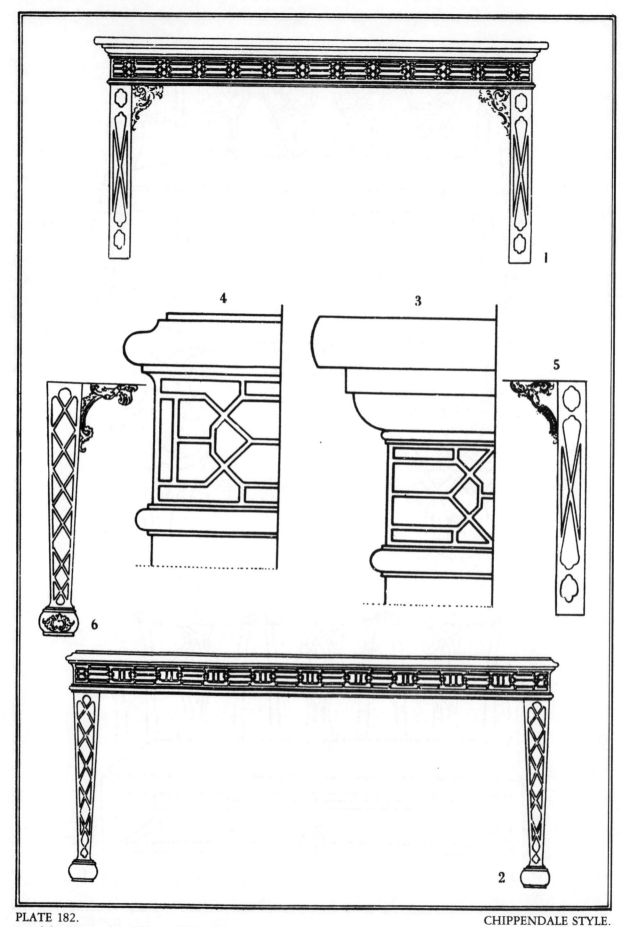

PLATE 182.   CHIPPENDALE STYLE.

1 and 2. Chippendale tables with Chinese motifs.   3. Moulding and frieze of first table.   4. Moulding and frieze of second table.   5 and 6. Details of their respective legs.

The Gentleman and Cabinet Maker's Director. T. Chippendale.

186

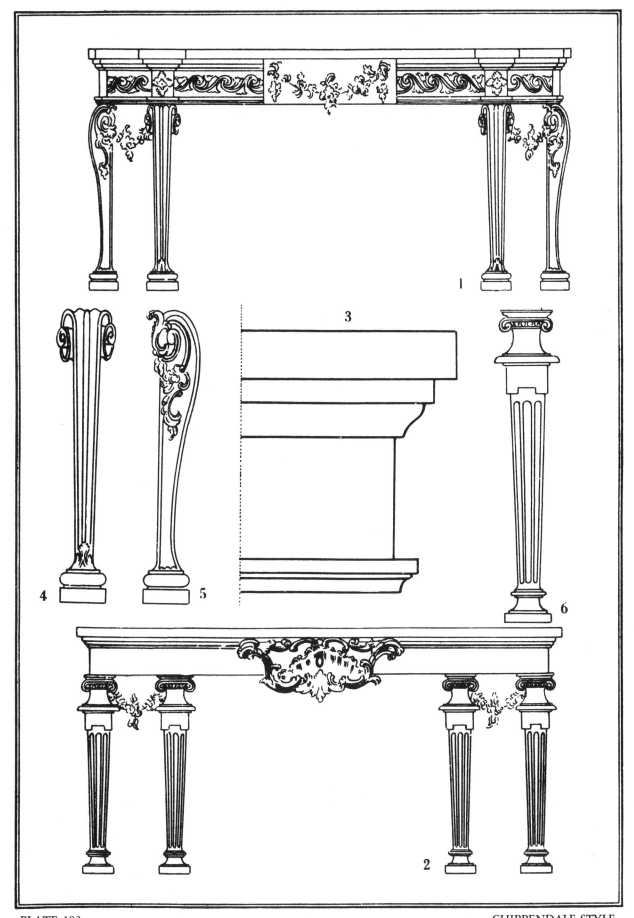

PLATE 183.

1 and 2. Elegant Chippendale tables. 3. Detail of first table's mouldings. 4 and 5. Decorations on legs of first table. 6. Same, second table.

CHIPPENDALE STYLE.

The Gentleman and Cabinet Maker's Director. T. Chippendale.

187

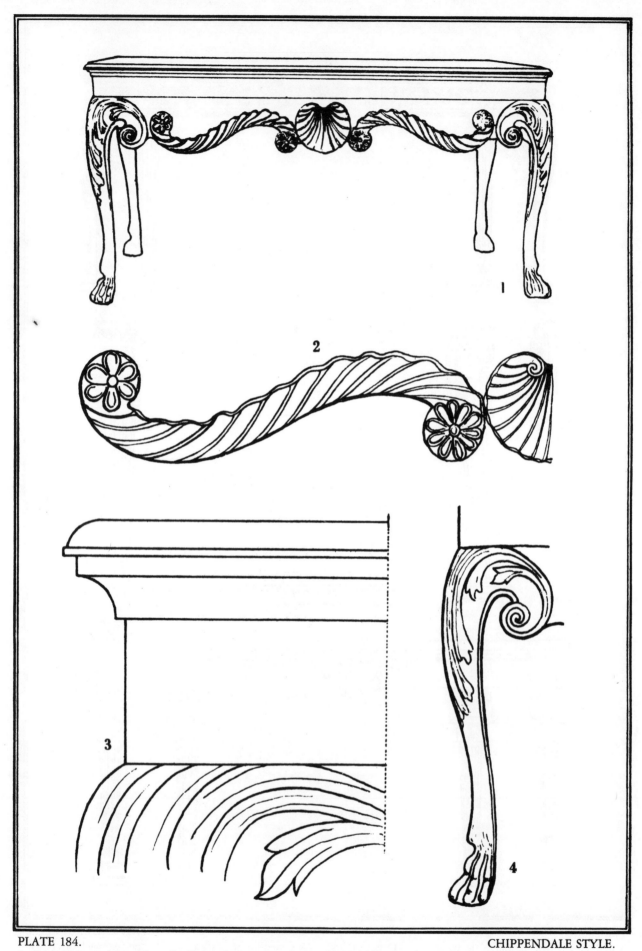

PLATE 184.   CHIPPENDALE STYLE.
1. Irish Chippendale table.   2. Decoration on crosspiece.   3. Mouldings and top of leg.   4. Decoration on legs.
Private collection.

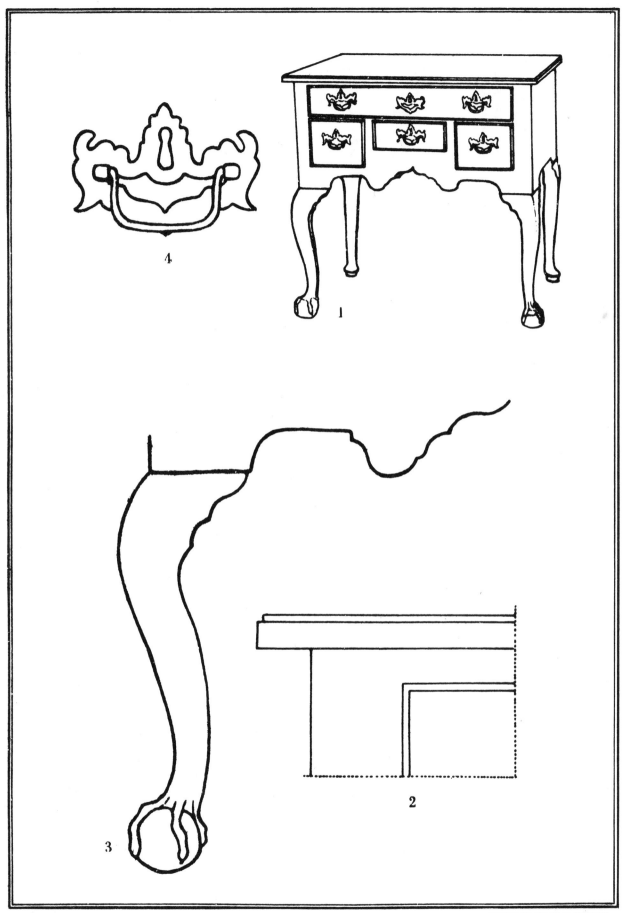

PLATE 185.   CHIPPENDALE STYLE.
1. Early Chippendale dressing table.   2. Detail of moulding.   3. Detail of leg and festoon on crosspiece.   4. Drawer
pull.

Private collection.

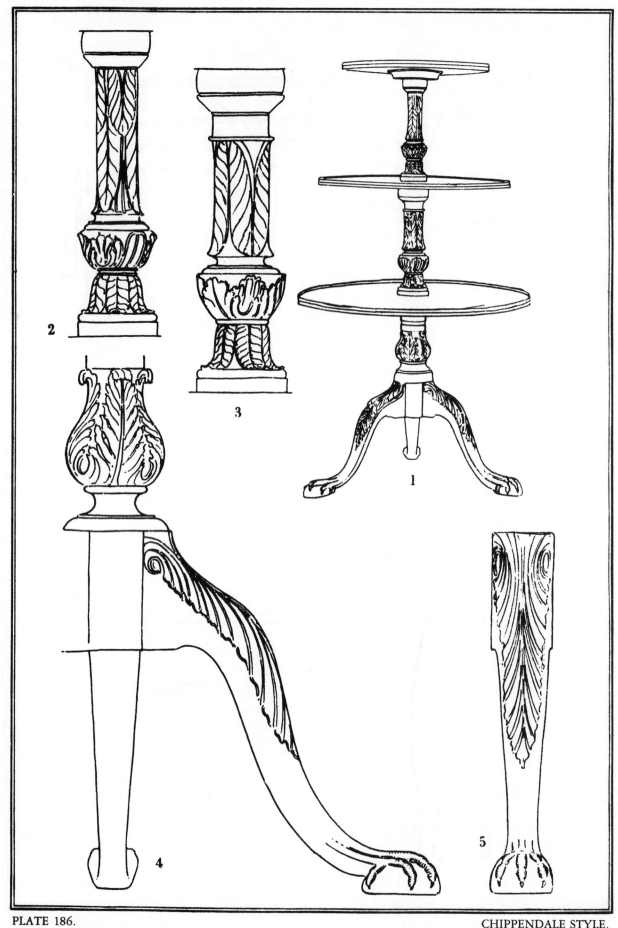

PLATE 186.   CHIPPENDALE STYLE.

1. Practical piece of furniture sometimes called a "silent butler."   2. Upper column.   3. Middle column.   4. Detail
of base.   5. Decoration on leg.

Private collection.

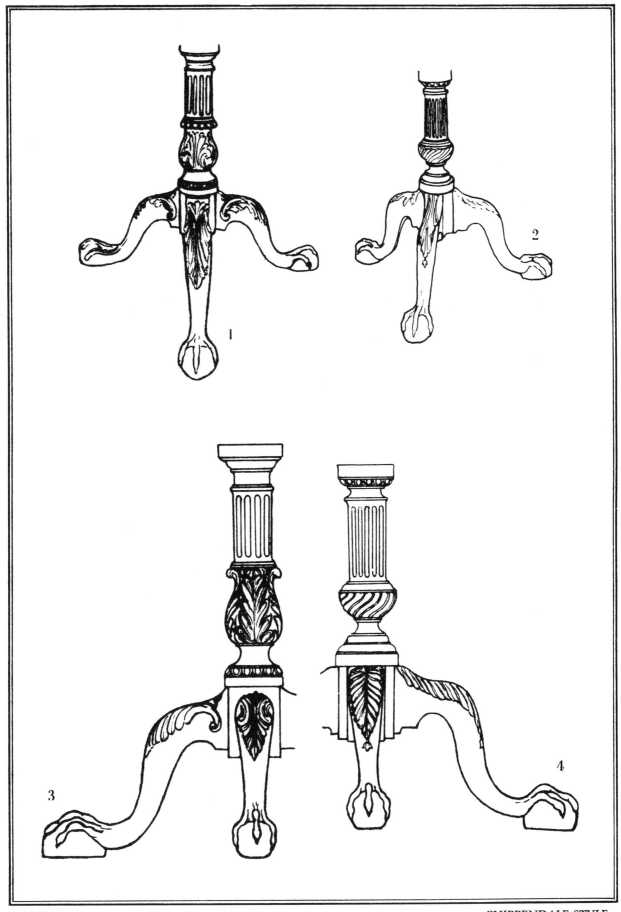

PLATE 187.

CHIPPENDALE STYLE.

1 and 2. Legs of pedestal tables.   3 and 4. Decorations on same.

Victoria and Albert Museum and private collection.

PLATE 188.

CHIPPENDALE STYLE.

1. Canopy bed.   2. Detail of post.   3, 4, 5 and 6. Posts of other beds in the same style.

The Gentleman and Cabinet Maker's Director. T. Chippendale.

PLATE 189.   CHIPPENDALE STYLE.
1. Simple commode with straight lines.   2. Detail of upper corner.   3. Detail of lower moulding and foot.
4. Escutcheon plate.   5. Drawer pull.

Private collection.

PLATE 190. CHIPPENDALE STYLE.
1. Simple commode with curved lines.   2. Detail of upper corner.   3. Frieze decoration on upright.   4. Lower moulding and foot.   5. Drawer pull.

Private collection.

PLATE 191.   CHIPPENDALE STYLE.

1. Tall commode with severe lines. 2. Cornice decoration. 3. Moulding at base of upper section. 4. Lower moulding and foot. 5. Drawer pull.

Private collection.

PLATE 192. CHIPPENDALE STYLE.
1 and 2. Desks designed by Chippendale.   3. Upper moulding of first desk.   4. Decoration on foot.   5. Detail of mouldings on second desk.   6 and 7. Drawer pulls on second desk.

The Gentleman and Cabinet Maker's Director. T. Chippendale.

PLATE 193.   CHIPPENDALE STYLE.

1 and 2. Desks designed by Chippendale.   3. Comparison of mouldings on the two desks.   4. Middle escutcheon plate of first desk.   5. Side escutcheon plate of second desk.   6. Drawer pull.

The Gentleman and Cabinet Maker's Director. T. Chippendale.

197

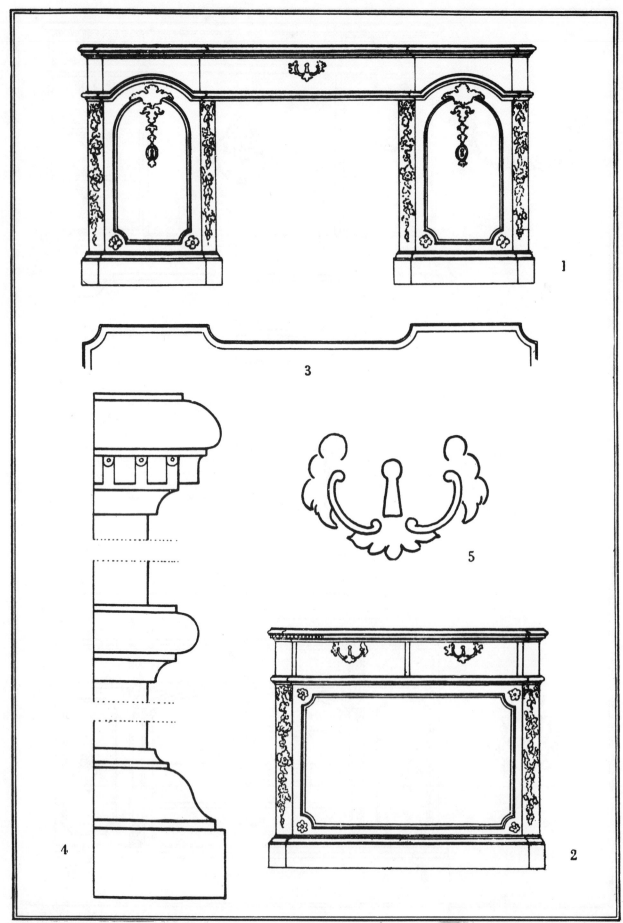

PLATE 194.   CHIPPENDALE STYLE.

1. Desk designed by Chippendale.   2. Side.   3. Silhouette of top.   4. Detail of cornice, mouldings and base.
5. Drawer pull.

The Gentleman and Cabinet Maker's Director. T. Chippendale.

198

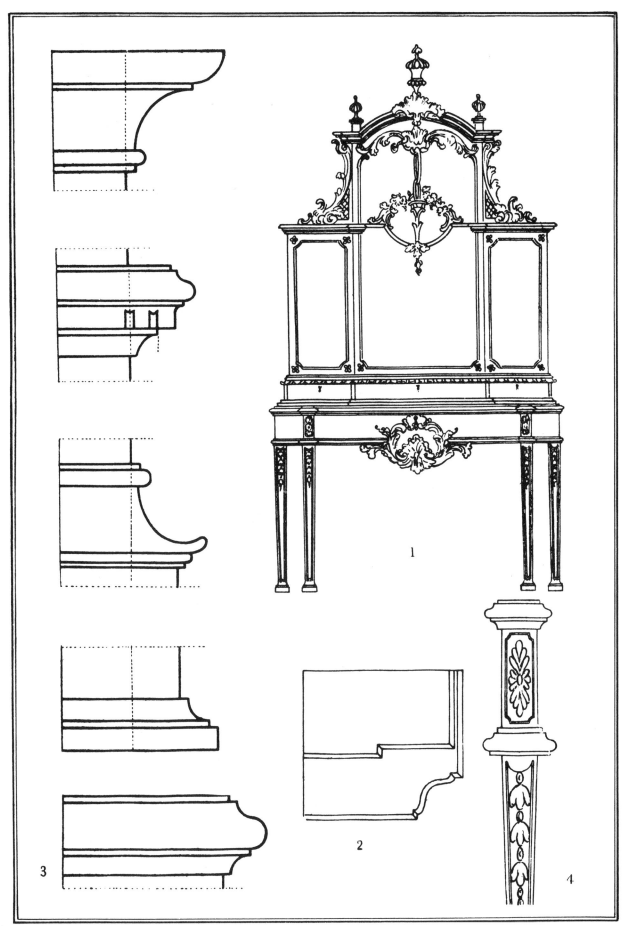

PLATE 195.   CHIPPENDALE STYLE.

1. Lady's desk designed by Chippendale.   2. Bottom of the table top and upper section.   3. Detail of cornices and
mouldings.   4. Decoration on legs.

The Gentleman and Cabinet Maker's Director. T. Chippendale.

PLATE 196.

CHIPPENDALE STYLE

1. Lady's secretary designed by Chippendale.   2. Bottom of tabletop and upper section.   3. Detail of cornices and mouldings.   4. Leg.

The Gentleman and Cabinet Maker's Director. T. Chippendale.

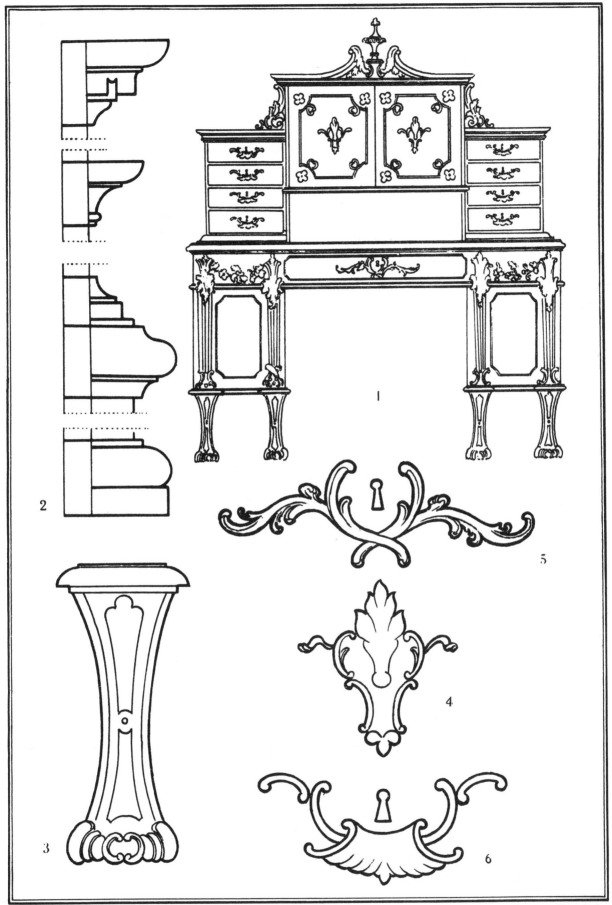

PLATE 197.   CHIPPENDALE STYLE.

1. Secretary designed by Chippendale.   2. Detail of cornices and mouldings.   3. Leg.   4. Central decoration on upper panels.   5 and 6. Escutcheon plates.

The Gentleman and Cabinet Maker's Director. T. Chippendale.

201

PLATE 198.   CHIPPENDALE STYLE.

1. Secretary designed by Chippendale.   2. Detail of cornices and mouldings.   3. Decoration on foot.

The Gentleman and Cabinet Maker's Director. T. Chippendale.

PLATE 199.   CHIPPENDALE STYLE.
1. Secretary designed by Chippendale.   2. Detail of cornices and mouldings.   3. Detail of middle section, covered
when secretary is closed.

The Gentleman and Cabinet Maker's Director. T. Chippendale.

203

PLATE 200.   CHIPPENDALE STYLE.

1. Secretary with architectonic frame designed by Chippendale.   2. Detail of cornice, mouldings and foot decoration.   3. Detail of middle section, covered when secretary is closed.   4. Drawer pull.

The Gentleman and Cabinet Maker's Director. T. Chippendale.

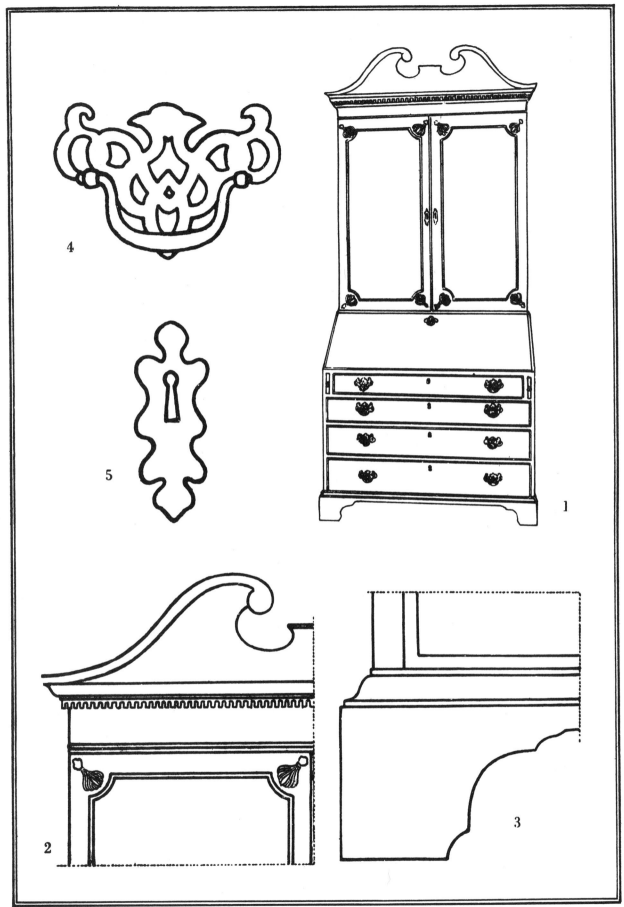

PLATE 201.   CHIPPENDALE STYLE.
1. Secretary.   2. Detail of crest and decoration.   3. Detail of foot.   4. Drawer pull.   5. Escutcheon plate.
Private collection.

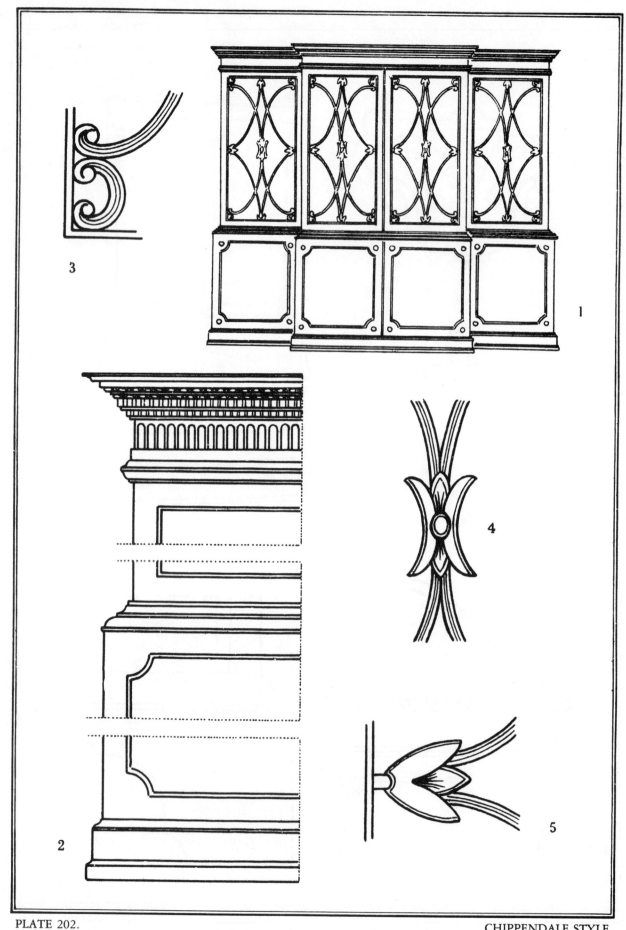

PLATE 202.   CHIPPENDALE STYLE.
1. Beautiful four-piece bookcase.   2. Detail of cornice, mouldings and socle.   3, 4 and 5. Decorations on glass doors.
Property of the Life Insurance Company, Norwich Union.

PLATE 203.

CHIPPENDALE STYLE.

1. Bookcase designed by Chippendale. 2. Cornice. 3. Crest. 4. Base and lower moulding of upper section. 5. Mouldings of lower section.

The Gentleman and Cabinet Maker's Director. T. Chippendale.

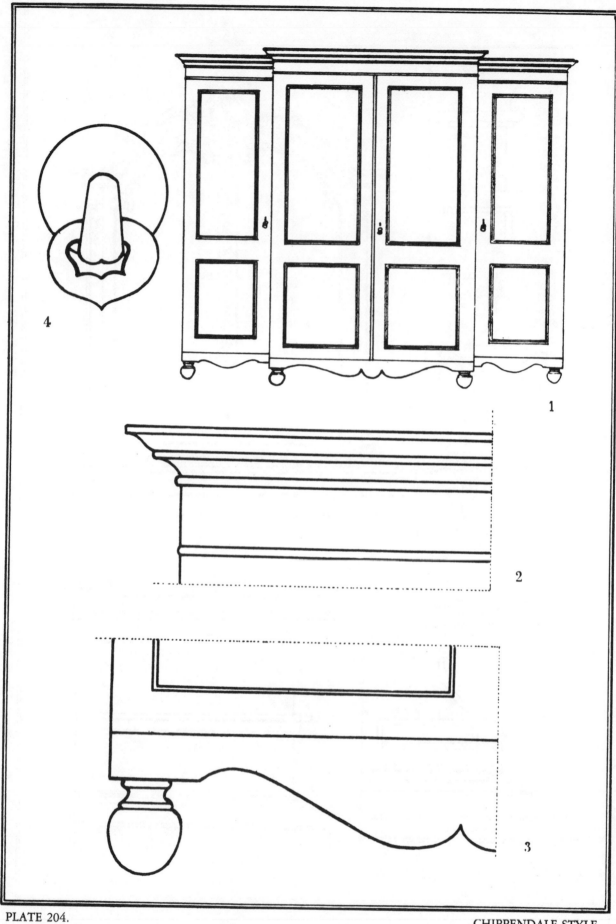

PLATE 204.

CHIPPENDALE STYLE.

1. Simple wardrobe.   2. Cornice.   3. Detail of foot and lower profile.   4. Door knob.

Private collection.

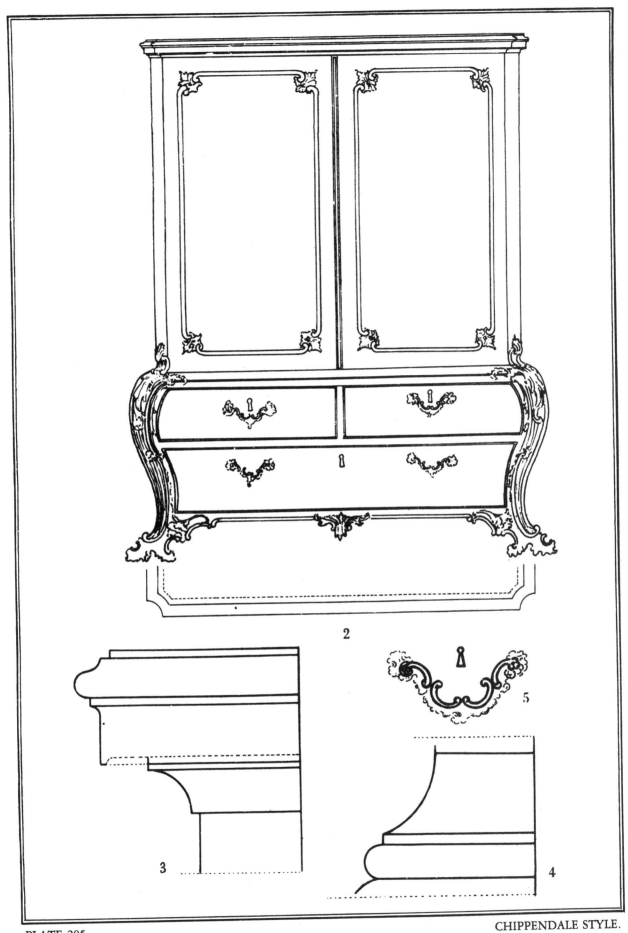

PLATE 205.

1. Wardrobe commode designed by Chippendale.   2. Base of lower section.   3. Cornice.   4. Moulding at base of upper section.   5. Drawer pull.

CHIPPENDALE STYLE.

The Gentleman and Cabinet Maker's Director. T. Chippendale.

PLATE 206.

1. Irish Chippendale showcase.   2. Decoration of crest, mouldings and glass panes.   3. Decoration on foot and lower crosspiece.   4. Drawer pull.

Private collection.

PLATE 207.
1 and 2. Mirrors with sprung frames.   3 and 4. Details of same.

CHIPPENDALE STYLE.

Private collection.

2

1

PLATE 208.

CHIPPENDALE STYLE.

1. Ornately decorated clock case. 2. Details of crest, face and mouldings.

Pennsylvania Museum, Philadelphia.

PLATE 209.

1. Irish Chippendale clock case.   2. Decoration of crest and mouldings.   3. Socle.

CHIPPENDALE STYLE.

Private collection.

PLATE 210.

1. Clock case with Chippendale traits.   2. Decorations, columns and mouldings.   3. Socle.

Private collection.

PLATE 211.   CHIPPENDALE STYLE.

1. Clock case with Chinese motifs, designed by Chippendale.   2. Decorations: crest, column, mouldings and socle.

The Gentleman and Cabinet Maker's Director. T. Chippendale.

2

1

PLATE 212.

1. Clock case designed by Chippendale. 2. Decorations: crest, frieze, pilaster, mouldings and foot.

The Gentleman and Cabinet Maker's Director. T. Chippendale.

PLATE 213.
1. Case for desk clock designed by Chippendale.   2. Decorations.   3. Base of upper cornice.   4. Lower base.

CHIPPENDALE STYLE.

The Gentleman and Cabinet Maker's Director. T. Chippendale.

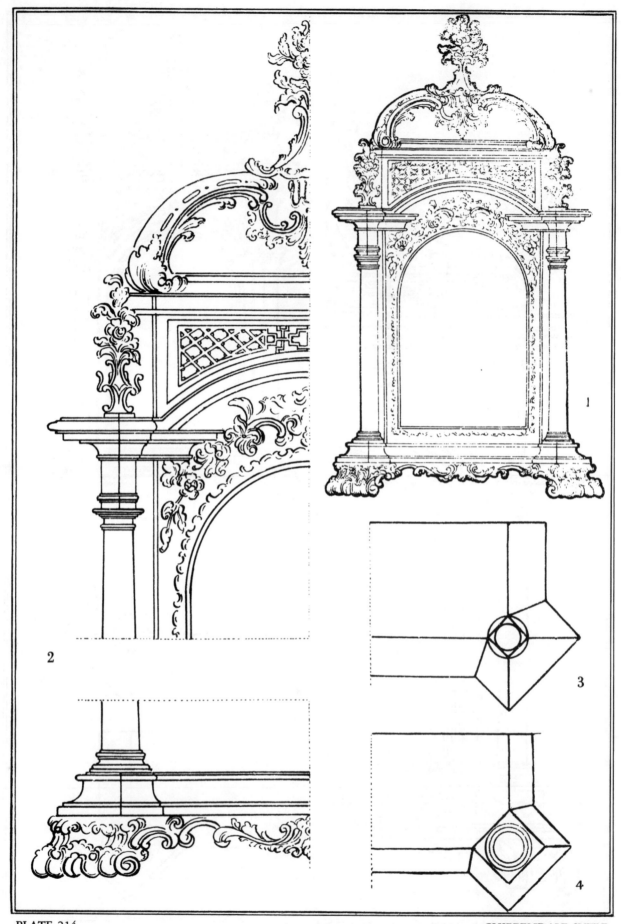

PLATE 214.
1. Case for desk clock designed by Chippendale.   2. Decorations.   3. Base of upper cornice.   4. Lower base.

CHIPPENDALE SYTLE.

The Gentleman and Cabinet Maker's Director. T. Chippendale.

218

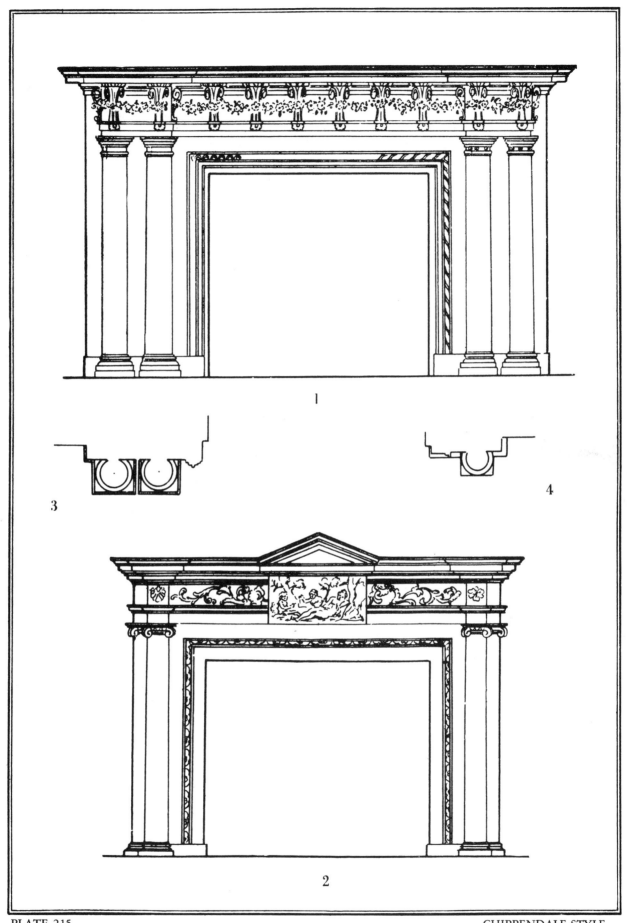

1

3

4

2

PLATE 215.   CHIPPENDALE STYLE.
1 and 2. Fireplaces designed by Chippendale.   3. Base of first fireplace.   4. Base of second fireplace.
The Gentleman and Cabinet Maker's Director. T. Chippendale.

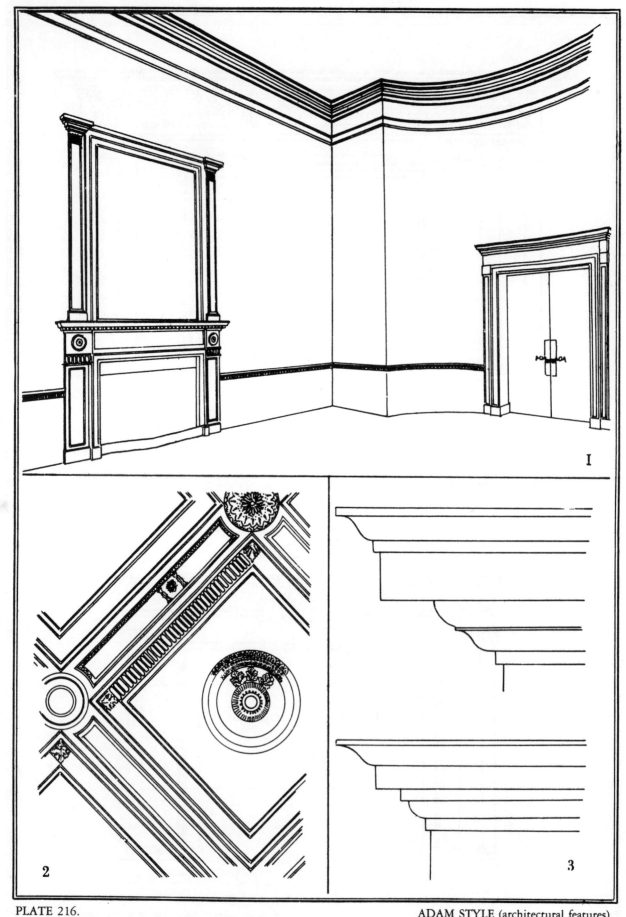

PLATE 216.

ADAM STYLE (architectural features).

1. Room designed by Adam, 20 St. James Square, London.   2. Ceiling section designed by Adam, foyer of Syon House.   3. Types of moulding used during period.

PLATE 217.   ADAM STYLE (architectural features).
1. Room designed by Adam, foyer of Kedleston.   2. Sketches by Robert Adam for door decorations.   3. Door, dining room at 20 St. James Square, London.   4. Type of Venetian window often used by Adam.   5. Window, pavilion of Hopeton House.

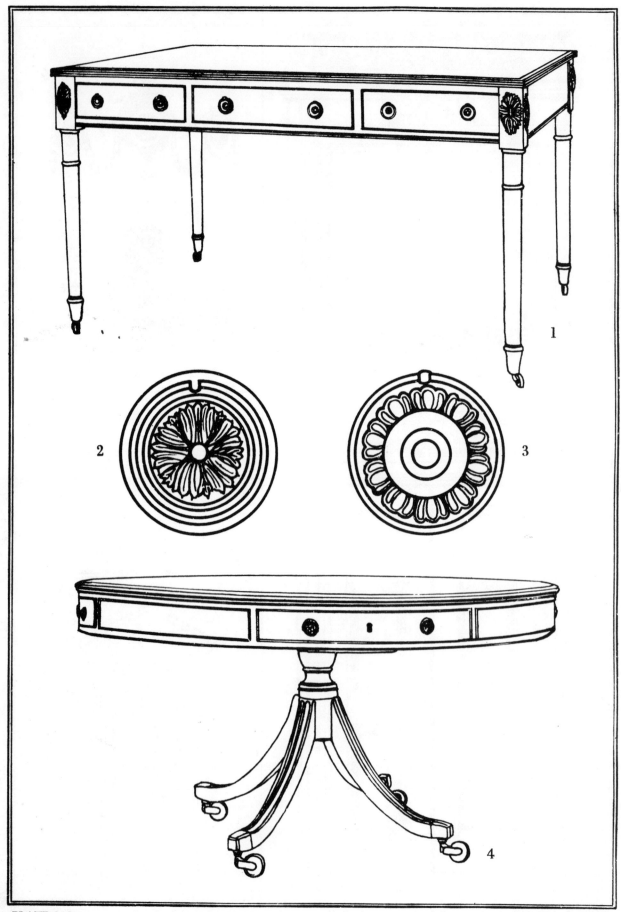

PLATE 218.
1 and 4. Adam tables.   2 and 3. Drawer pulls.

ADAM STYLE.

Private collections.

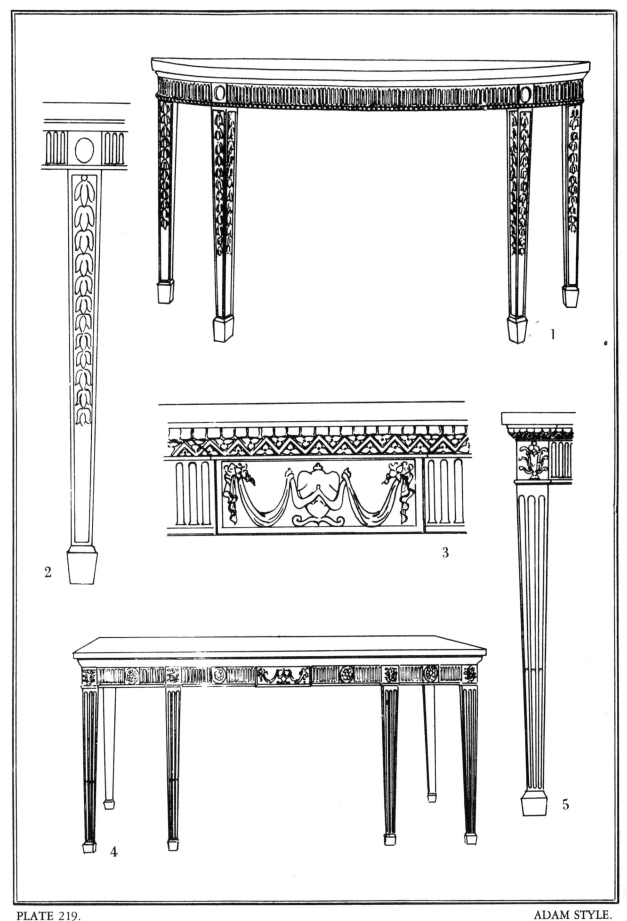

PLATE 219.   ADAM STYLE.

1 and 4. Adam console tables.   2 and 5. Decorations on their respective legs.   3. Central detail of frieze on second table.

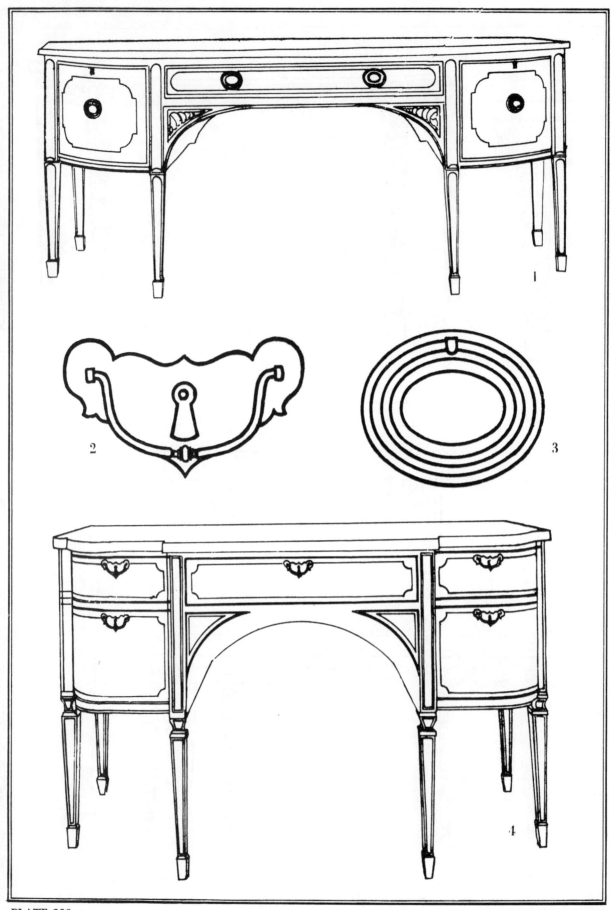

PLATE 220.
1 and 4. Adam credenzas.   2 and 3. Drawer pulls.

ADAM STYLE.

Private collection.

224

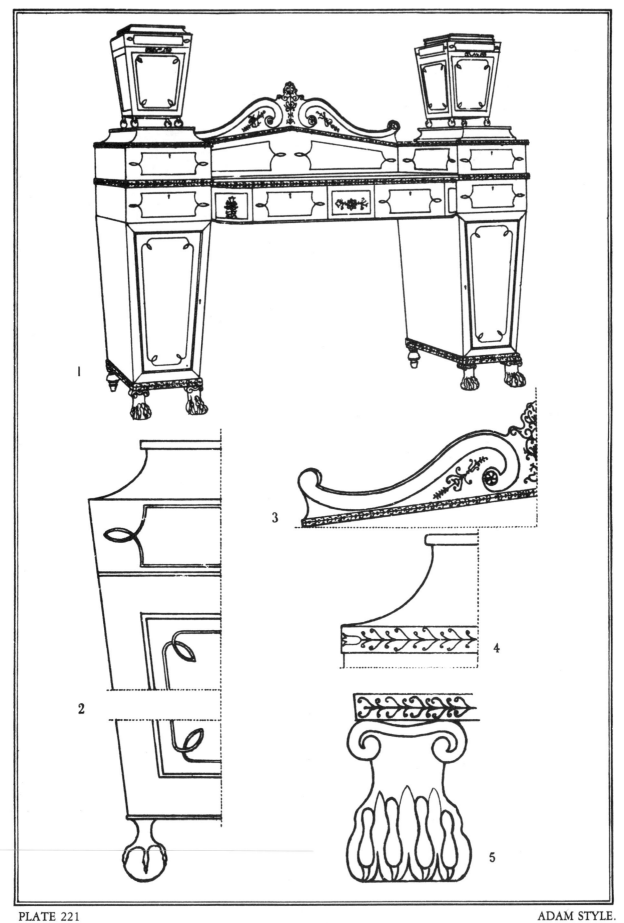

PLATE 221   ADAM STYLE.

1. Adam desk.   2. Detail of urns.   3. Detail of crest.   4. Detail of base for urns.   5. Leg.

Victoria and Albert Museum.

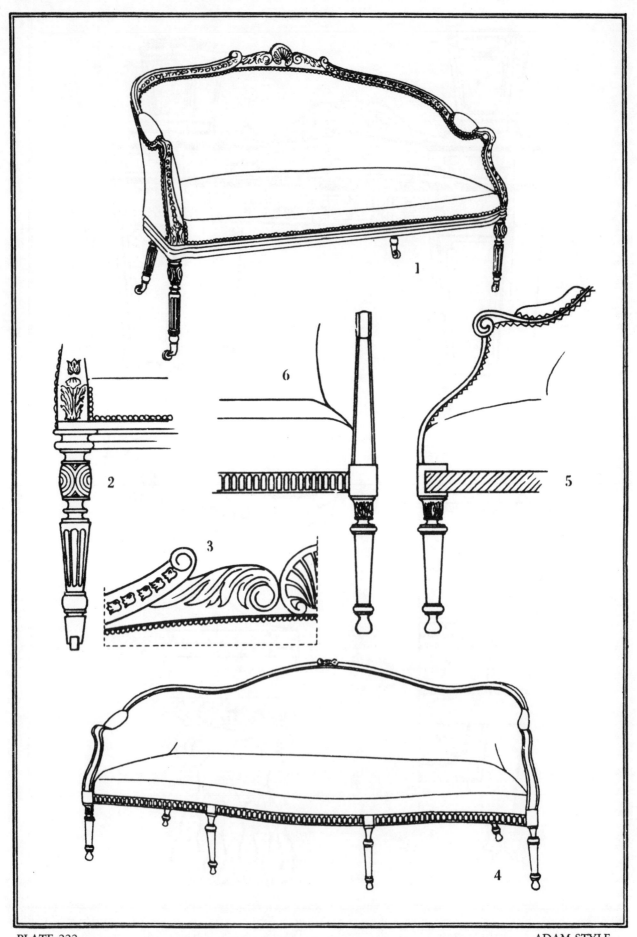

PLATE 222.   ADAM STYLE.
1 and 4. Adam sofas.   2 and 3. Decorations on first sofa—leg and crest.   5 and 6. Decorations on second sofa—leg and arm.

Property of F. W. Phillips.

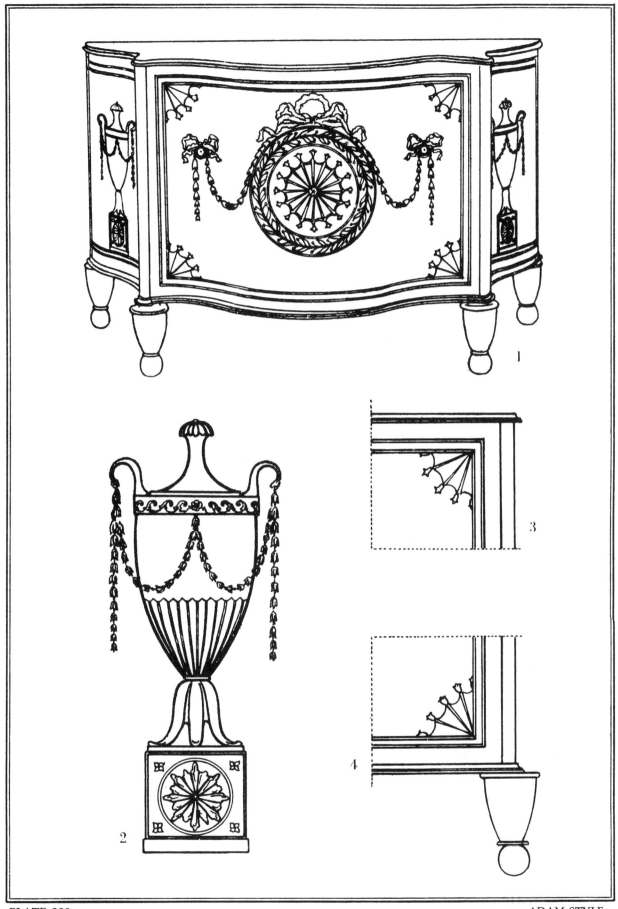

PLATE 223.   ADAM STYLE.

1. Adam commode.   2. Decoration on side panels.   3 and 4. Decorations on corners and leg.

Victoria and Albert Museum.

227

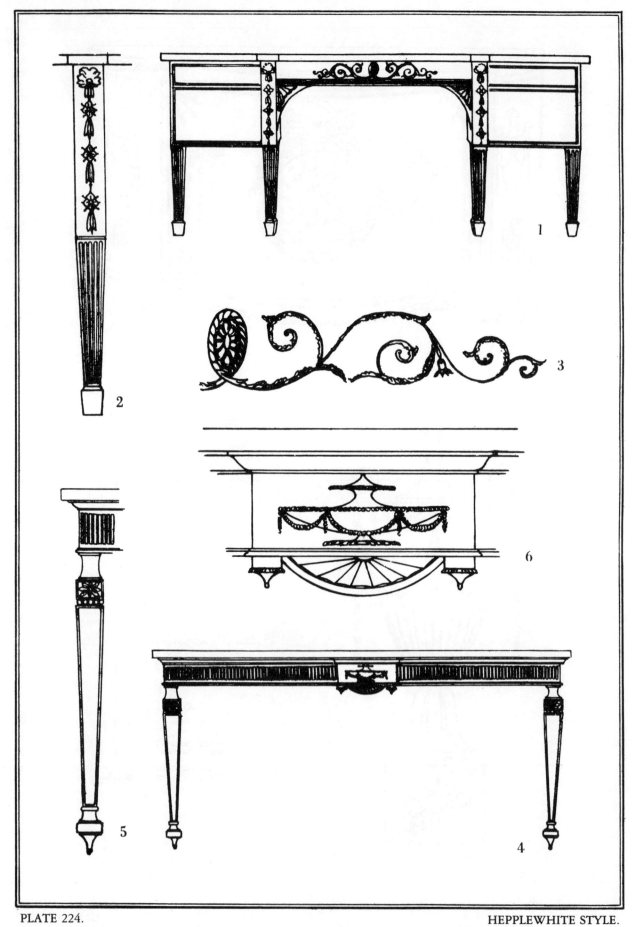

PLATE 224.   HEPPLEWHITE STYLE.

1 and 4. Hepplewhite console tables. 2 and 5. Decorations on legs. 3. Central detail of frieze on first table. 6. Central detail of frieze on second table.

The Cabinet-Maker and Upholsterer's Guide. G. Hepplewhite.

228

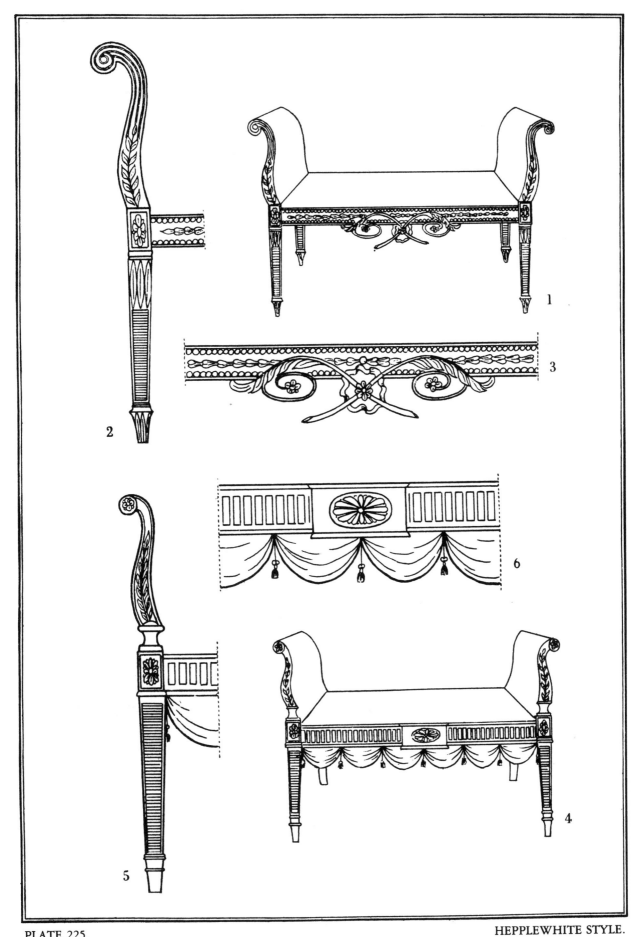

PLATE 225.   HEPPLEWHITE STYLE.

1 and 4. Hepplewhite benches.   2 and 3. Decorations on first one—leg, arm and crosspiece.   5 and 6. Decorations on second one—leg, arm and crosspiece.

The Cabinet-Maker and Upholsterer's Guide. G. Hepplewhite.

229

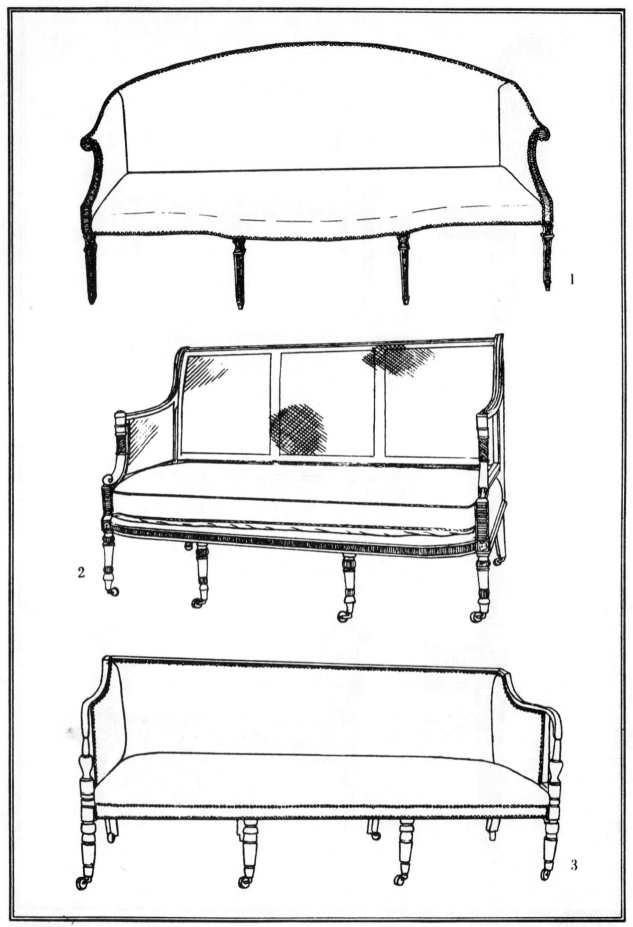

PLATE 226.   HEPPLEWHITE STYLE.

Hepplewhite sofas: 1. From *The Cabinet-Maker and Upholsterer's Guide*. 2. Property of F. W. Phillips. 3. Private collection.

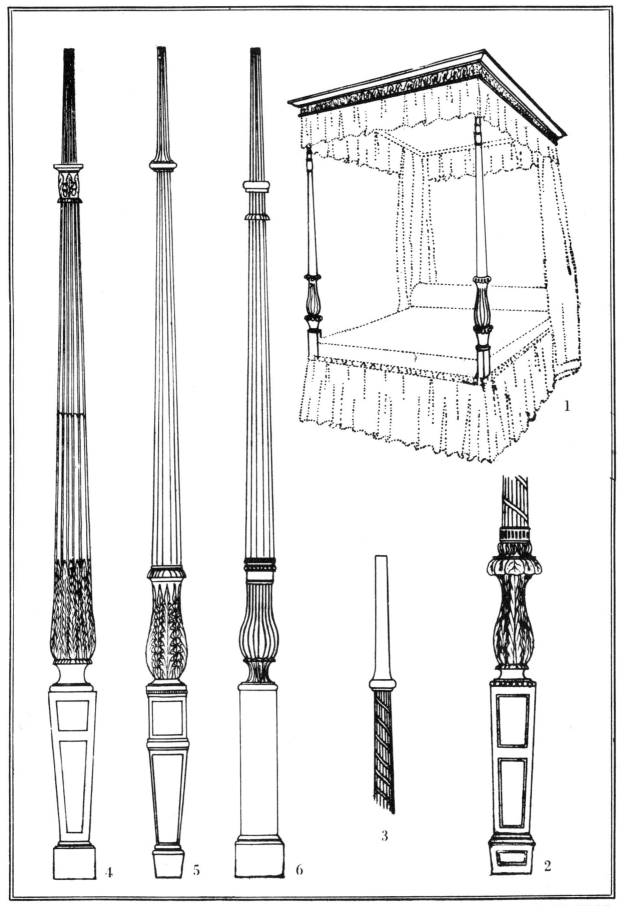

1. Hepplewhite canopy bed.   2 and 3. Details of post.   4, 5 and 6. Other posts in the same style.

The Cabinet-Maker and Upholsterer's Guide. G. Hepplewhite.

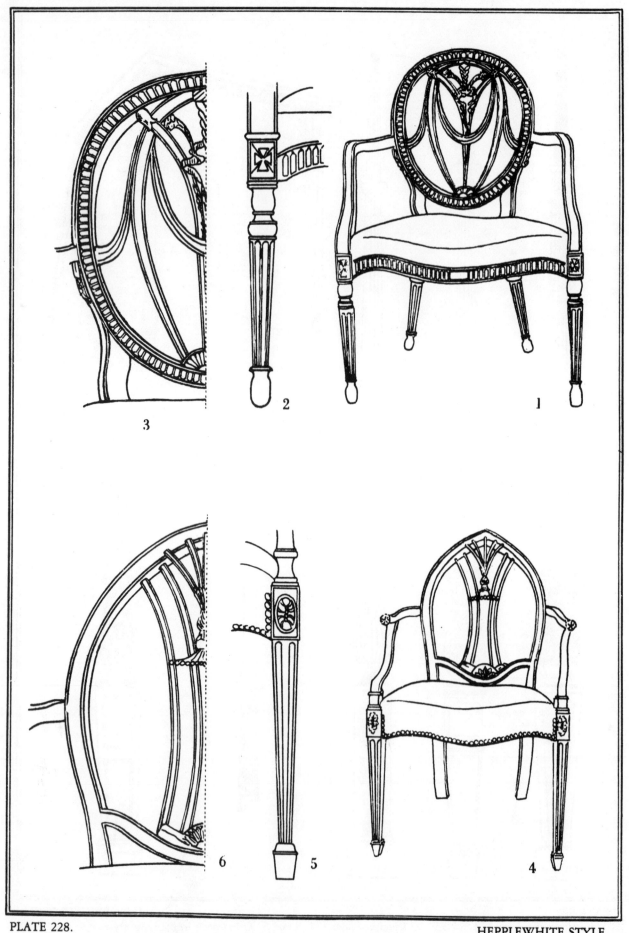

PLATE 228.   HEPPLEWHITE STYLE.
1. Hepplewhite armchair.   2. Detail of leg.   3. Detail of back.   4. Hepplewhite armchair.   5. Detail of leg.
6. Detail of back.

Victoria and Albert Museum and property of F. W. Phillips.

232

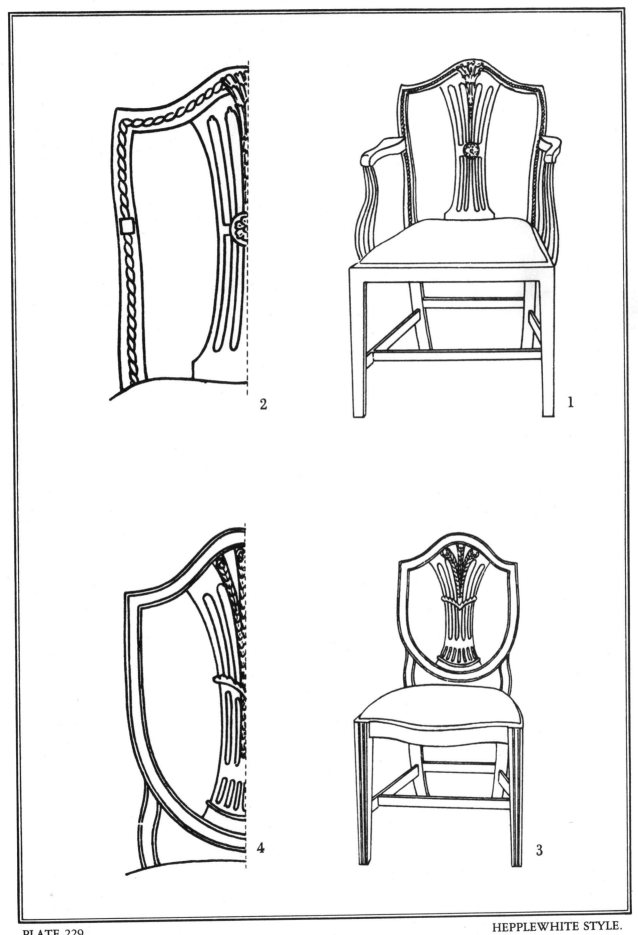

PLATE 229.
1. Hepplewhite armchair.   2. Detail of back.   3. Hepplewhite chair.   4. Detail of back.

Private collection and property of F. W. Phillips.

HEPPLEWHITE STYLE.

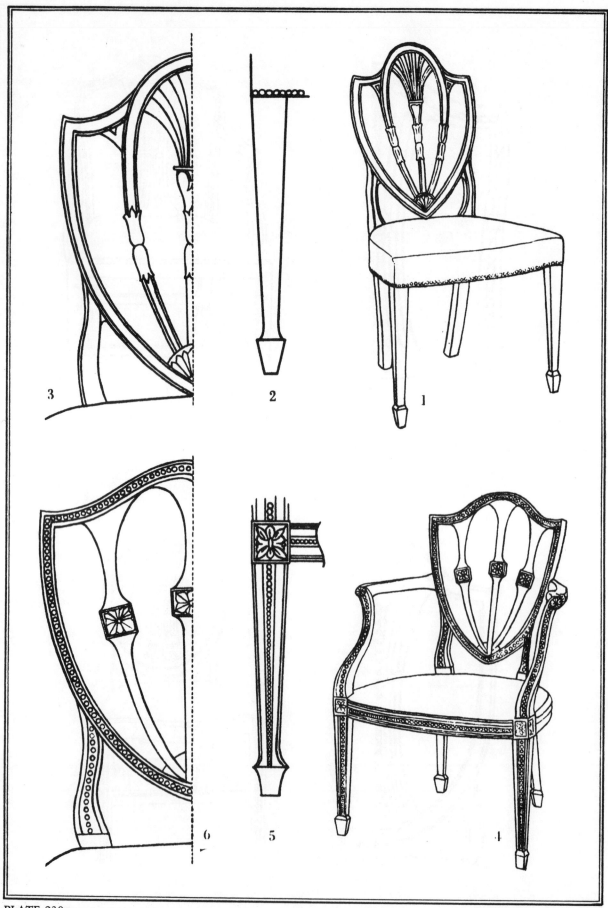

PLATE 230.

HEPPLEWHITE STYLE.

1. Hepplewhite armchair with shield-shaped back.   2. Front leg.   3. Detail of back.   4. Hepplewhite armchair with shield back.   5. Front leg.   6. Detail of back.

Metropolitan Museum of Art.

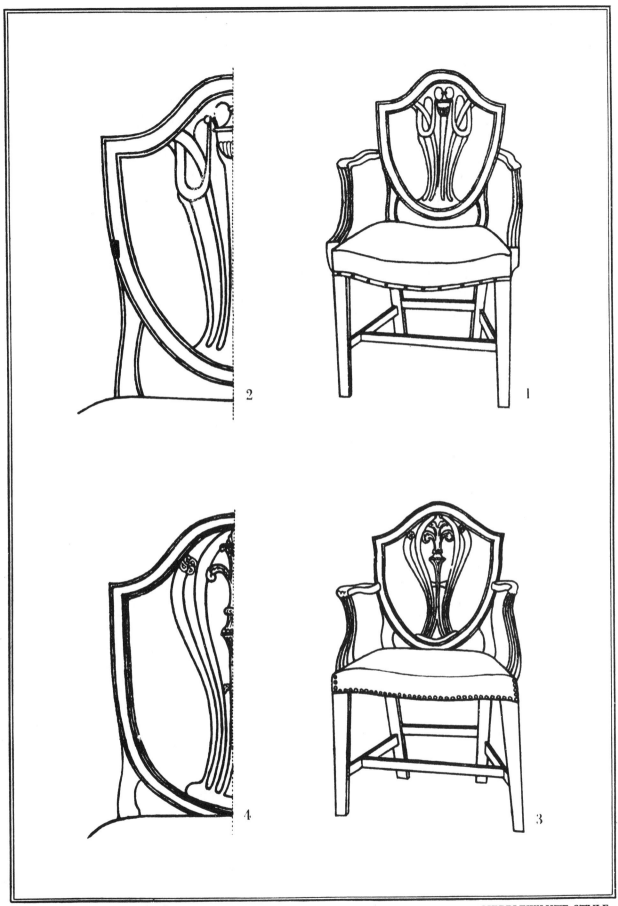

PLATE 231.   HEPPLEWHITE STYLE.

1. Hepplewhite armchair with shield back.   2. Detail of back.   3. Hepplewhite armchair with shield back.   4. Detail of back.

Private collection and Victoria and Albert Museum.

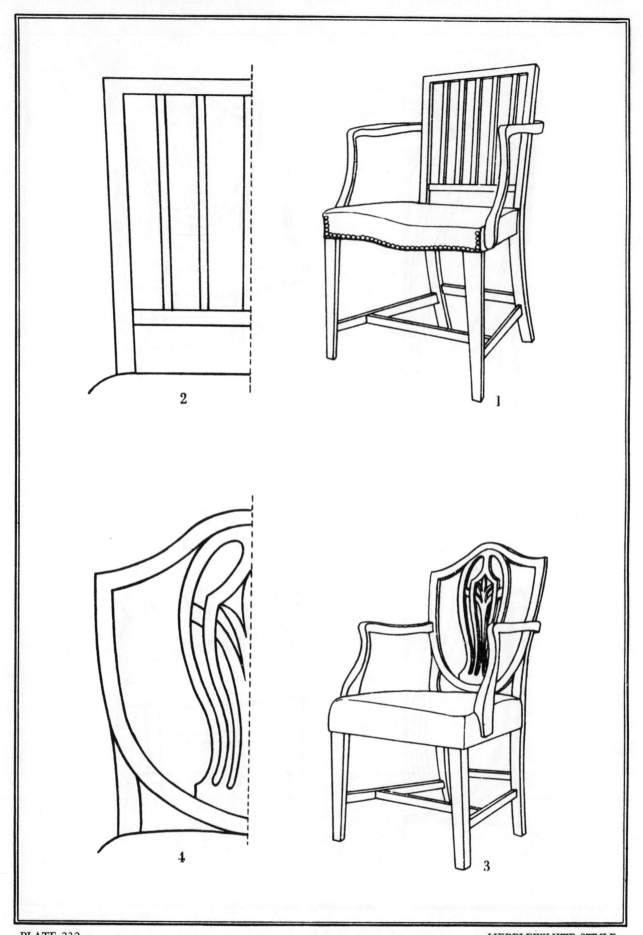

PLATE 232.   HEPPLEWHITE STYLE.
1. Hepplewhite armchair.   2. Detail of back.   3. Hepplewhite armchair with shield back.   4. Detail of back.
Private collection and North Ockenden Hall, Essex.

236

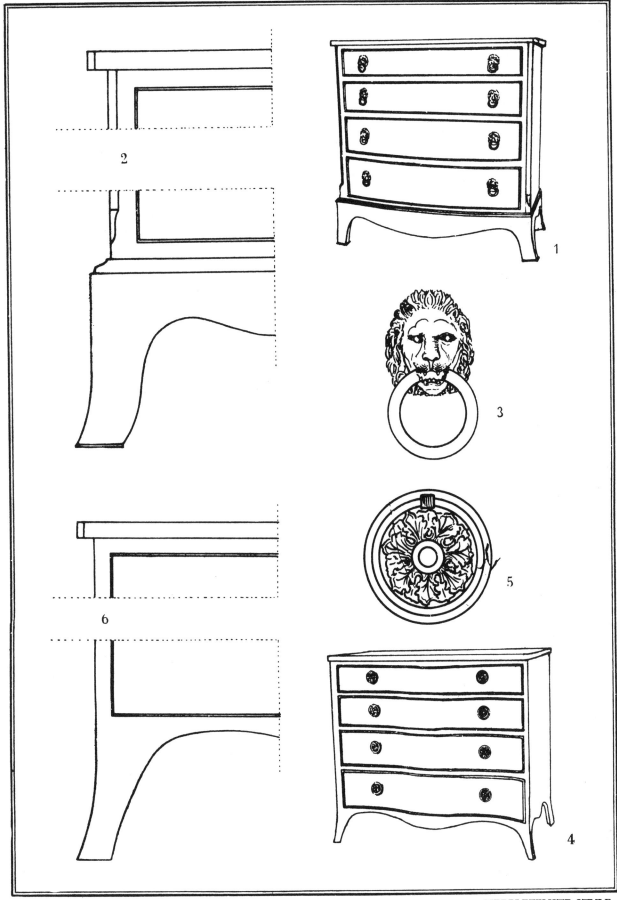

PLATE 233.   HEPPLEWHITE STYLE.

1 and 4. Hepplewhite commodes.   2 and 3. Details of first commode; moulding, foot and drawer pull.   5 and
6. Details of second commode: drawer pull and foot.

Private collection.

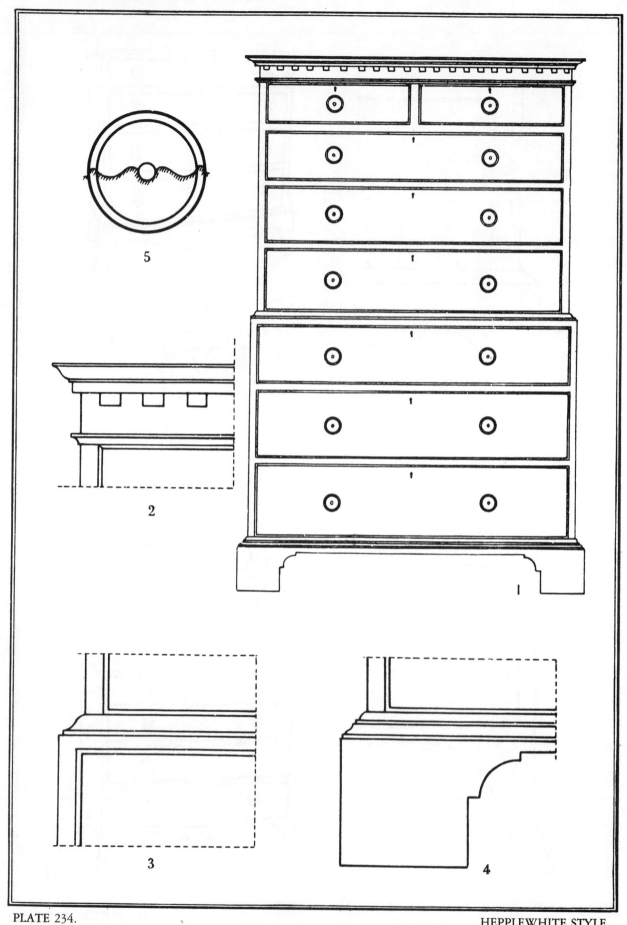

PLATE 234.   HEPPLEWHITE STYLE.
1. Tall Hepplewhite commode.   2. Cornice.   3. Base of upper section.   4. Mouldings at base of lower section and
foot.   5. Drawer pull.

The Cabinet-Maker and Upholsterer's Guide. G. Hepplewhite.

PLATE 235.

1. Hepplewhite secretary. 2. Detail of middle section of secretary, covered when closed. 3. Crest, cornice and glass decoration. 4. Base of lower section and foot. 5. Drawer pull.

HEPPLEWHITE STYLE.

The Cabinet-Maker and Upholsterer's Guide. G. Hepplewhite.

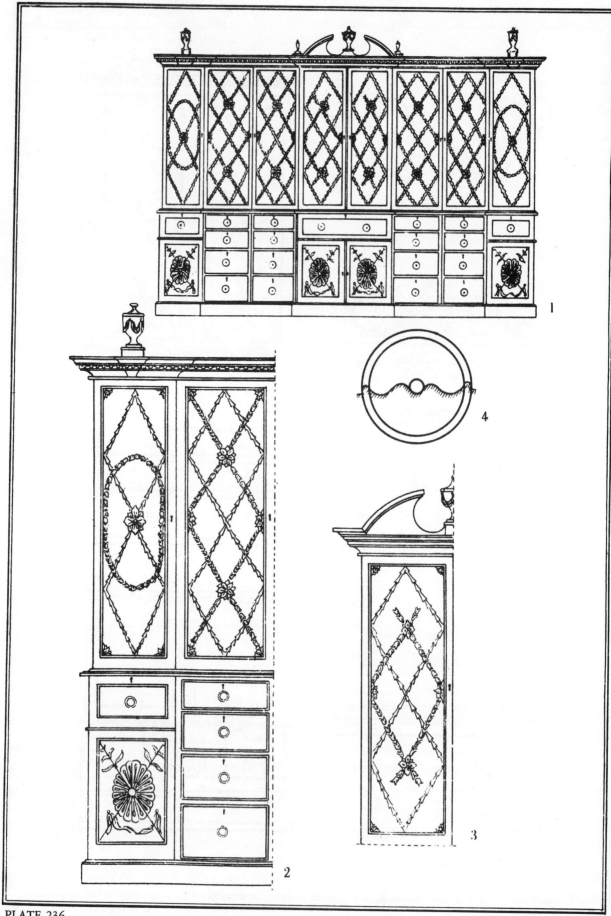

PLATE 236.

1. Hepplewhite bookcase.   2. Detail of side sections.   3. Detail of glass pane central finial.   4. Drawer pull.

HEPPLEWHITE STYLE.

The Cabinet-Maker and Upholsterer's Guide. G. Hepplewhite.

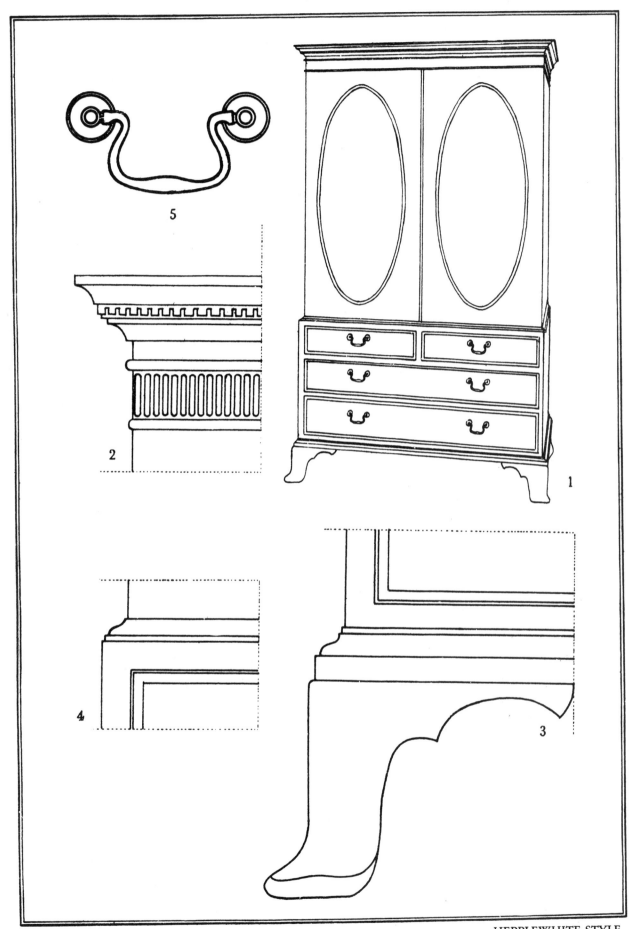

PLATE 237.   HEPPLEWHITE STYLE.
1. Hepplewhite wardrobe commode.   2, 3 and 4. Decorations: cornice, frieze, mouldings and leg.   5. Drawer pull.
Property of F. W. Phillips.

Sheraton

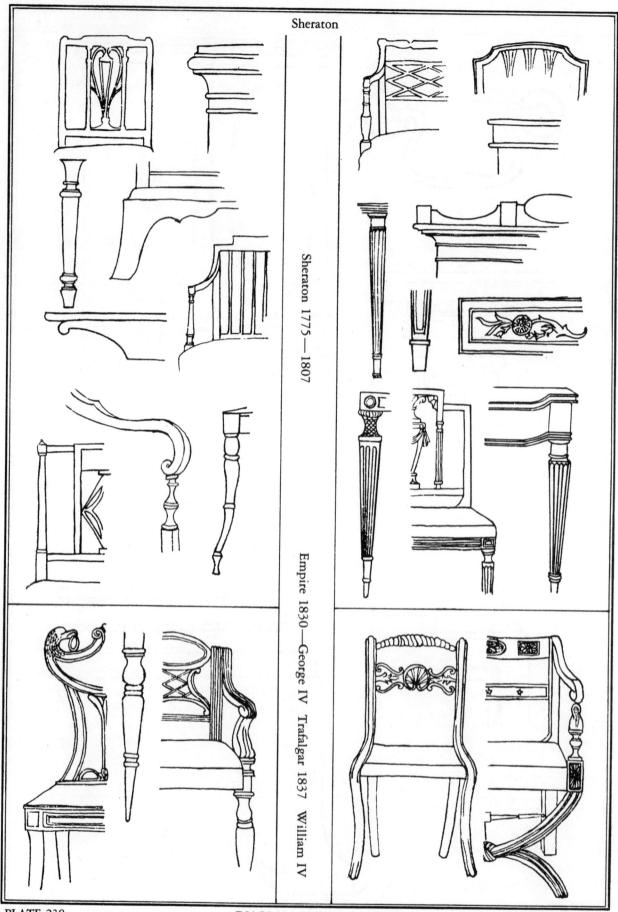

Sheraton 1775—1807

Empire 1830—George IV Trafalgar 1837 William IV

PLATE 238.

DIAGRAM OF THE DEVELOPMENT OF THE SHERATON STYLE.

242

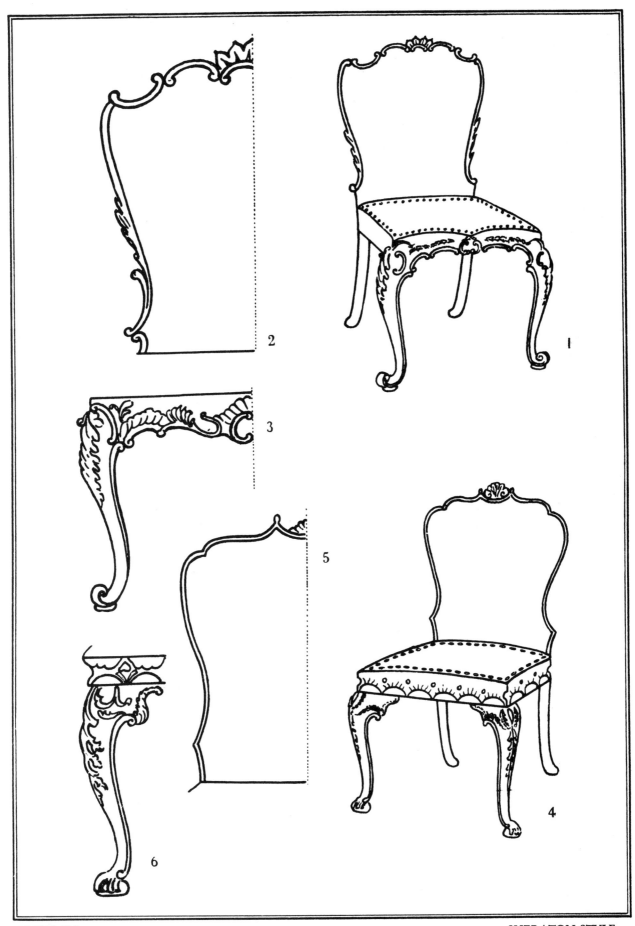

PLATE 239   SHERATON STYLE.

1 and 4. Chairs with upholstered backs and seats.   2 and 5. Detail of their respective backs.   3. Decoration on leg
and edge of seat of first chair.   6. Decoration on leg of second chair.

Universal Systems of Household Furniture 1762, Ince and Mayhew.

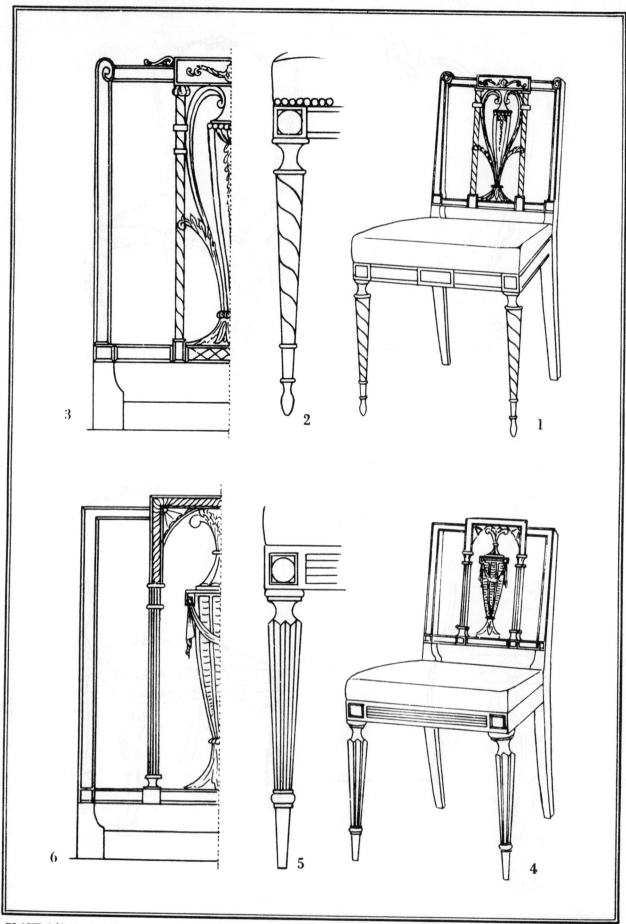

PLATE 240.

SHERATON STYLE.

1 and 4. Sheraton chairs with urn design on backs.   2 and 5. Details of front legs.   3 and 6. Details of backs.

Album of designs by Sheraton.

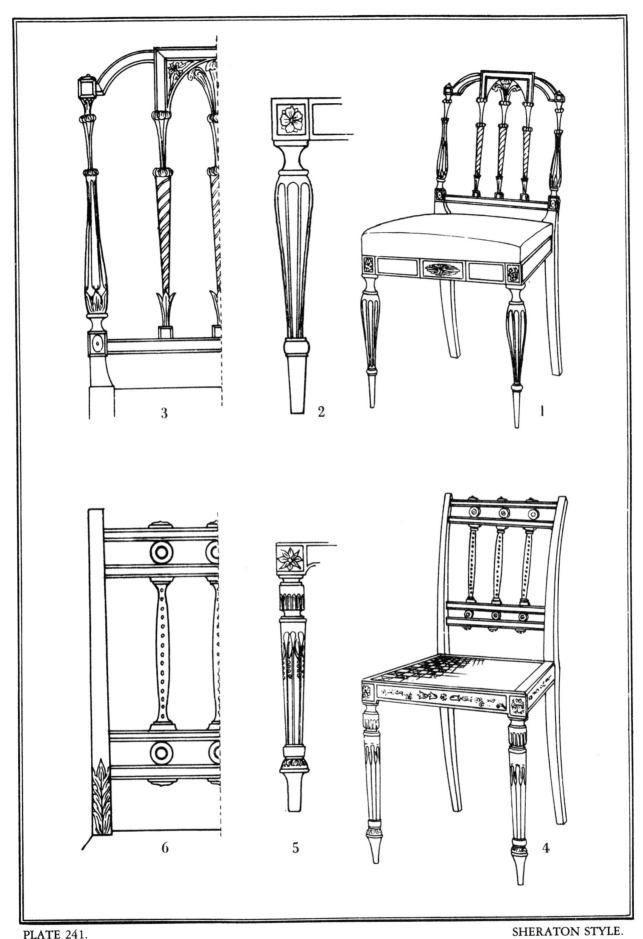

PLATE 241.   SHERATON STYLE.
1. Sheraton chair.   2. Front leg.   3. Detail of back.   4. Sheraton chair.   5. Front leg.   6. Detail of back.
Album of designs by Sheraton and collection of George Stoner, West Wickham, Kent.

245

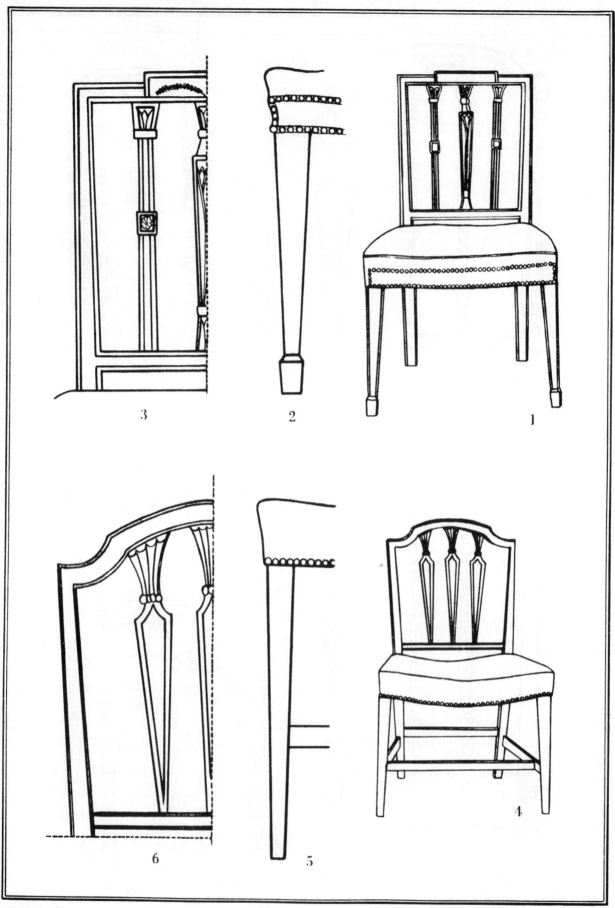

PLATE 242.   SHERATON STYLE.
1 and 4. Sheraton chairs showing Hepplewhite influence.   2 and 5. Front legs.   3 and 6. Details of backs.

Private collection.

246

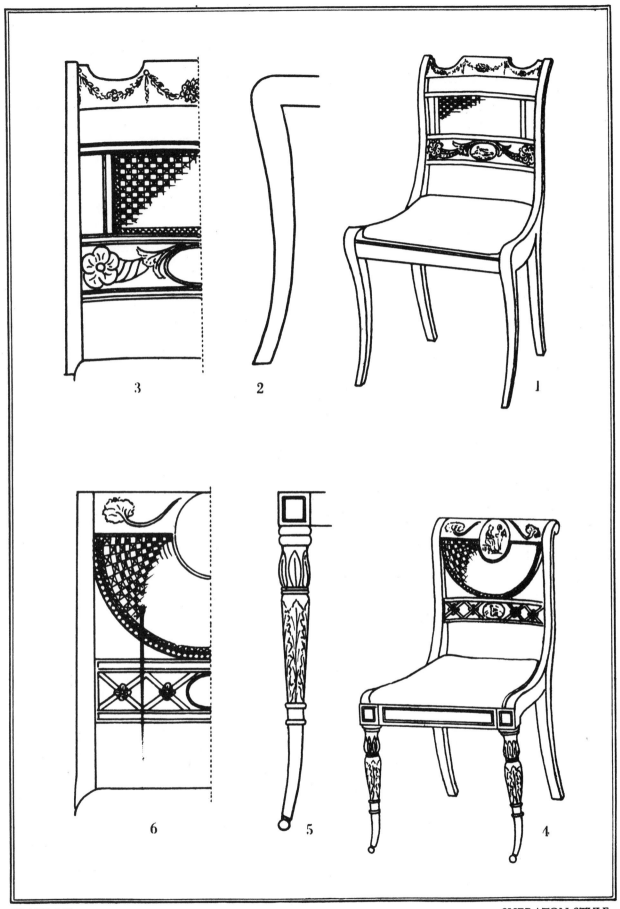

3 2 1

6 5 4

PLATE 243. SHERATON STYLE.
1 and 4. Sheraton chairs. 2 and 5. Front legs. 3 and 6. Details of backs.

Collection of George Stoner, West Wickham, Kent.

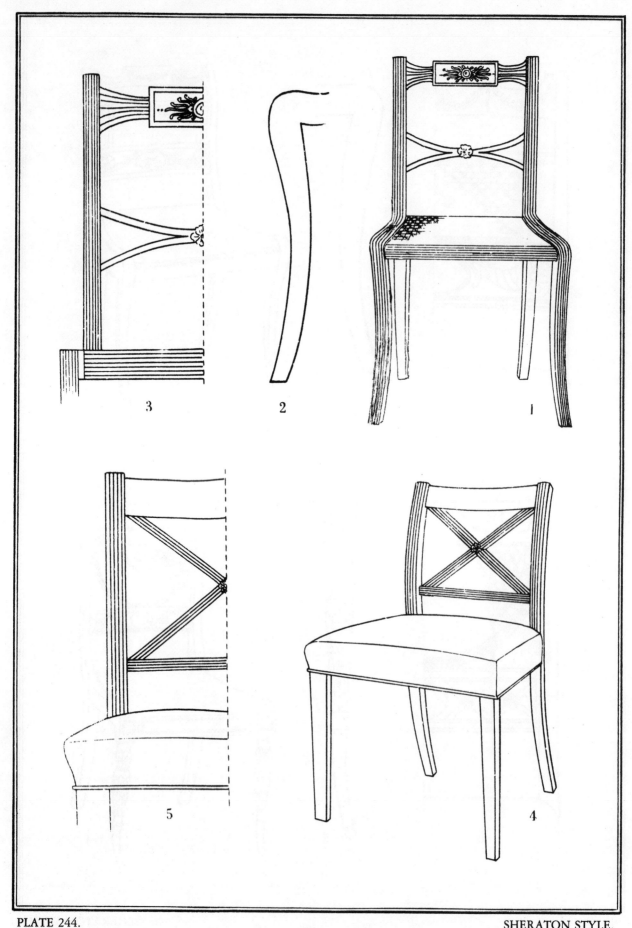

PLATE 244.   SHERATON STYLE.

1. Sheraton chair showing influence of Adam.   2. Front leg.   3. Detail of back.   4. Sheraton chair showing influence of Adam.   5. Detail of back.

Property of Sir Spencer Ponsonby-Fane and a private collection.

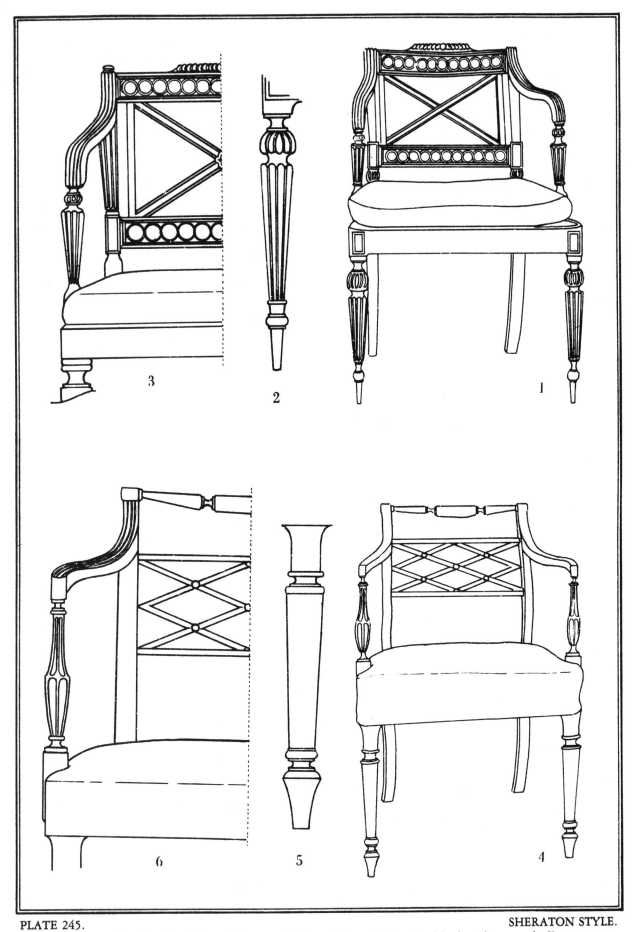

PLATE 245.   SHERATON STYLE.
1. Sheraton armchair showing Adam influence. 2. Front leg. 3. Details of back and arm. 4. Sheraton arm-chair. 5. Front leg. 6. Details of back and arm.

Victoria and Albert Museum (private property) and a private collection.

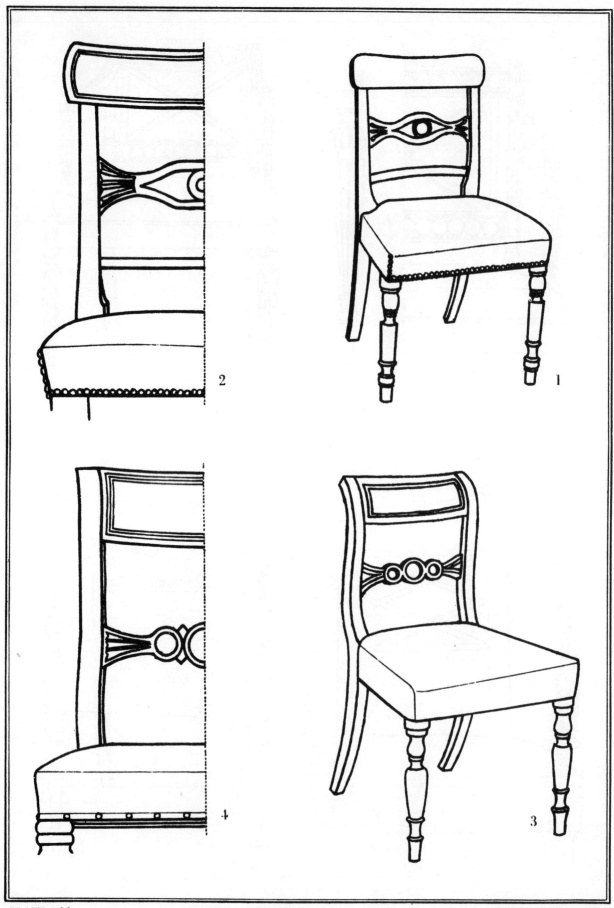

PLATE 246.

SHERATON STYLE.

1 and 3. Chairs from the last Sheraton period, early 19th century.   2 and 4. Detail of backs.

Victoria and Albert Museum.

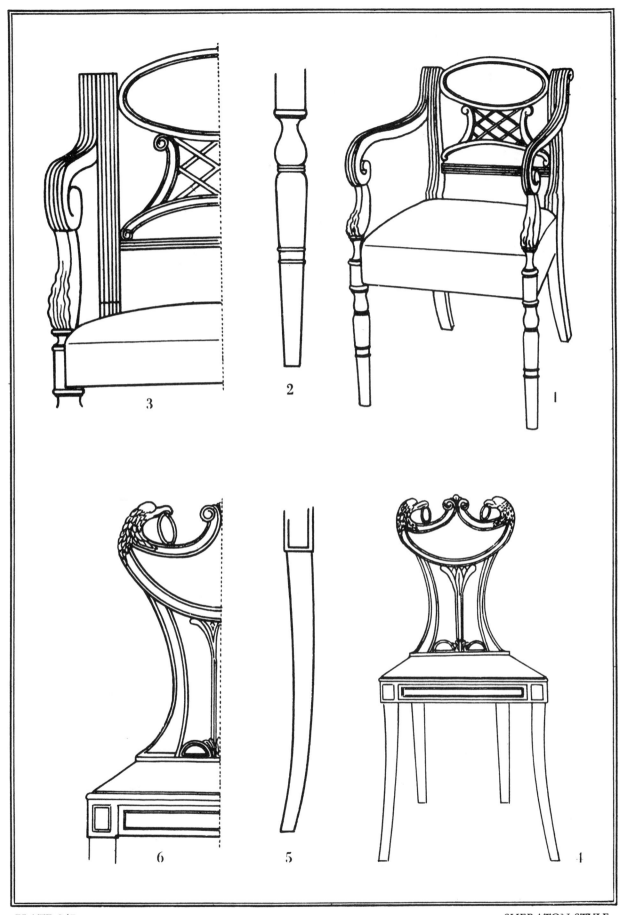

PLATE 247.   SHERATON STYLE.

1. Armchair in English Empire style.   2. Front leg.   3. Detail of back and arm.   4. Chair in English Empire
style.   5. Front leg.   6. Detail of back.

Private collection and Victoria and Albert Museum.

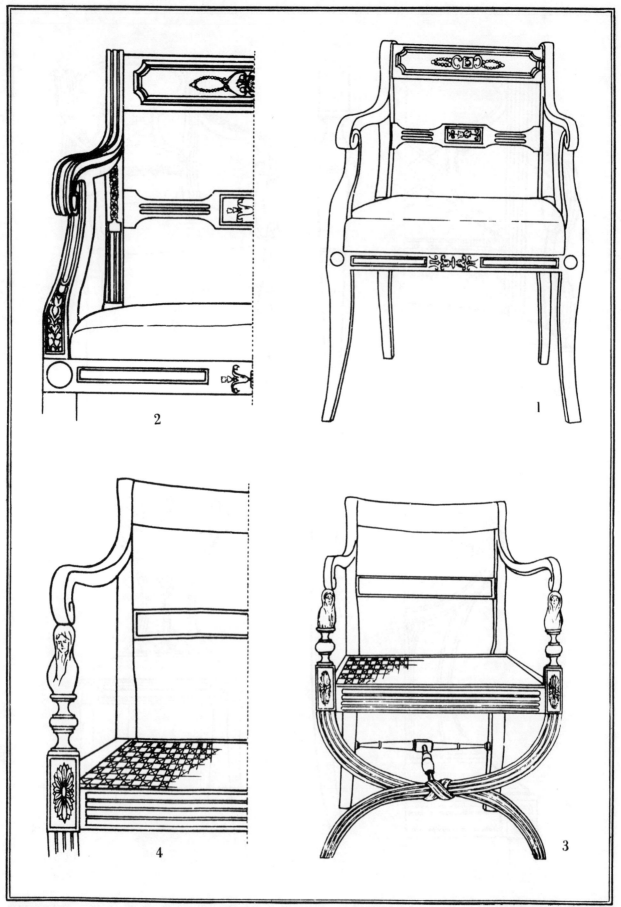

PLATE 248.

SHERATON STYLE.

1 and 3. Sheraton armchairs showing Adam and Trafalgar influence. 2 and 4. Details of backs and arms.

Property of Sir Spencer Ponsonby-Fane.

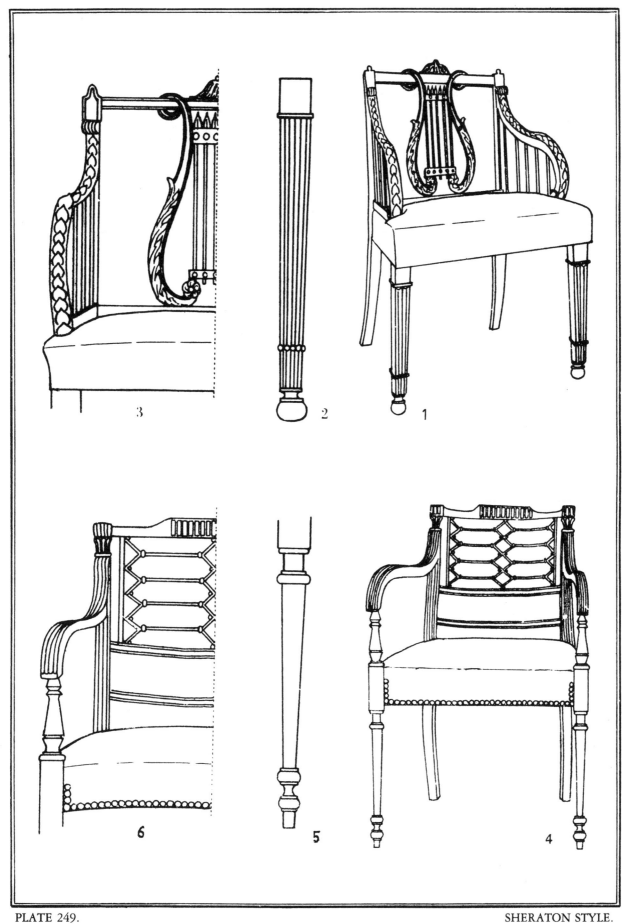

PLATE 249.   SHERATON STYLE.

1. Sheraton armchair.   2. Front leg.   3. Details of back and arm.   4. Sheraton armchair.   5. Front leg.   6. Details
of back and arm.

Victoria and Albert Museum and property of Henry Willet of Brighton.

253

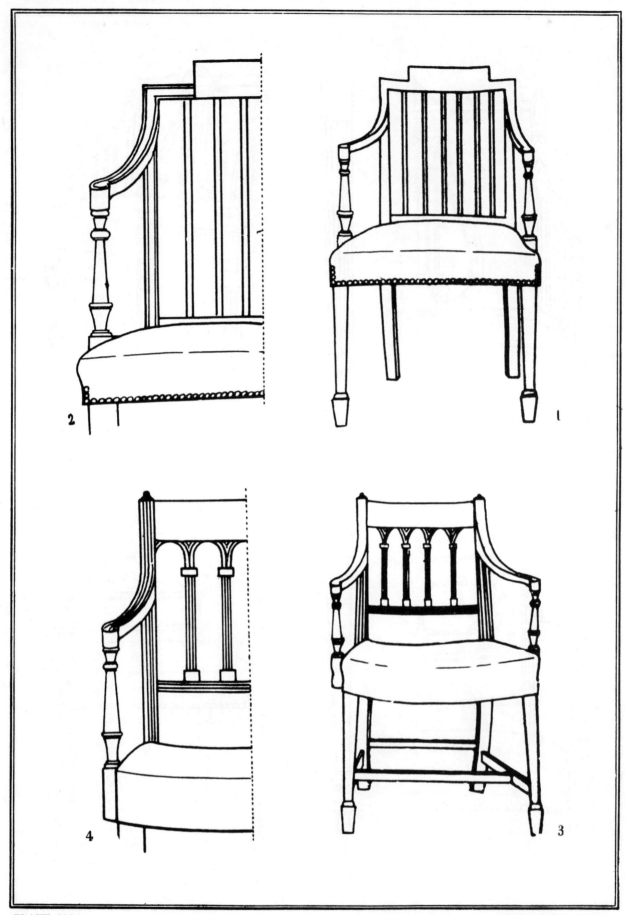

PLATE 250.   SHERATON STYLE.
1. Sheraton armchair.   2. Details of back and arm.   3. Sheraton armchair.   4. Details of back and arm.
Property of E. Hugh Spottiswoode and Victoria and Albert Museum.

PLATE 251.   SHERATON STYLE.

1 and 4. Sheraton armchairs.   2 and 5. Front legs.   3 and 6. Detail of backs.

Album of designs by Sheraton.

PLATE 252.   SHERATON STYLE
1 and 4. Sheraton armchairs.   2 and 5. Front legs.   3 and 6. Details of backs.

Victoria and Albert Museum.

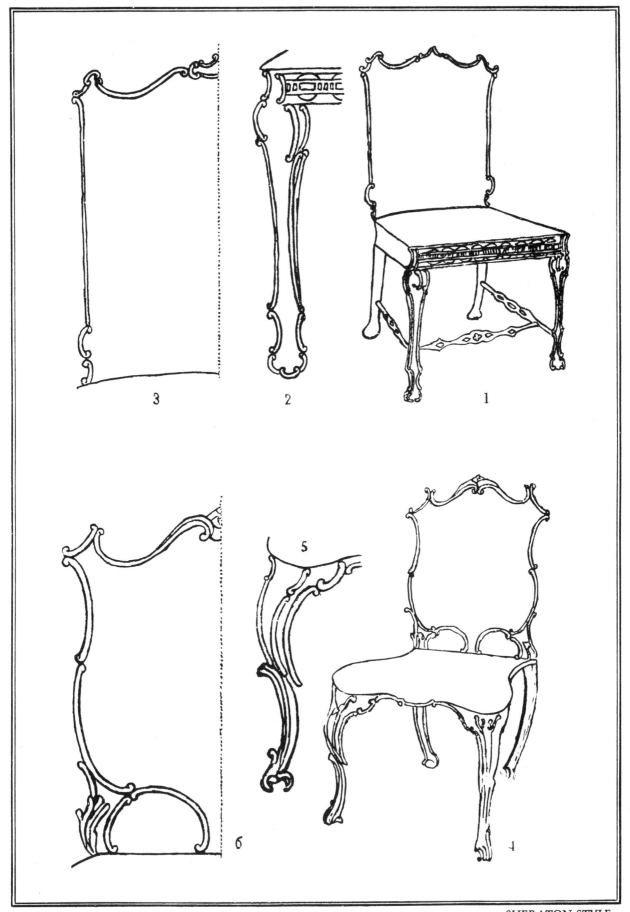

PLATE 253.   SHERATON STYLE.
1 and 4. Sketches of chairs.   2 and 5. Details of legs.   3 and 6. Details of backs.
The Universal System of Household Furniture 1762. Ince and Mayhew.

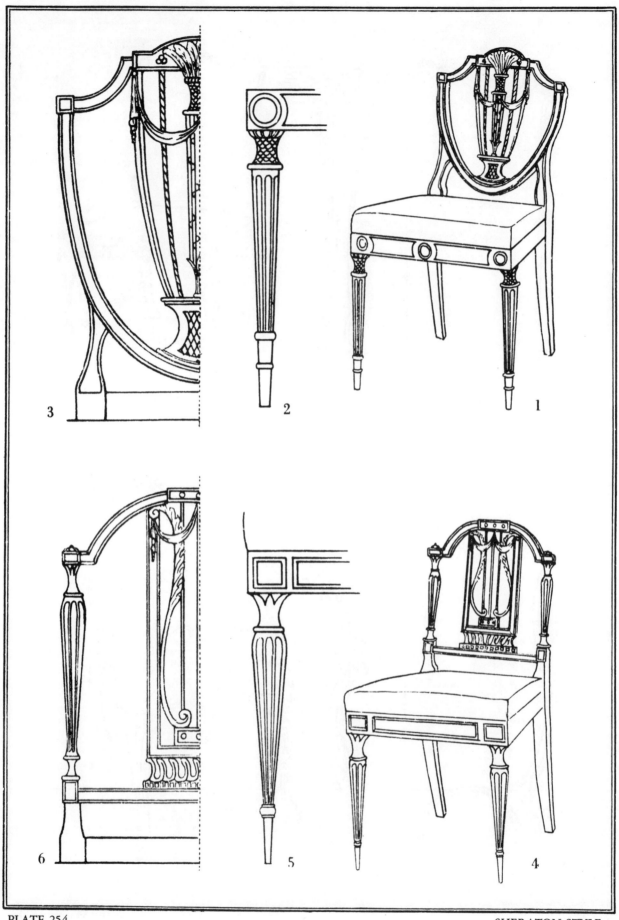

PLATE 254.

SHERATON STYLE.

1 and 4. Sheraton chairs. 2 and 5. Detail of front legs. 3 and 6. Detail of backs.

Album of designs by Sheraton.

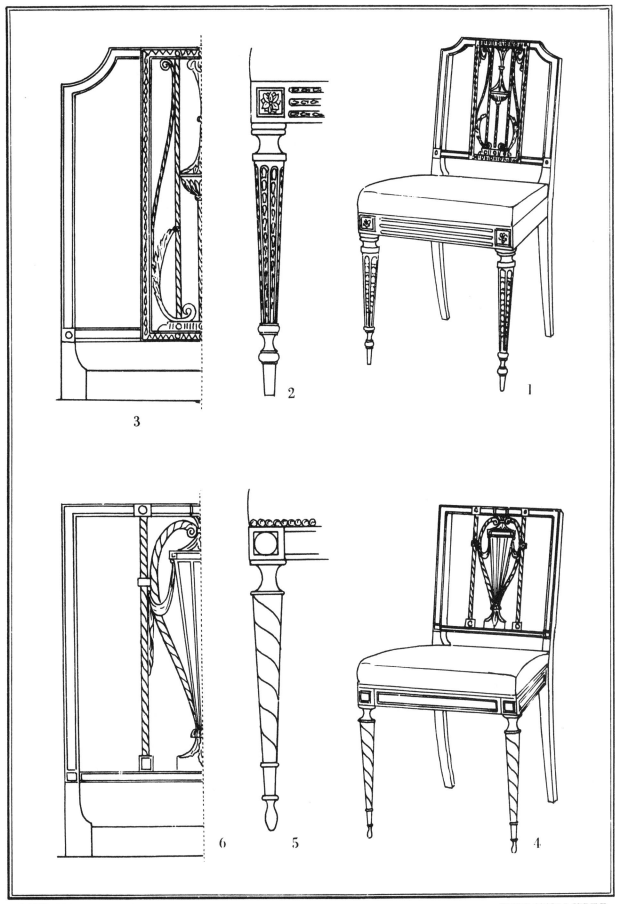

PLATE 255.
1 and 4. Sheraton chairs.   2 and 5. Detail of front legs.   3 and 6. Detail of backs.

SHERATON STYLE.

Album of designs by Sheraton.

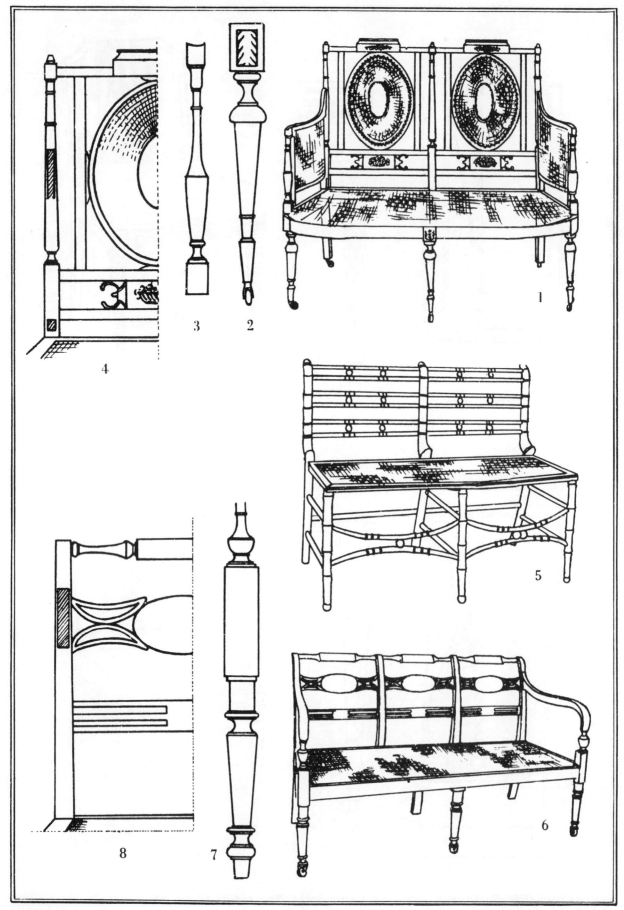

PLATE 256.   SHERATON STYLE.

1. Sheraton sofa.   2. Leg.   3. Arm support.   4. Detail of back.   5. Sheraton sofa.   6. Sheraton sofa.   7. Leg.
8. Detail of back.

Property of Mr. Edward; a private collection and property of F. W. Phillips.

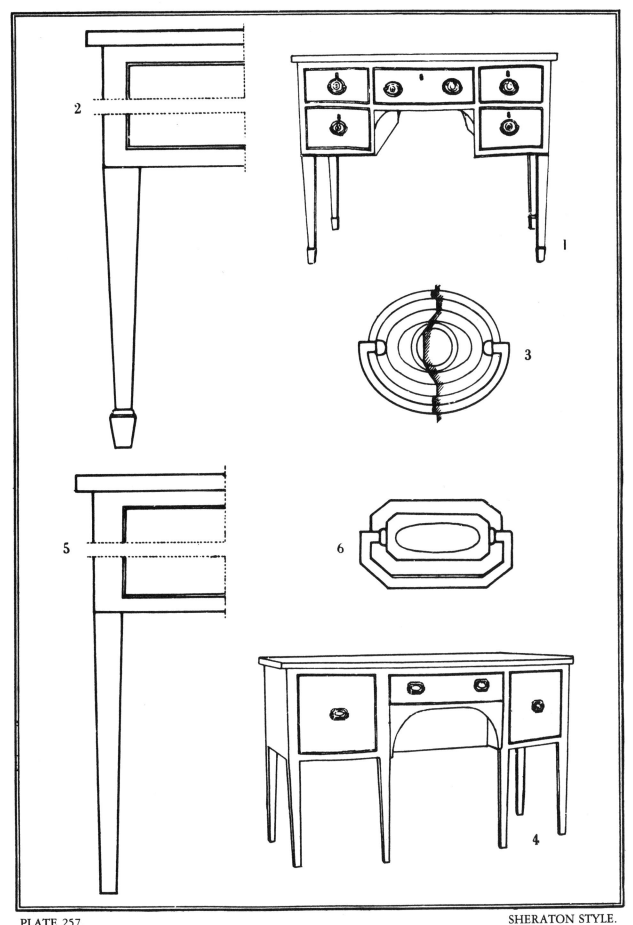

PLATE 257.   SHERATON STYLE.

1. Sheraton desk.   2. Detail.   3. Drawer pull.   4. Sheraton desk.   5. Detail.   6. Drawer pull.

Property of F. W. Phillips, Hitchin and J. H. Springett, Rochester.

PLATE 258.   SHERATON STYLE.
1. Sheraton cabinet. 2. Drawer pull. 3. Escutcheon plate. 4. Sheraton cabinet. 5. Details of leg and upright. 6. Drawer pull.

Property of George Stoner, West Wickham, Kent and Victoria and Albert Museum.

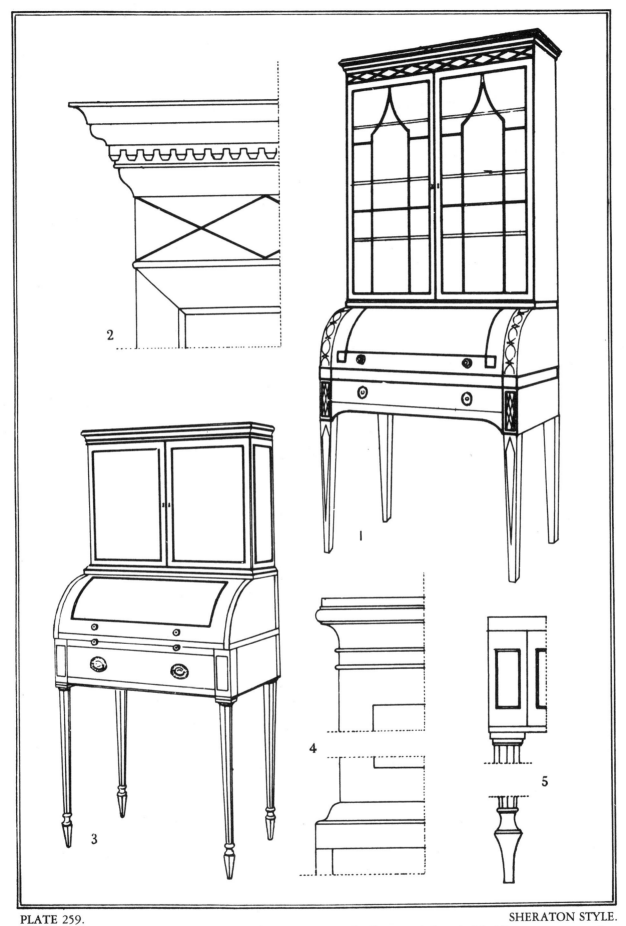

PLATE 259.   SHERATON STYLE.

1. Sheraton desk.   2. Details of cornice and upper corner.   3. Sheraton desk.   4. Moulding on upper section.
5. Detail of leg.

Victoria and Albert Museum and property of George Stoner, West Wickham, Kent.

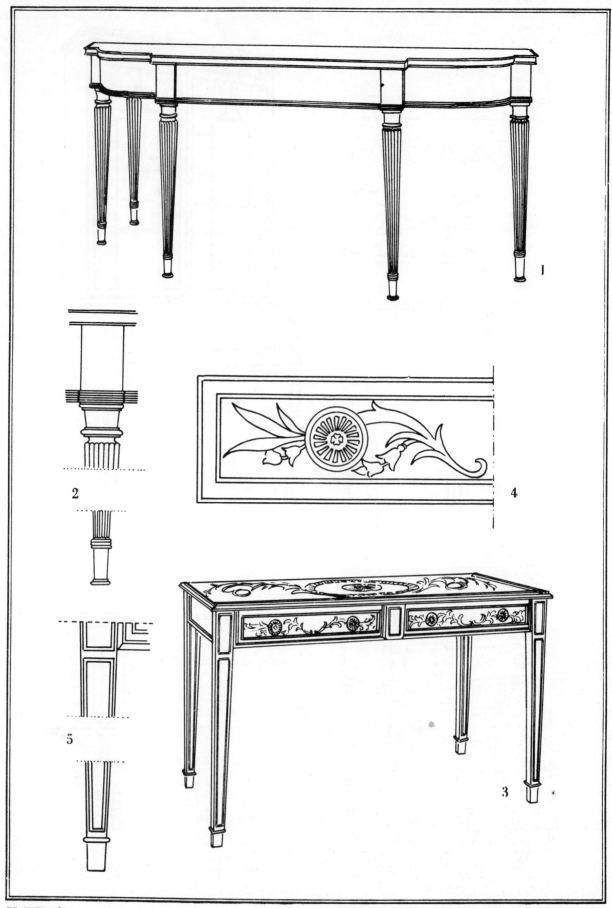

PLATE 260.   SHERATON STYLE.
1. Sheraton console table.   2. Detail of mouldings and leg.   3. Sheraton console table.   4. Decoration on drawer
panels.   5. Leg.

Victoria and Albert Museum and property of C. J. Charles.

264

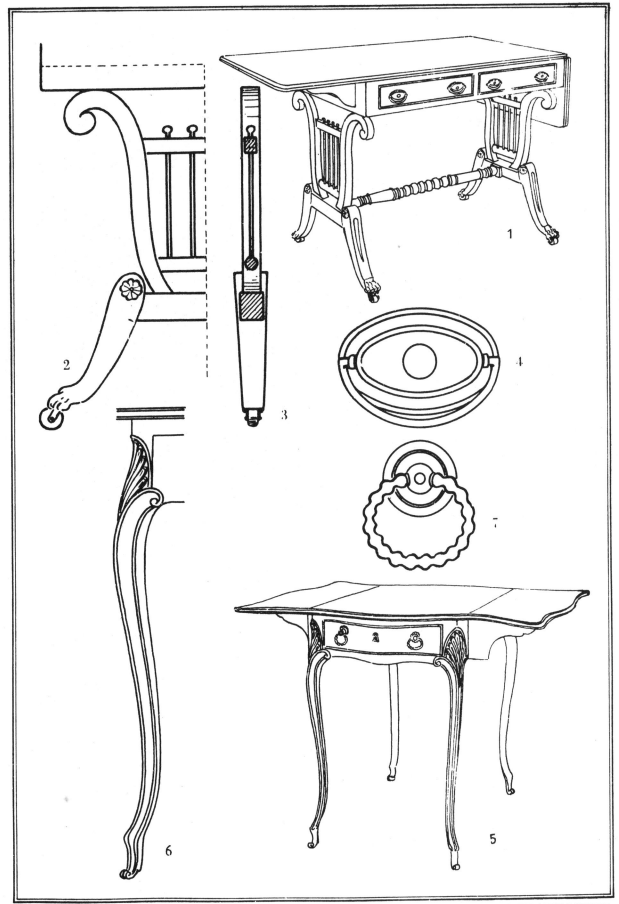

PLATE 261.   SHERATON STYLE.
1. Sheraton table.   2. Decoration on support.   3. Detail of support construction.   4. Drawer pull.   5. Sheraton
table.   6. Leg.   7. Drawer pull.

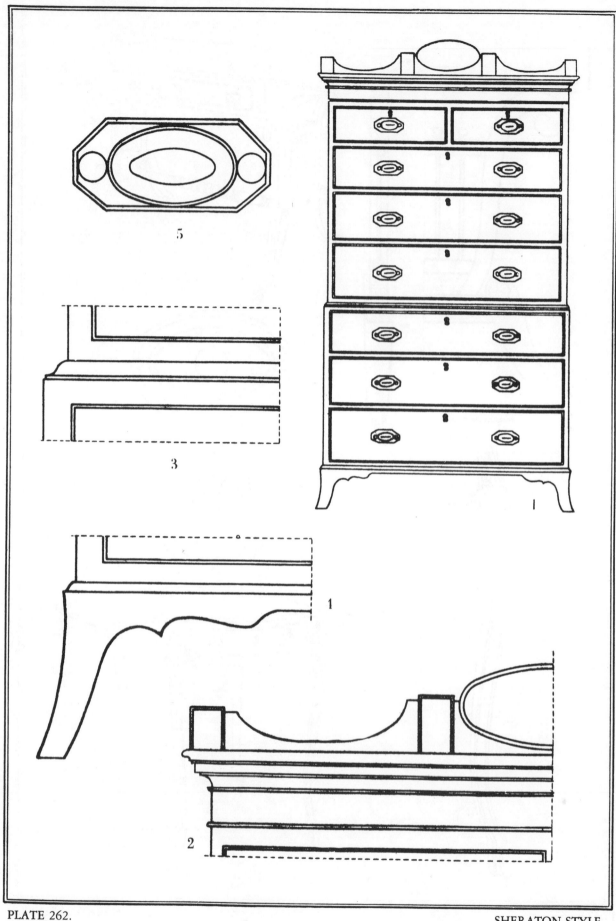

PLATE 262.   SHERATON STYLE.
1. Tall Sheraton commode.   2. Cornice and crest.   3. Base of upper section.   4. Foot.   5. Drawer pull.

Property of J. H. Springett of Rochester.

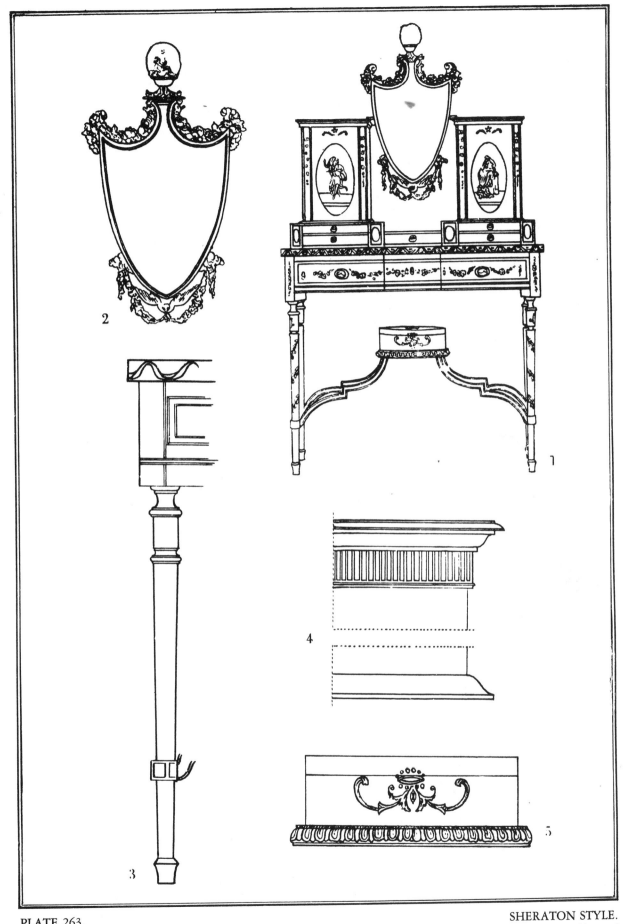

PLATE 263.

1. Sheraton dressing table with delicate paintings by Angelica Kauffman.   2. Detail of mirror.   3. Details of leg and corner of table.   4. Mouldings and frieze.   5. Small box supported by crosspieces.

SHERATON STYLE.

Victoria and Albert Museum.

PLATE 264.   SHERATON STYLE.

1. Intricately designed Sheraton clock case. 2. Details of crest, face and upper section. 3. Decoration at bottom of middle section. 4. Detail of lower section.

Album of designs by Sheraton.

PLATE 265.

SHERATON STYLE.

1. Sheraton clock case.   2. Crest and face.   3. Detail of top of middle section.   4. Side column.   5. Detail of lower section.   6. Decorative motif at bottom of middle section.

Album of designs by Sheraton.

PLATE 266.   SHERATON STYLE.
1 and 5. Shearer desks.   2. Decoration on first desk: mouldings at top and base, and upright.   3. Drawer pull of
second desk.   4. Drawer pull of first desk.   6. Detail of base of leg, second desk.

From Shearer catalogue.

PLATE 267.   SHERATON STYLE.

1. Shearer bookcase.   2 and 3. Decoration: crest, cornices, mouldings and base.   4. Drawer pull.

From Shearer catalogue.

PLATE 268.

SHERATON STYLE.

1. Shearer bookcase, 2, 3 and 4. Decorations: crest, cornice, mouldings, glass panes and base. 5. Rosette.

Shearer catalogue.

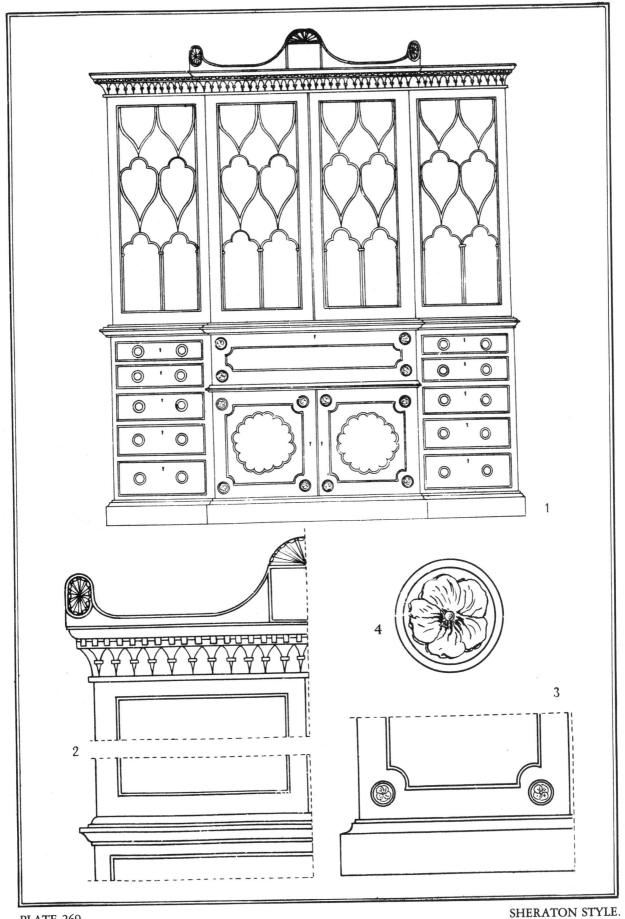

PLATE 269.

SHERATON STYLE.

1. Shearer bookcase with two sections. 2 and 3. Decoration: crests, cornice, mouldings and base. 4. Rosette.

Shearer catalogue.

PLATE 270.

COLONIAL STYLE (architectural features).

1. Living room of a Colonial house.   2. Typical Colonial foyer.   3. Simple Colonial dining room.   4. Another dining room with typical decorations.   5 and 6. Stairway balustrades.

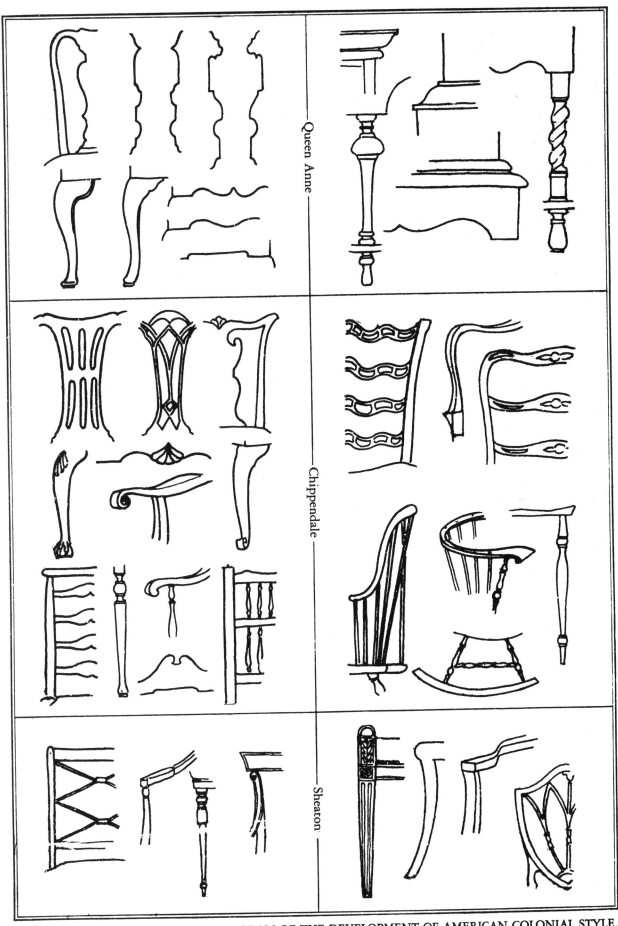

Queen Anne

Chippendale

Sheaton

PLATE 271.　DIAGRAM OF THE DEVELOPMENT OF AMERICAN COLONIAL STYLE.

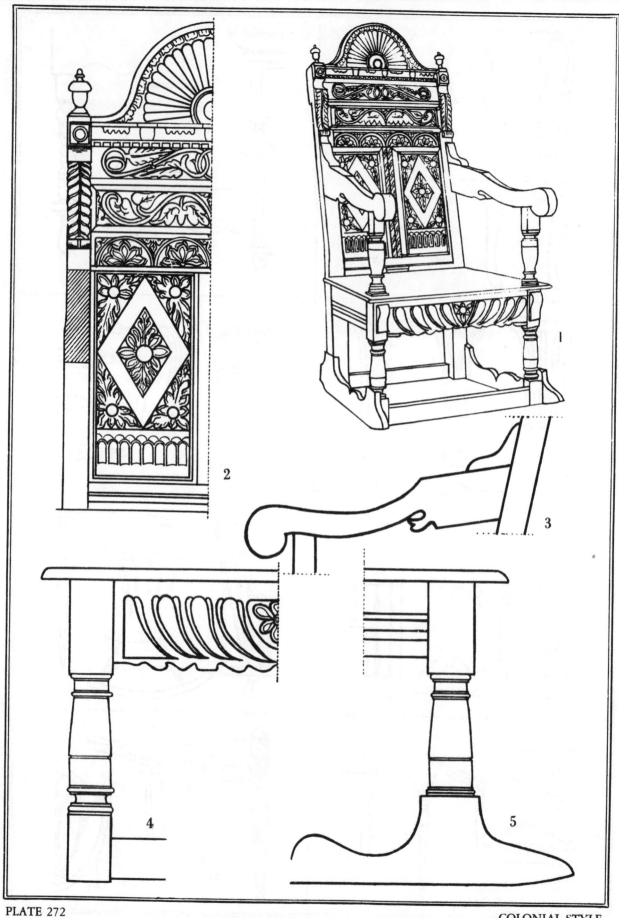

PLATE 272

COLONIAL STYLE.

1. Tudor-style armchair. 2. Detail of back. 3. Detail of arm. 4. Front view of leg and crosspiece. 5. Side view of leg and rocker.

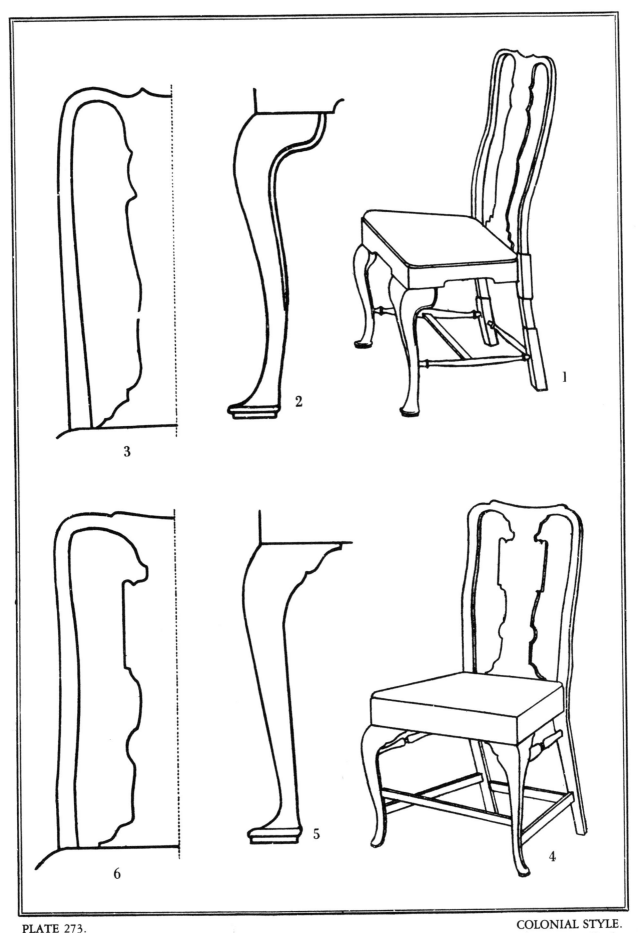

PLATE 273.   COLONIAL STYLE.
1. Queen Anne style chair.   2. Leg.   3. Detail of back.   4. Queen Anne style chair.   5. Leg.   6. Detail of back.
Private collection and the residence of Lady Jowitt.

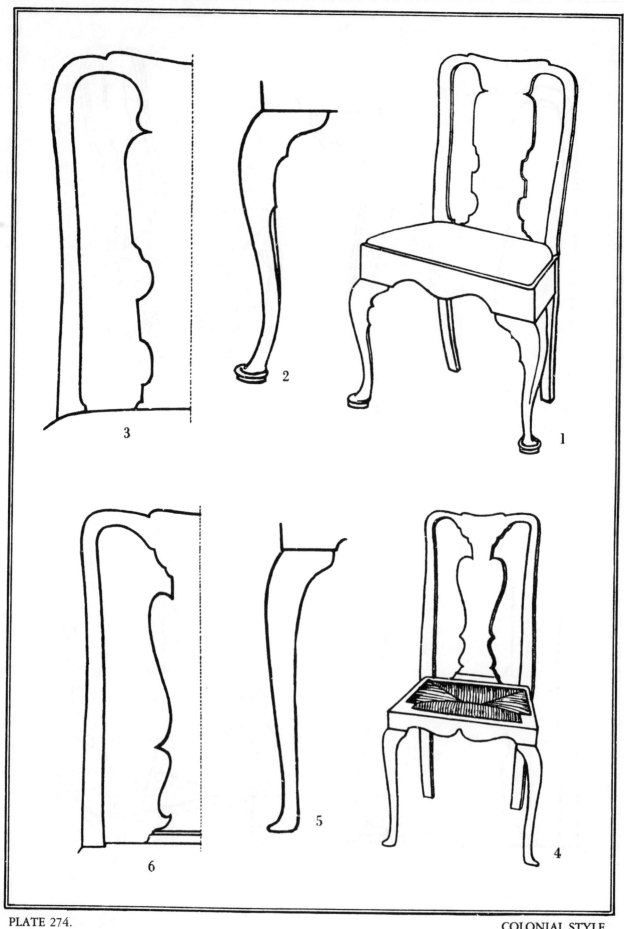

PLATE 274.

1 and 4. Chairs with Queen Anne traits.   2 and 5. Legs.   3 and 6. Details of backs.

COLONIAL STYLE.

Private collection.

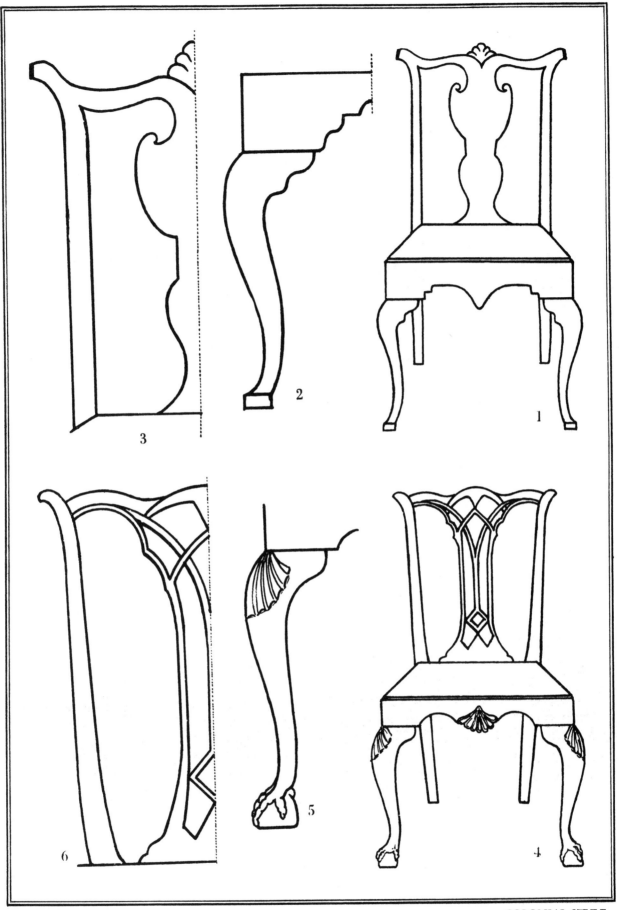

PLATE 275.

1 and 4. Chippendale style chairs.   2 and 5. Legs.   3 and 6. Details of backs.

COLONIAL STYLE.

Private collections.

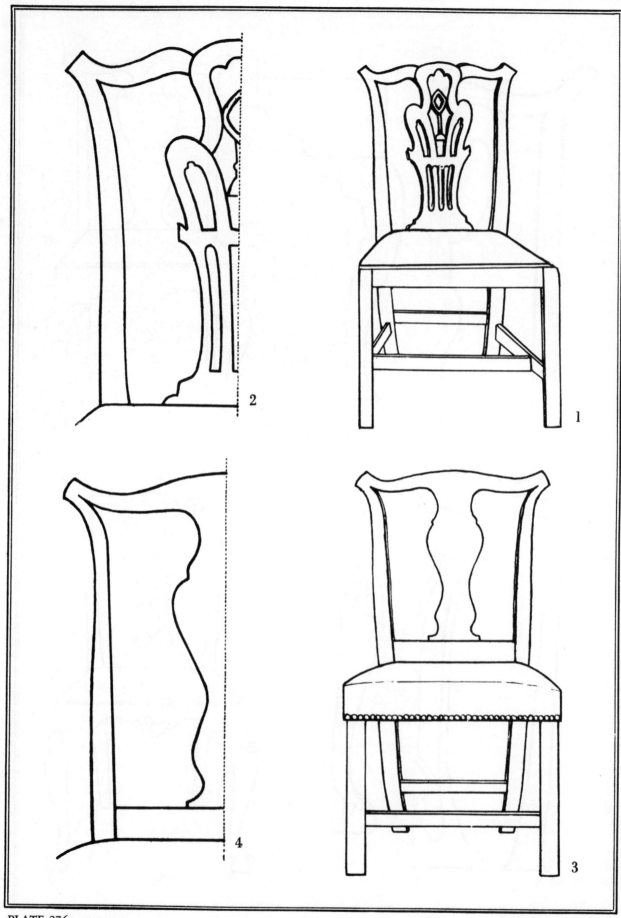

PLATE 276.
1 and 3. Chippendale style chairs.   2 and 4. Detail of backs.

COLONIAL STYLE.

Private collections.

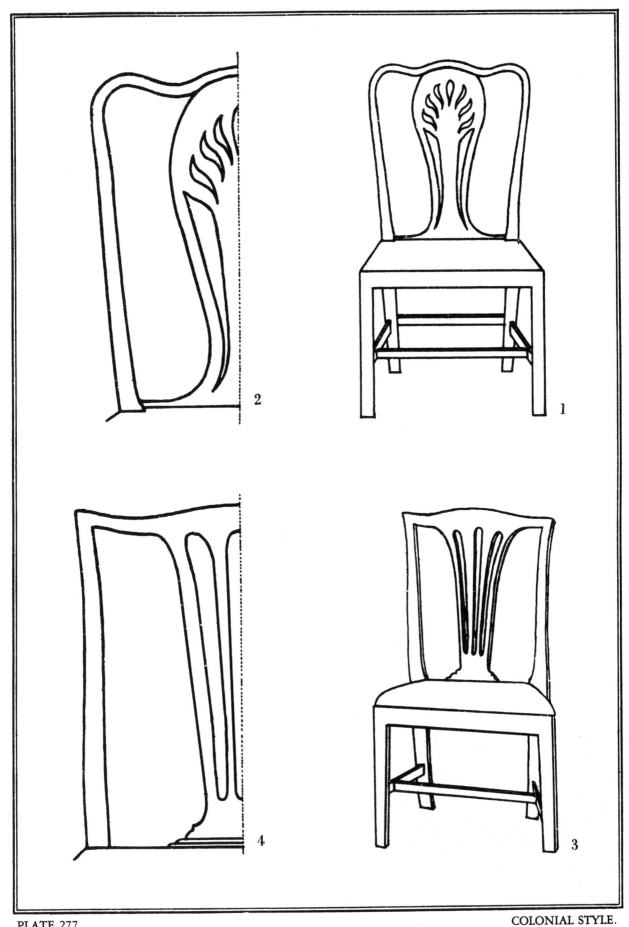

PLATE 277.
1 and 3. Chippendale style chairs with straight backs.   2 and 4. Detail of backs.

COLONIAL STYLE.

Private collectinos.

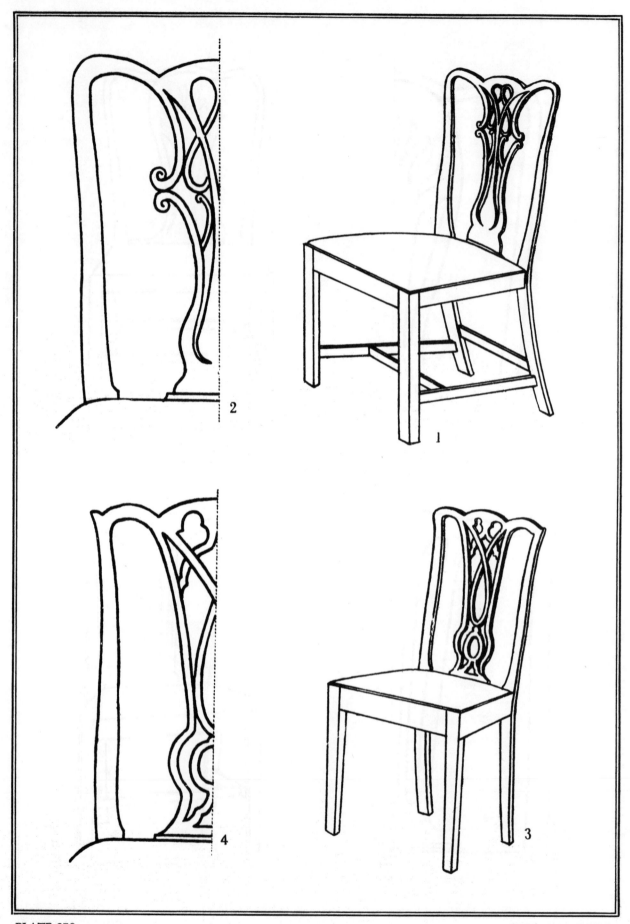

PLATE 278.   COLONIAL STYLE.
1. Chippendale style chair.   2. Detail of back.   3. Chippendale style chair.   4. Detail of back.
Private collection and the residence of James P. Magill.

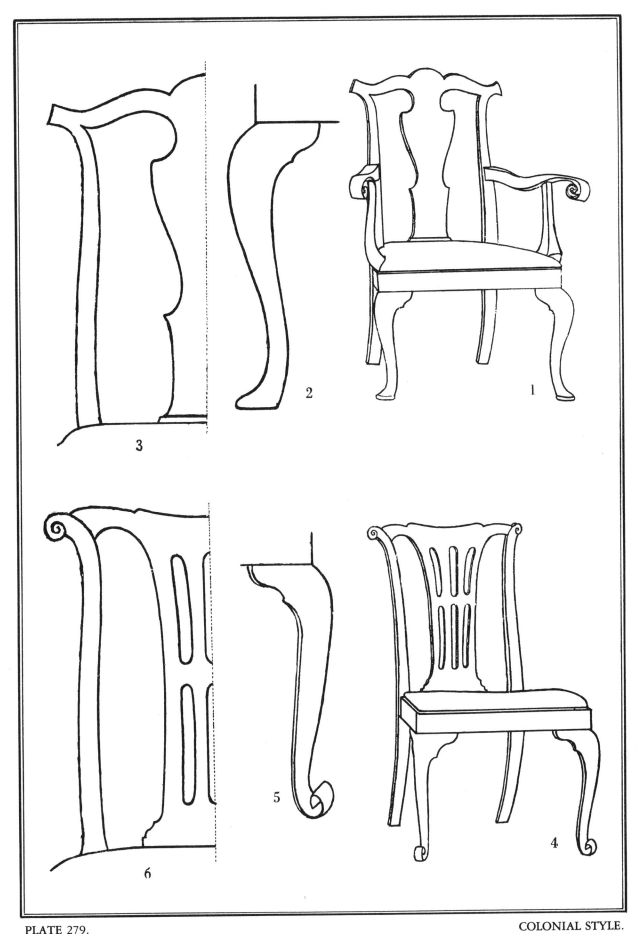

PLATE 279.   COLONIAL STYLE.

1. Free interpretation of Chippendale style armchair.   2. Leg.   3. Detail of back.   4. Free interpretation of Chippendale style chair.   5. Leg.   6. Detail of back.

From the residence of Bruce MacLeish and a private collection.

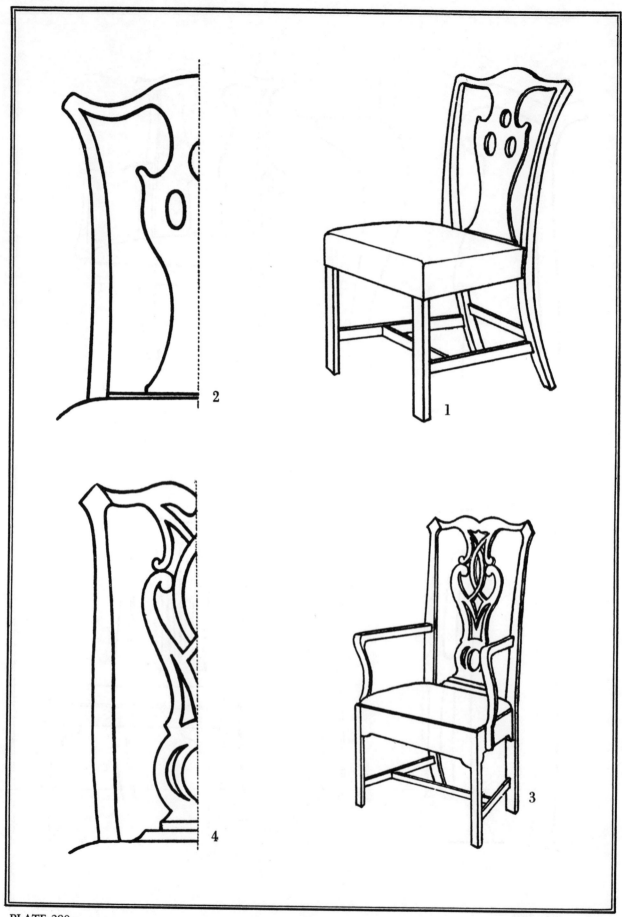

PLATE 280.
1. Chippendale style chair.   2. Detail of back.   3. Chippendale style armchair.   4. Detail of back.

COLONIAL STYLE.

Private collections.

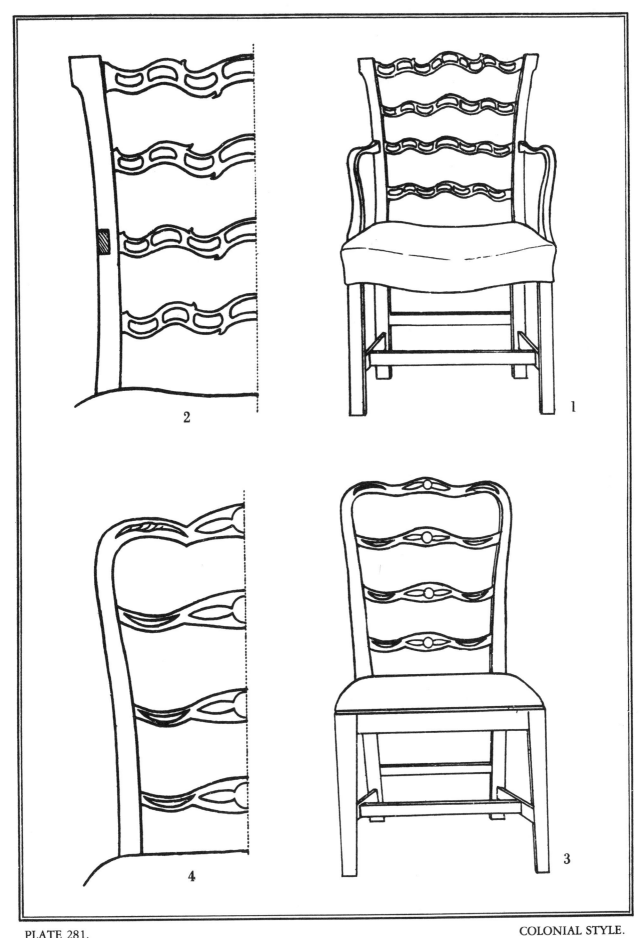

PLATE 281.   COLONIAL STYLE.
1. Chippendale style armchair with horizontal ladder back.   2. Detail of back.   3. Chippendale style chair with
horizontal ladder back.   4. Detail of back.

Private collections.

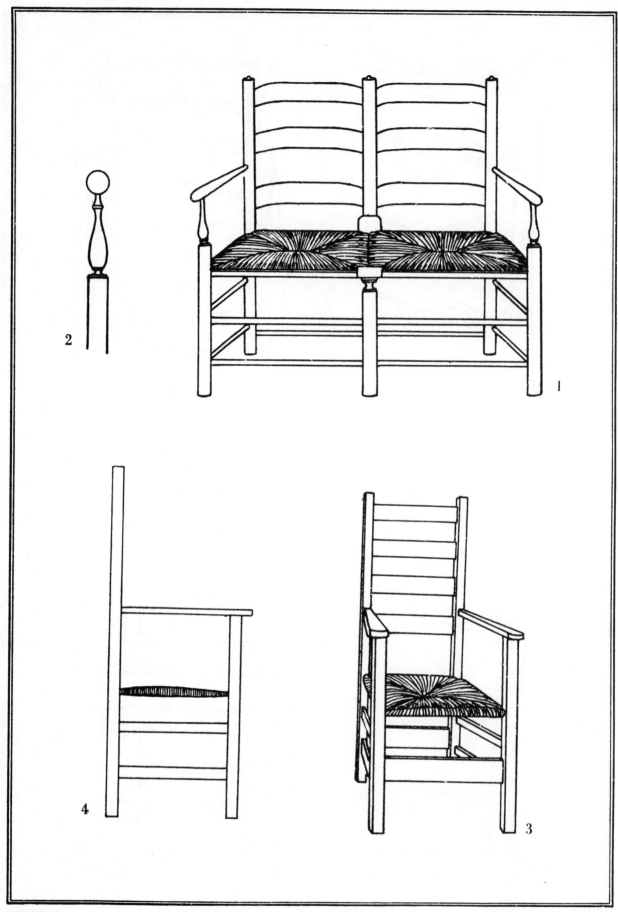

PLATE 282.   COLONIAL STYLE.
1. Sofa in rustic Chippendale style.   2. Detail of arm support.   3. Armchair in rustic Chippendale style.   4. Detail of structure.

Private collections.

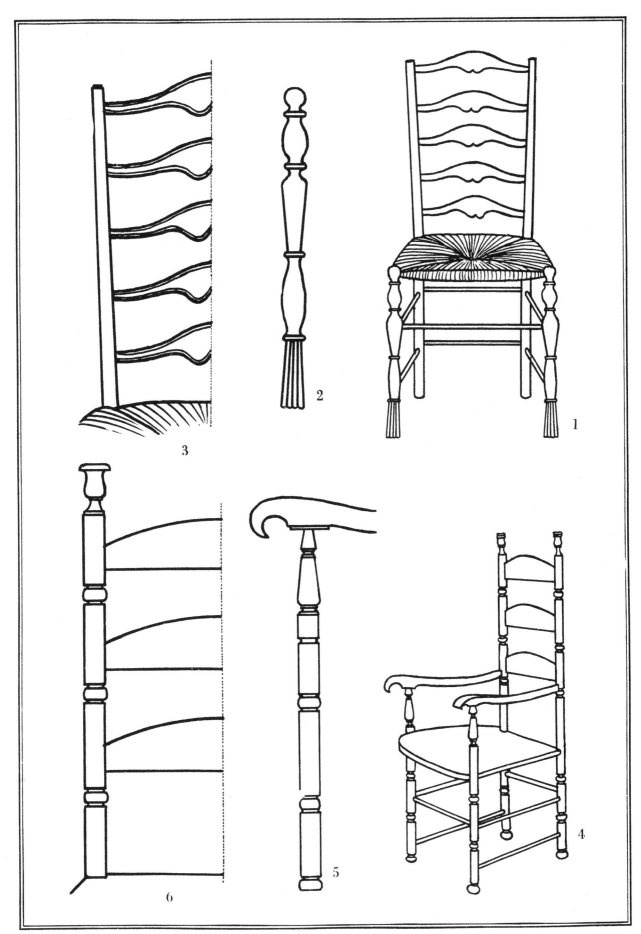

PLATE 283. COLONIAL STYLE.

1. Chippendale style chair with turned legs and horizontal back.   2. Turned leg.   3. Detail of back.   4. Chippendale style armchair with turned posts and horizontal back.   5. Turned leg.   6. Detail of back and turned upright.

Private collections.

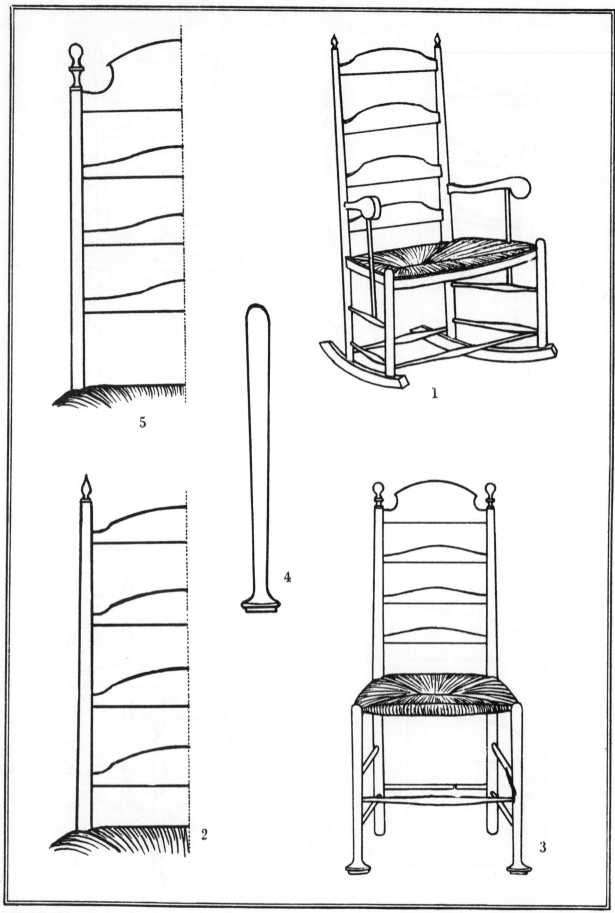

PLATE 284.

COLONIAL STYLE.

1. Simple rocking chair.   2. Detail of back.   3. Simple chair.   4. Front leg.   5. Detail of back.

Private collections.

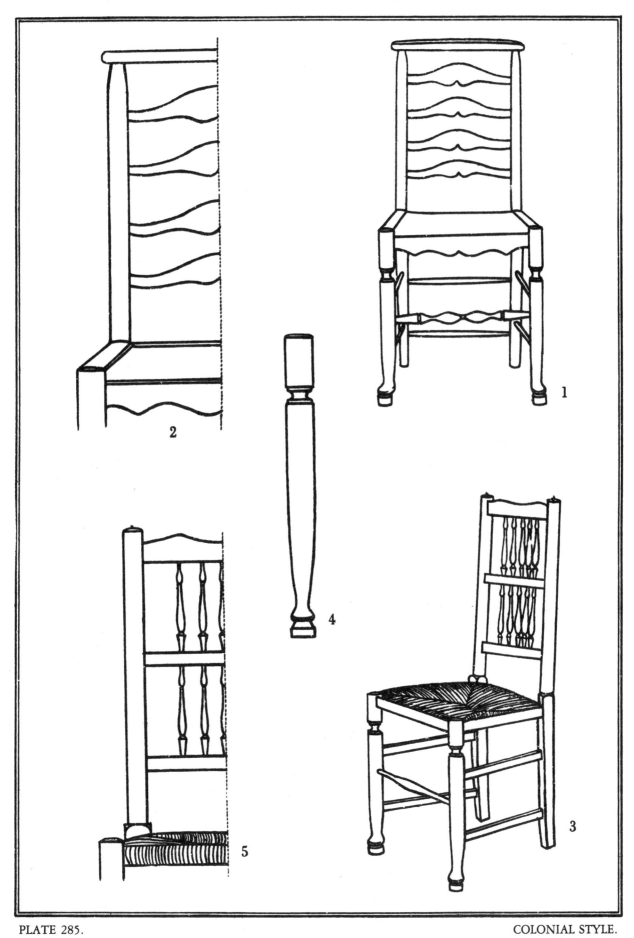

PLATE 285.   COLONIAL STYLE.
1. Chair with horizontal back.   2. Detail of back.   3. Chair with horizontal back and spindles.   4. Turned leg.   5. Detail of back.

Private collections.

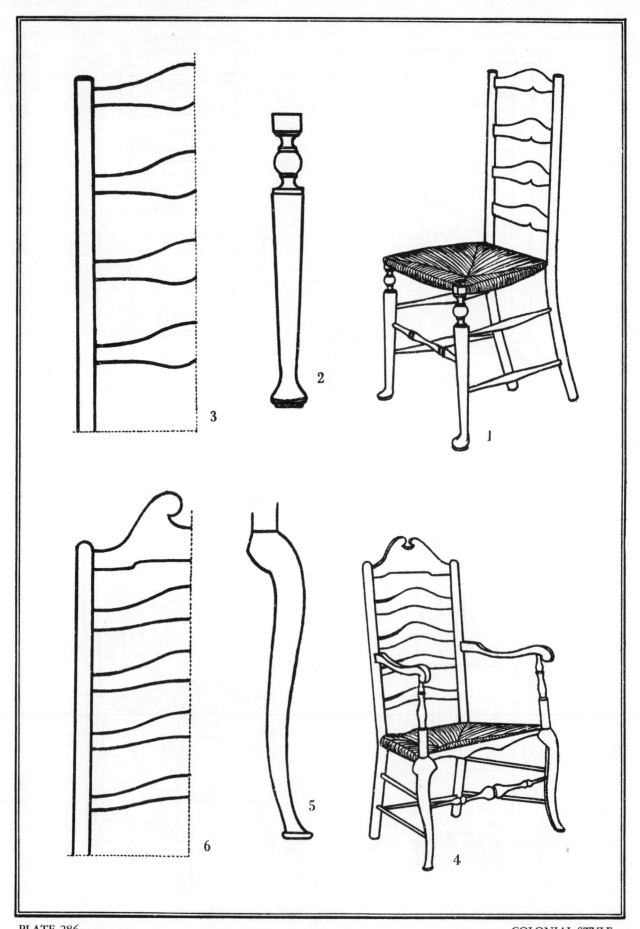

PLATE 286   COLONIAL STYLE.
1. Chair with horizontal back.   2. Turned leg.   3. Detail of back.   4. Armchair with horizontal back.   5. Front
leg.   6. Detail of back.

Private collections.

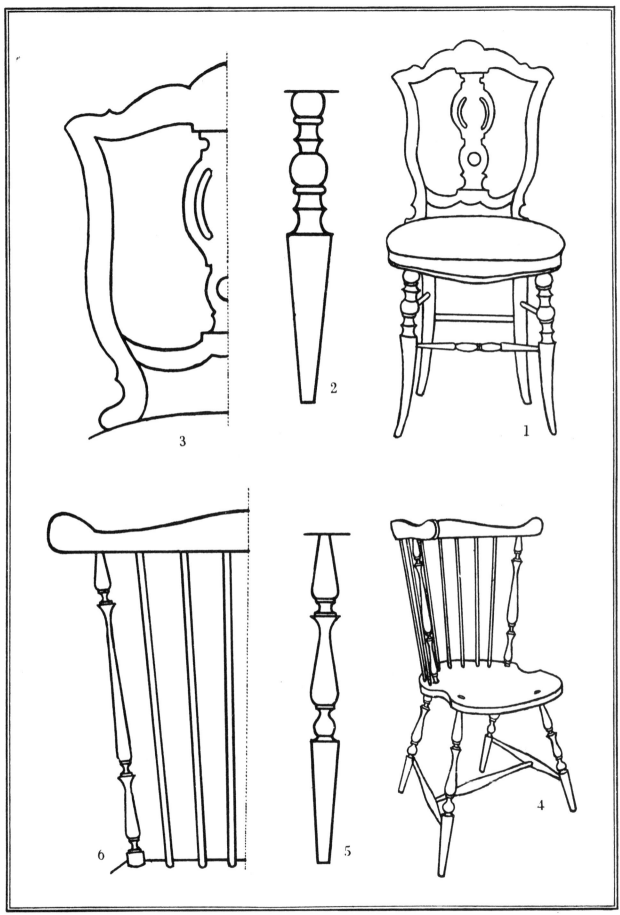

PLATE 287.   COLONIAL STYLE.

1. Chair with whimsical lines.   2. Turned leg.   3. Detail of back.   4. Typical colonial chair.   5. Turned leg.
6. Detail of back.

Private collections.

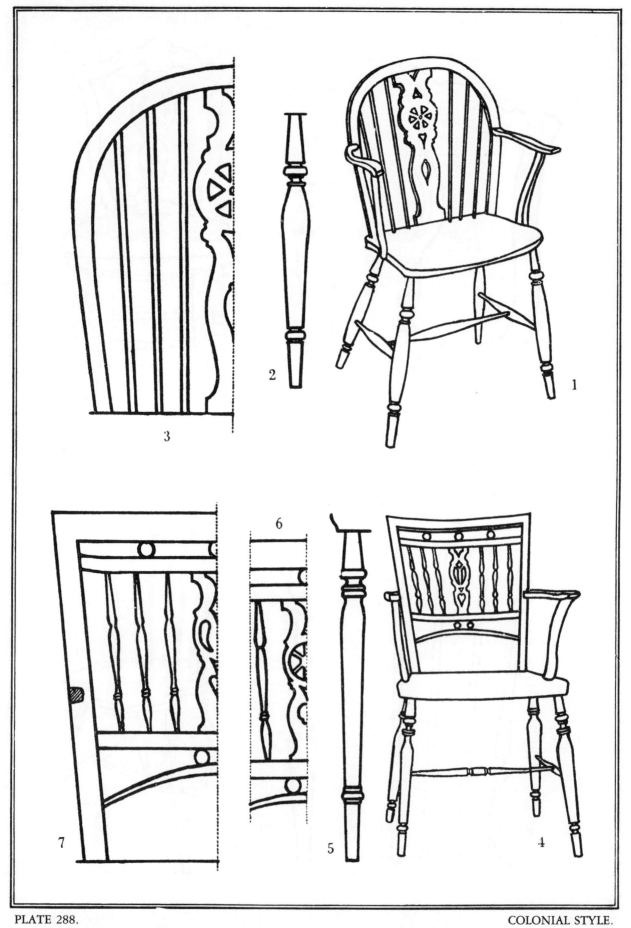

PLATE 288.   COLONIAL STYLE.
1. Colonial chair.   2. Turned leg.   3. Detail of back.   4. Chair of distinctly Sheraton style.   5. Turned leg.
6 and 7. Details of back.

Private collections.

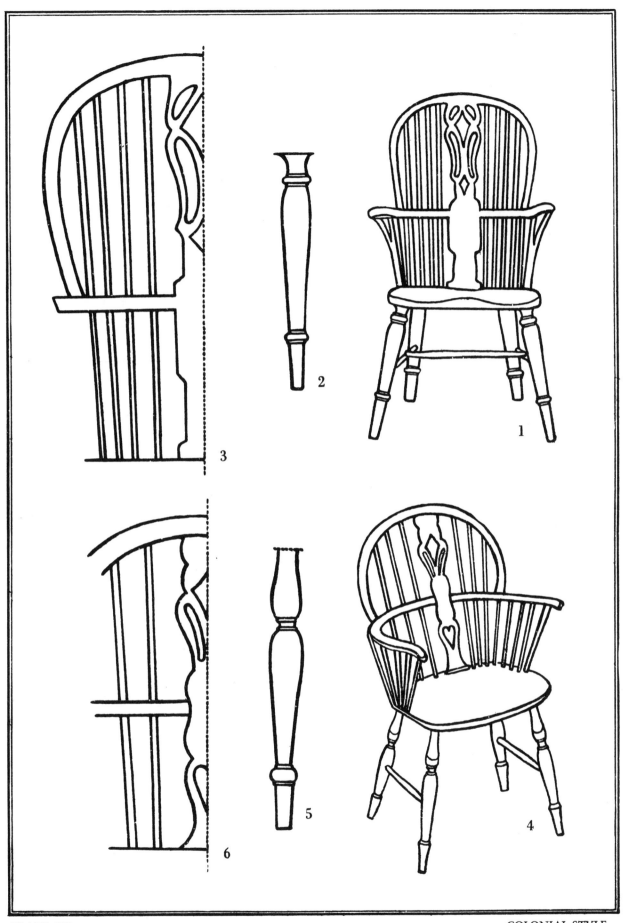

PLATE 289   COLONIAL STYLE.
1 and 4. Typical Colonial chairs.   2 and 5. Respective turned legs.   3 and 6. Detail of backs.

Private collections.

PLATE 290.   COLONIAL STYLE.
1. Windsor chair.   2. Turned leg.   3. Arm.   4. Detail of back.   5. Windsor chair.   6. Turned leg.   7. Detail of back.

From the residences of Thomas Evans and Paul Pulliani.

PLATE 291.   COLONIAL STYLE.

1. Simple chair.   2. Detail of back.   3. Simple chair.   4. Turned leg.   5. Detail of back.

Private collections.

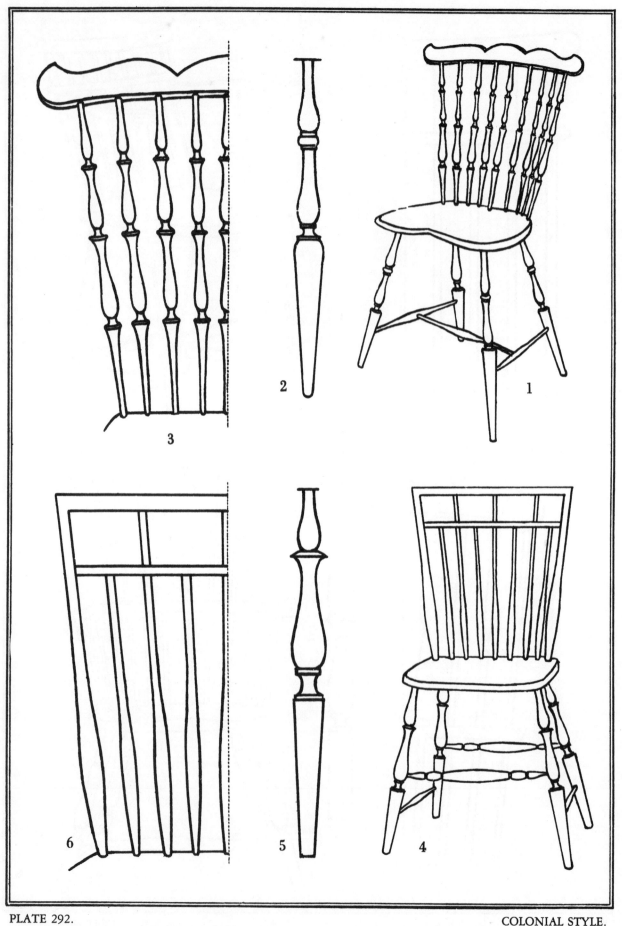

PLATE 292.
1 and 4. Chairs with turned posts.　2 and 5. Turned legs.　3 and 6. Detail of backs.

COLONIAL STYLE.

Private collections.

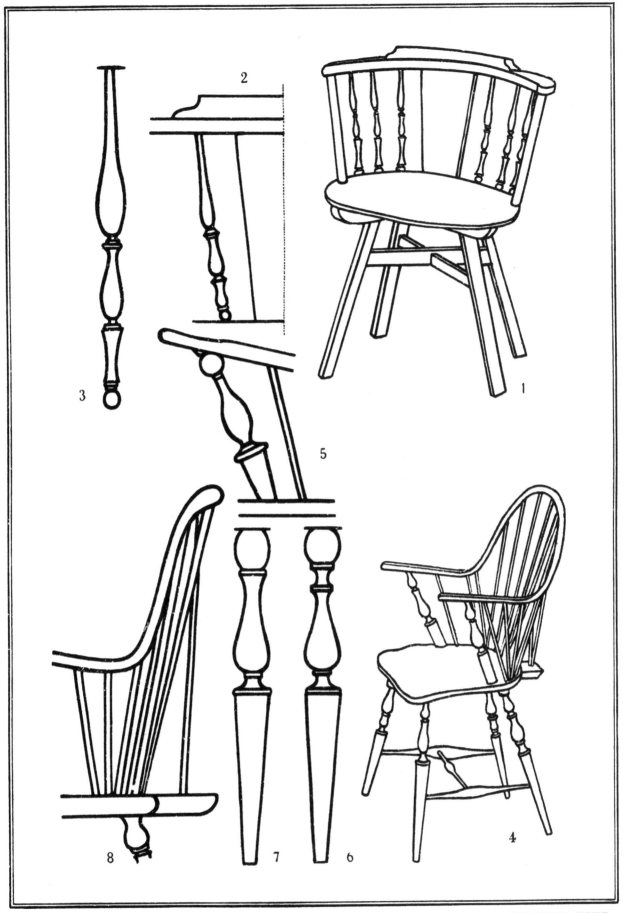

PLATE 293.   COLONIAL STYLE.
1. Typical Colonial chair.   2. Detail of back.   3. Turned spindle.   4. Typical Colonial chair.   5. Detail of end of
arm.   6 and 7. Turned legs.   8. Detail of back structure.

Private collections.

297

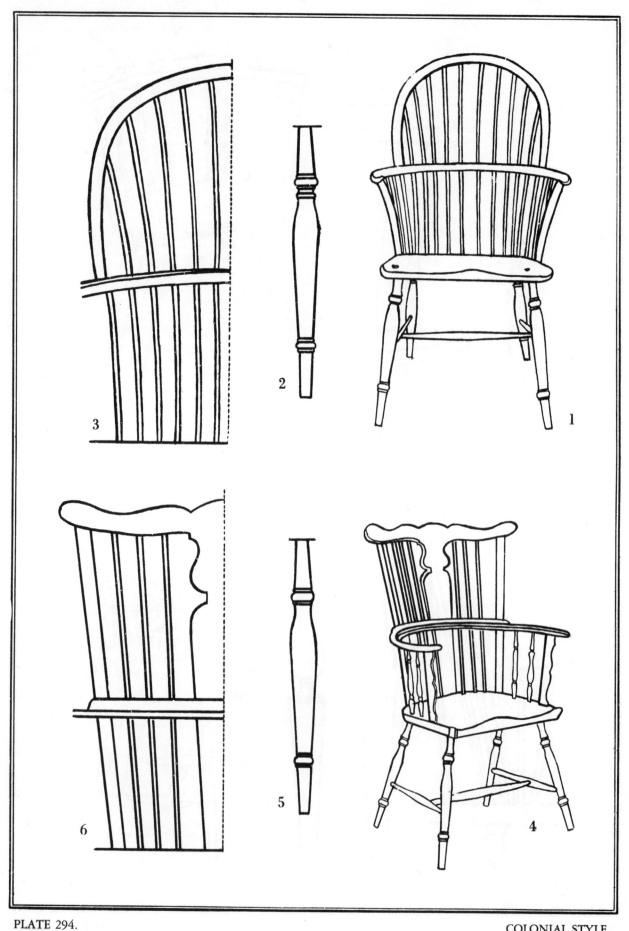

PLATE 294.

1 and 4. High backed chairs.   2 and 5. Turned legs.   3 and 6. Details of backs.

COLONIAL STYLE.

Private collections.

298

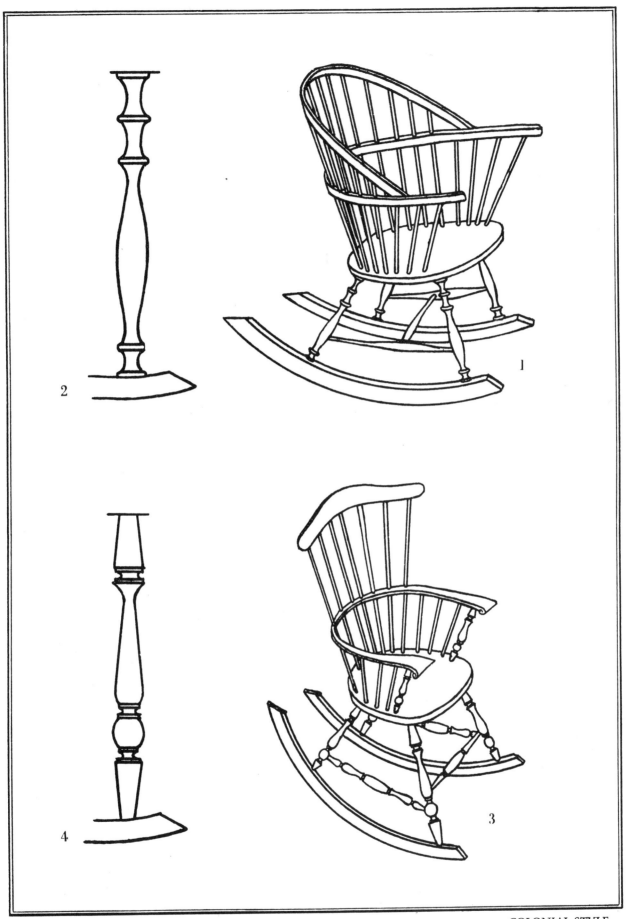

PLATE 295.

COLONIAL STYLE.

1 and 3. Rocking chairs with graceful lines. 2 and 4. Turned legs.

Private collections.

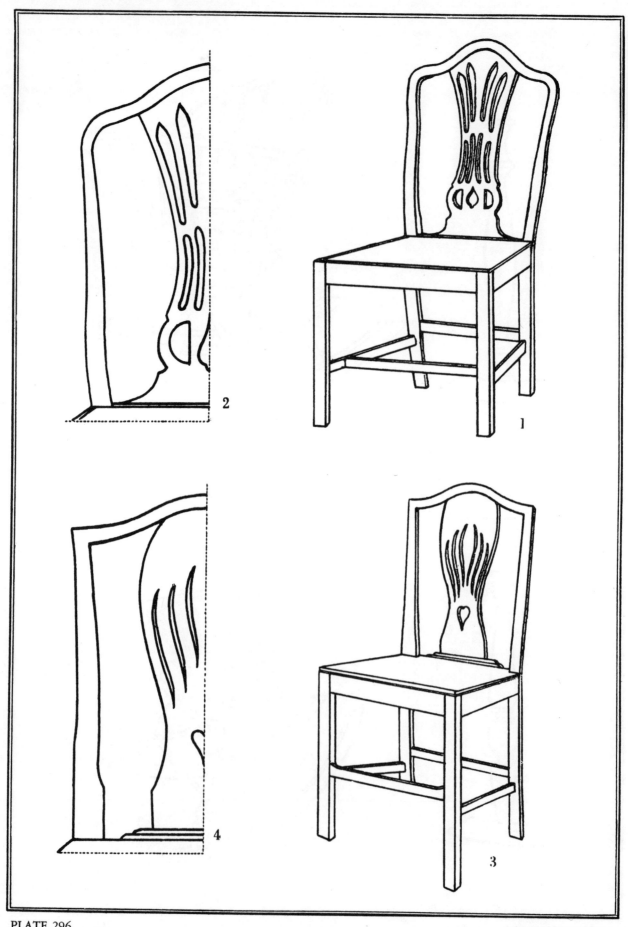

PLATE 296.
1 and 3. Chairs which are suggestive of the Hepplewhite style.   2 and 4. Detail of backs.

COLONIAL STYLE.

Private collections.

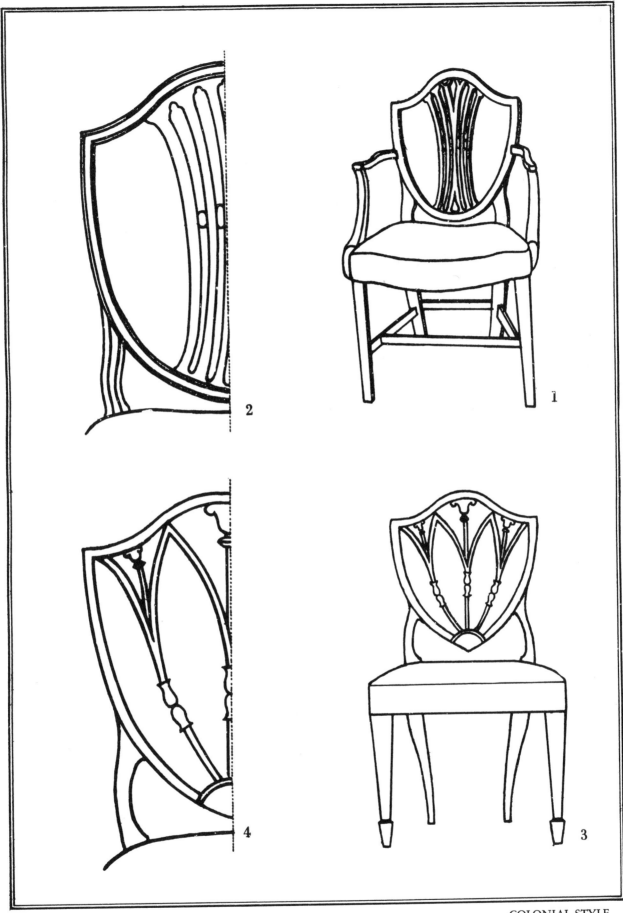

PLATE 297.
1. Hepplewhite style armchair.   2. Detail of back.   3. Hepplewhite style chair.

Private collections.

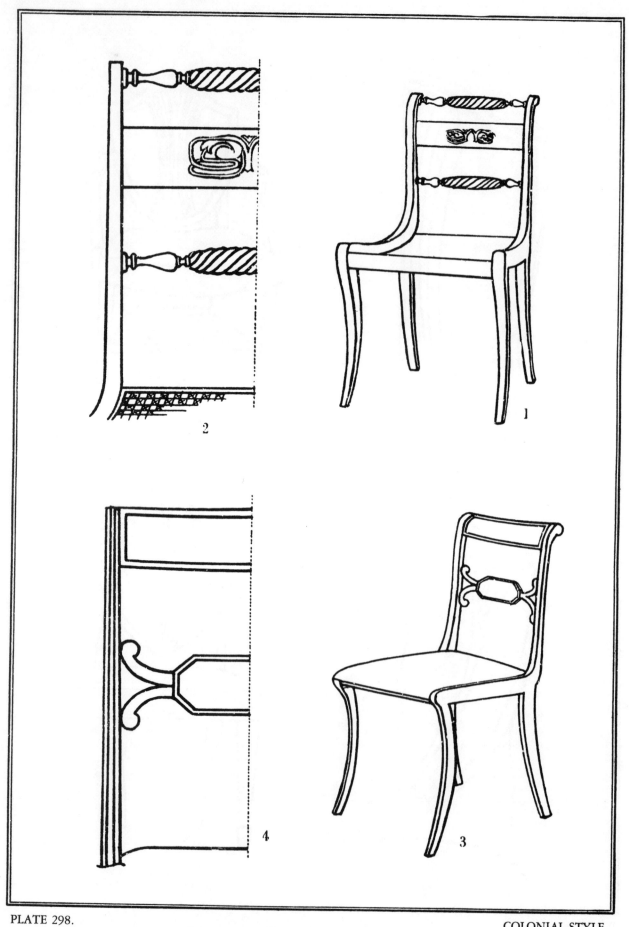

PLATE 298.

COLONIAL STYLE.

1 and 3. Chairs of Sheraton and Adam (Duncan Phyfe) style.   2 and 4. Detail of backs.

Private collections.

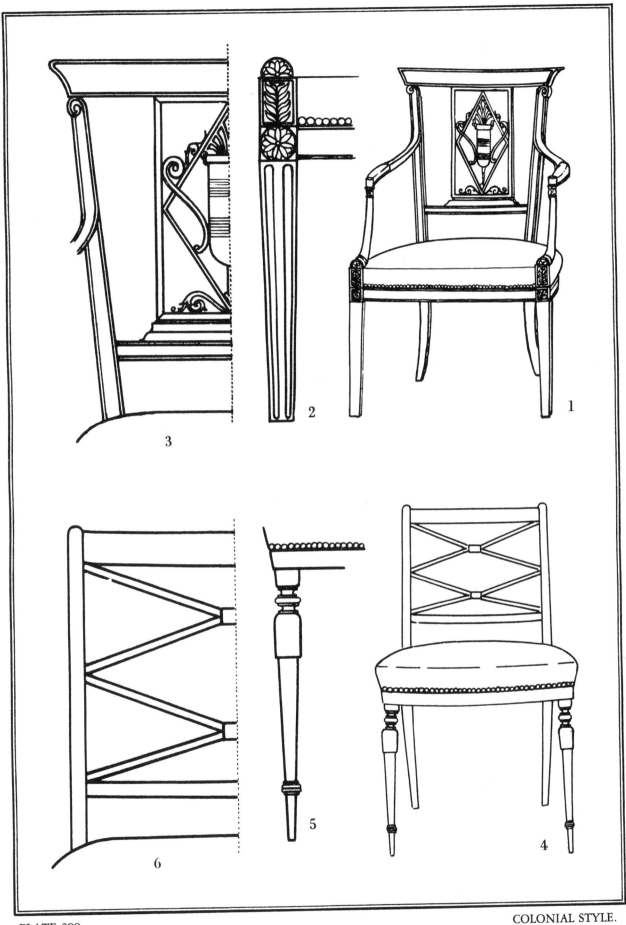

PLATE 299.

COLONIAL STYLE.

1. Armchair of Sheraton and Adam (Duncan Phyfe) style. 2. Leg decoration. 3. Detail of back. 4. Chair of Sheraton and Adam (Duncan Phyfe) style. 5. Turned leg. 6. Detail of back.

Private collections.

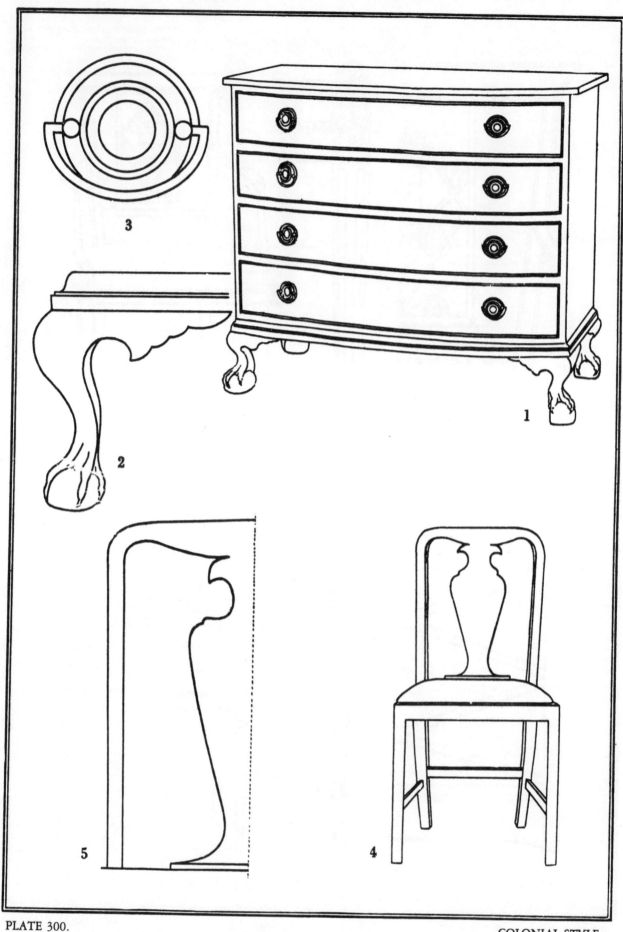

PLATE 300.   COLONIAL STYLE.
1. Colonial commode.   2. Detail of leg.   3. Drawer pull.   4. Colonial chair.   5. Detail of back.
Metropolitan Museum of Art and a private collection.

PLATE 301.   COLONIAL STYLE.
1. William and Mary style highboy.   2. Drawer pull.   3. Detail of moulding.   4. Turned leg.

Private collection.

PLATE 302.

COLONIAL STYLE.

1. William and Mary style highboy. 2. Drawer pull. 3. Turned leg. 4. Decoration: cornice, moulding and profile of crosspiece.

Private collection.

PLATE 303.   COLONIAL STYLE.
1. William and Mary style highboy.   2. Detail of moulding.   3. Turned leg.   4. Drawer pull.

Private collection.

307

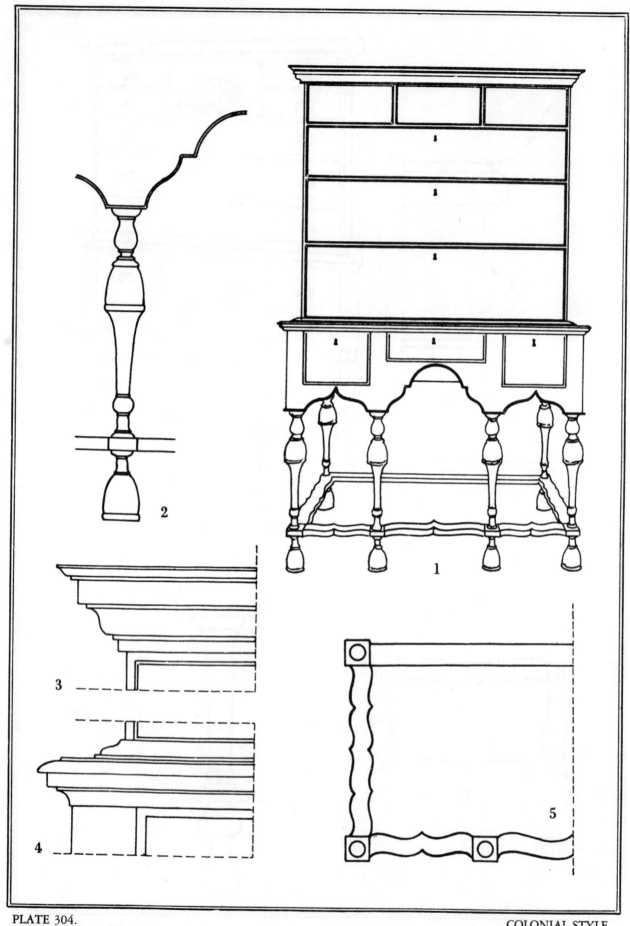

PLATE 304.

1. William and Mary style highboy.   2. Turned leg and front profile of support.   3 and 4. Details of mould-ing.   5. Profile of crosspieces.

Private collection.

PLATE 305.   ENGLISH MINORCAN STYLE (architectural features).
1. Foyer of a Minorcan manor.   2. Ceiling with whitewashed exposed beams.   3. Living room of Minorcan house.   4. Typical Minorcan sashed window.   5. Balcony showing neoclassical influence.   6. Type of iron stairway, which was very popular in Minorca.

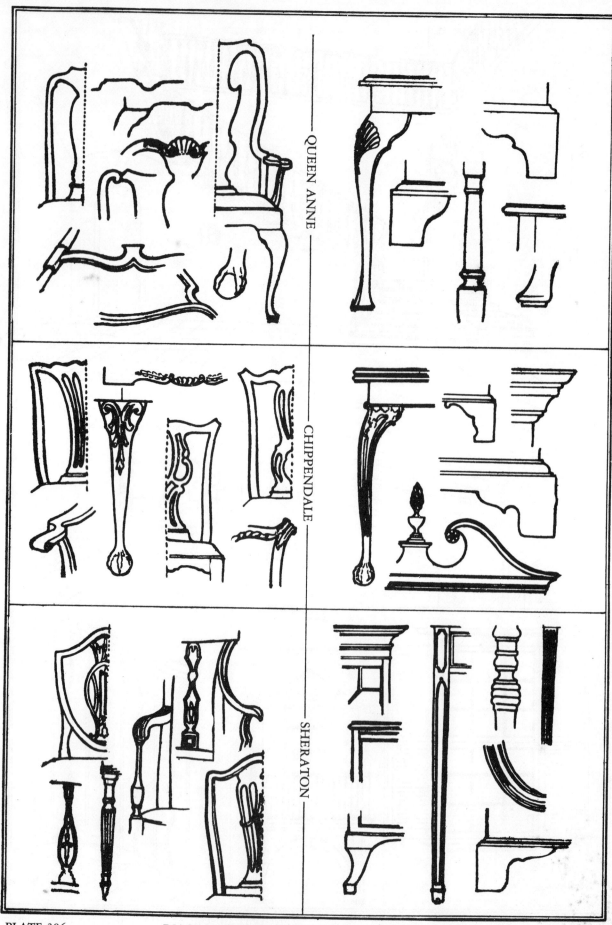

QUEEN ANNE

CHIPPENDALE

SHERATON

PLATE 306.

DIAGRAM SHOWING THE DEVELOPMENT OF ENGLISH MINORCAN STYLE.

310

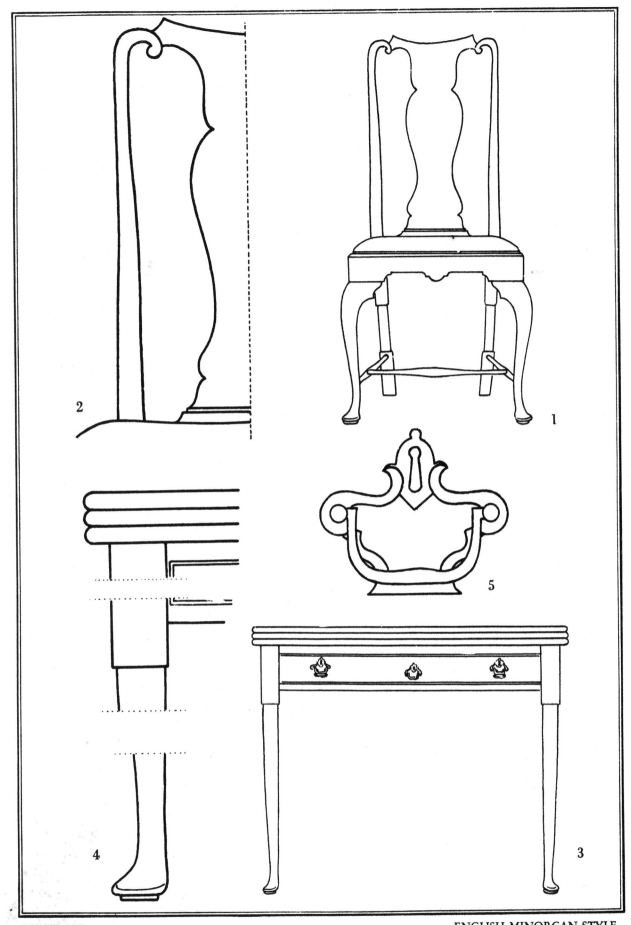

PLATE 307.

1. Queen Anne style chair. 2. Detail of back. 3. Queen Anne style table. 4. Details of moulding and legs. 5. Drawer pull.

From the residence of Cosme Trebol Pons. Alayor.

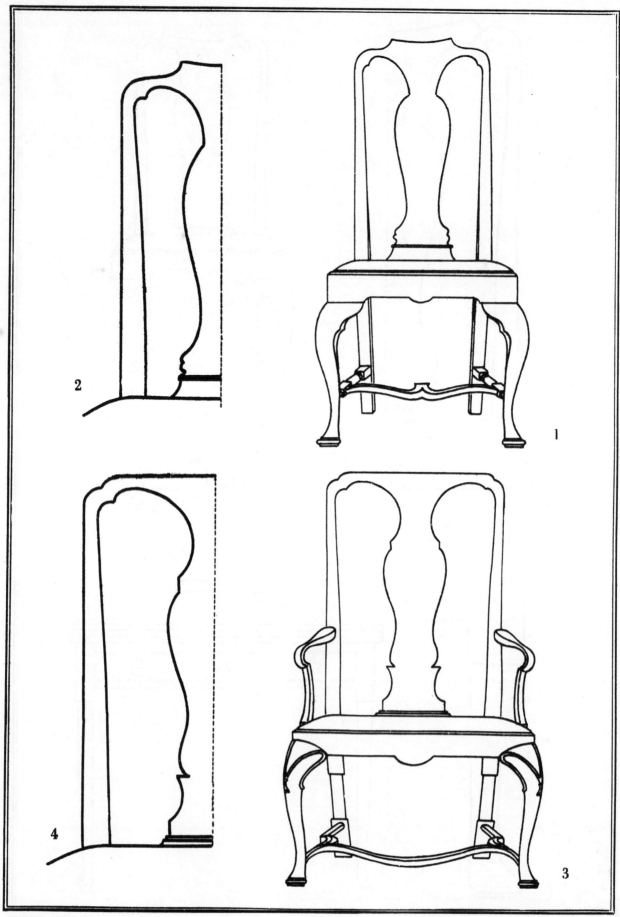

PLATE 308.   ENGLISH MINORCAN STYLE.
1. Queen Anne style chair.   3. Queen Anne style armchair.   2 and 4. Detail of backs.
From the residence of Ignacio Saura Sintas, Mahon.

312

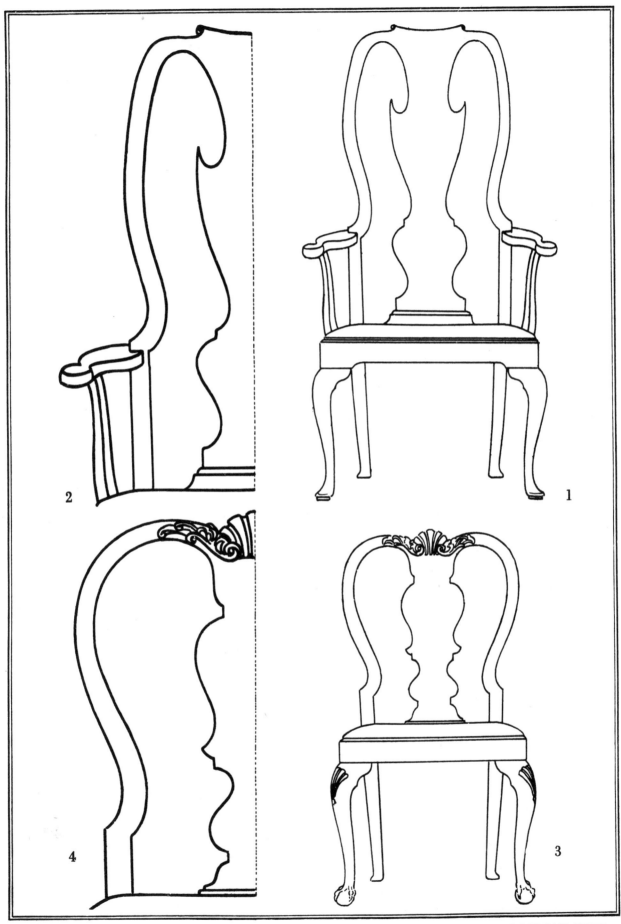

PLATE 309.

ENGLISH MINORCAN STYLE.

1. Queen Anne style armchair.   3. Queen Anne style chair.   2 and 4. Details of backs.

From the residence of Simon Vidal Sintas, Mahon.

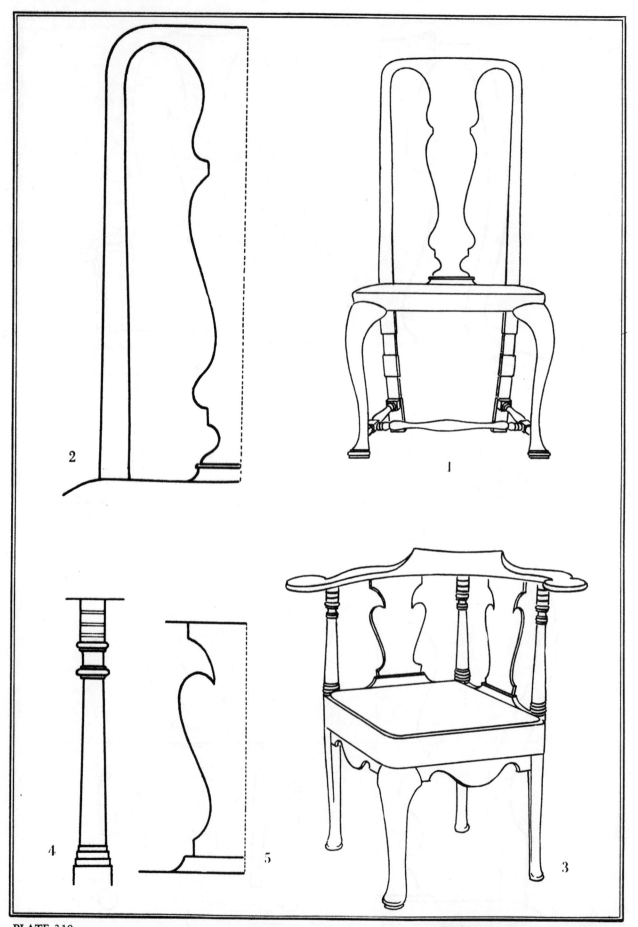

PLATE 310.

ENGLISH MINORCAN STYLE.

1. Queen Anne style chair. 2. Detail of back. 3. Corner armchair. 4 and 5. Details of back.

From "Sa Cudia Cremada," the residence of Francisca Martorell.

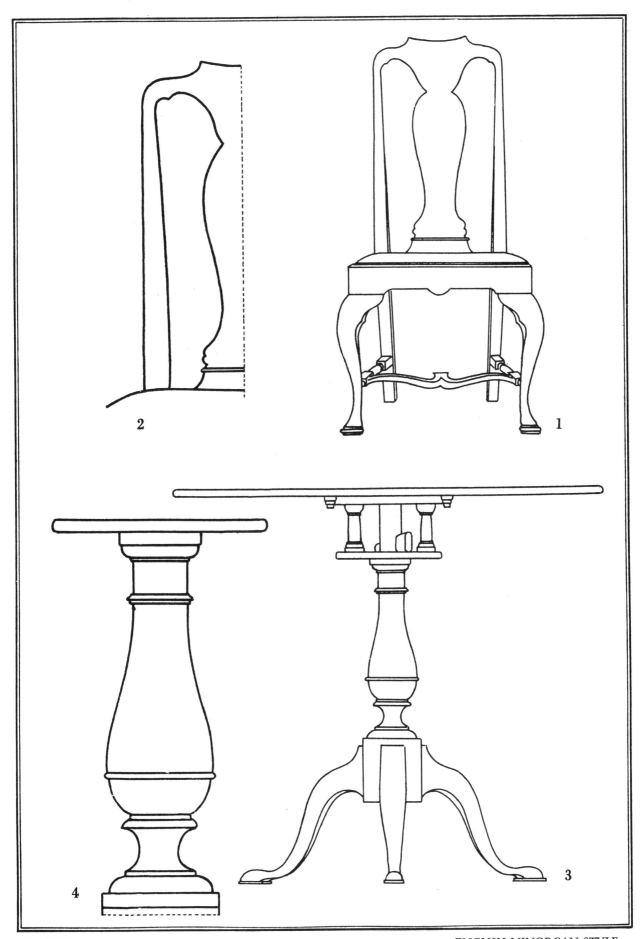

PLATE 311.   ENGLISH MINORCAN STYLE.
1. Queen Anne style chair.   2. Detail of back.   3. Queen Anne style table.   4. Turned central column.
From the residence of Simon de Oliver Canet, Baron of Leuriach, Ciudadela.

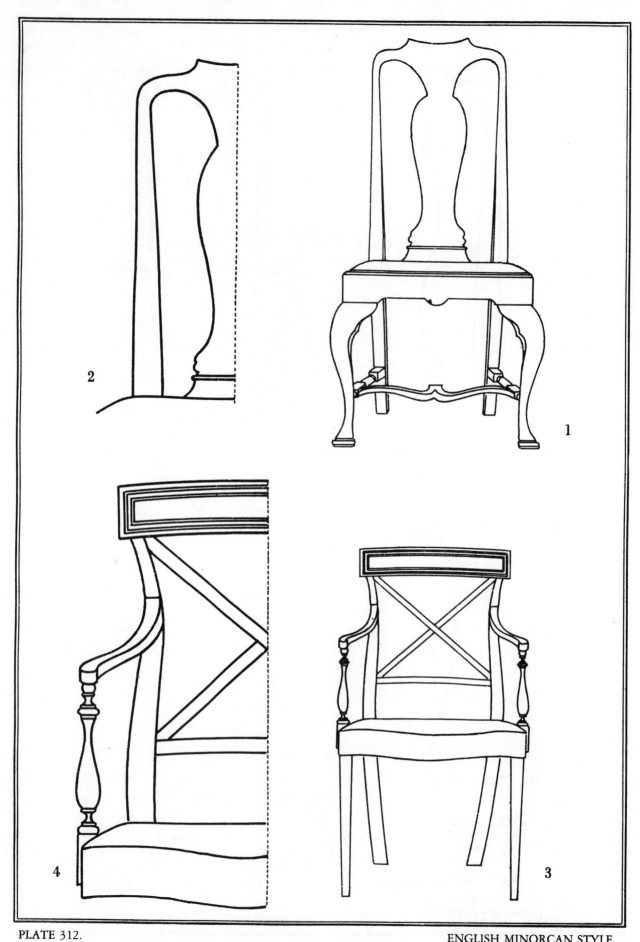

PLATE 312.   ENGLISH MINORCAN STYLE.
1. Queen Anne style chair.   2. Detail of back.   3. Sheraton style armchair.   4. Detail of back and arm.
From the residence of Carlos de Olivar de Olives. Ciudadela.

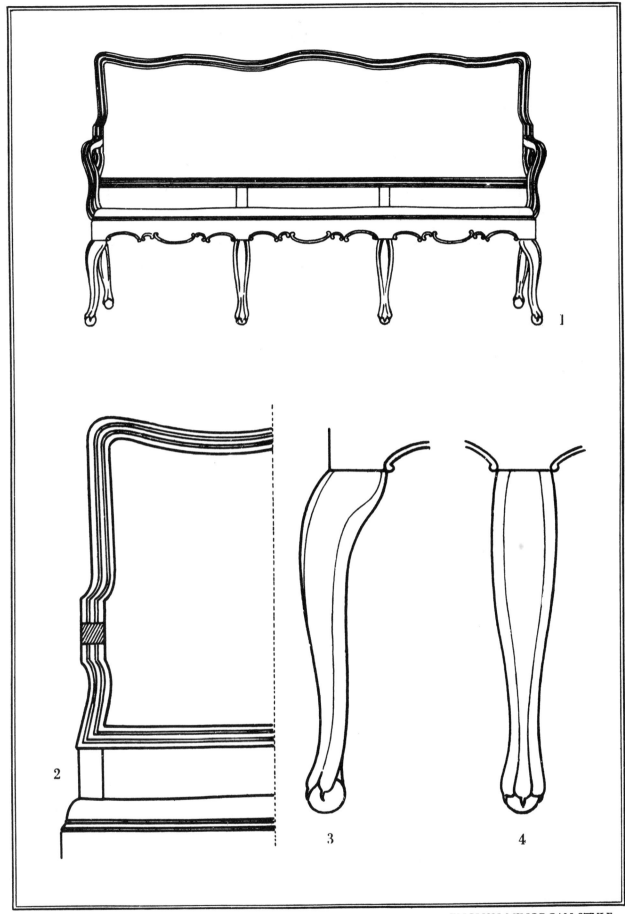

PLATE 313.   ENGLISH MINORCAN STYLE.
1. Sofa.   2. Detail of back.   3. End leg.   4. Middle leg.

From the residence of Francisco Terres Coll. Mahon

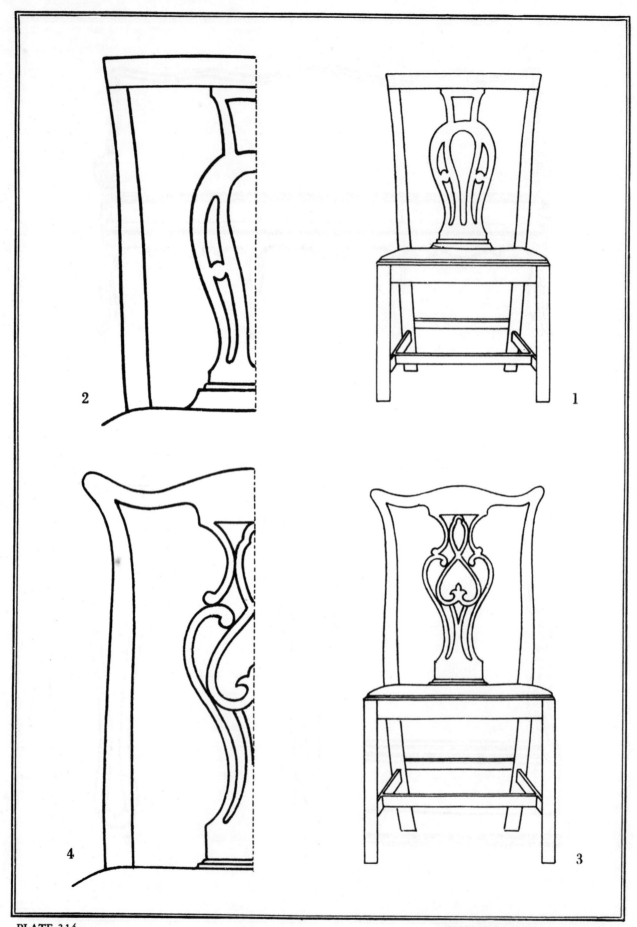

PLATE 314.   ENGLISH MINORCAN STYLE.
1. Chippendale style chair.   2. Detail of back.   3. Chippendale style chair.   4. Detail of back.
From the residences of Juana Pons Guinart de Salort, Alayor and Lorenzo de Salort de Martorell, Ciudadela.

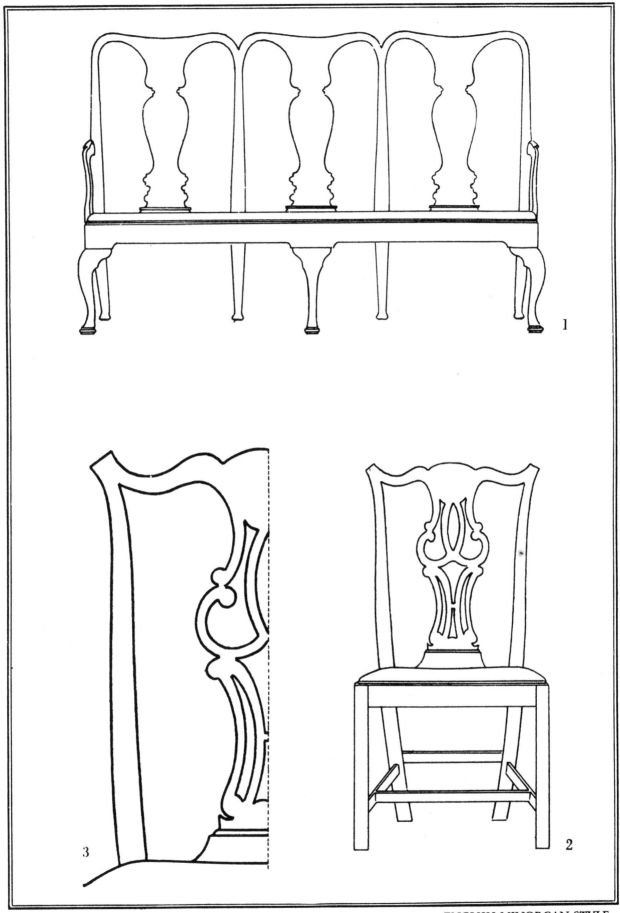

PLATE 315.

ENGLISH MINORCAN STYLE.

1. Queen Anne sofa. 2. Chippendale style chair. 3. Detail of chair back.

From the residence of Ignacio Saura de Sintas, Ciudadela.

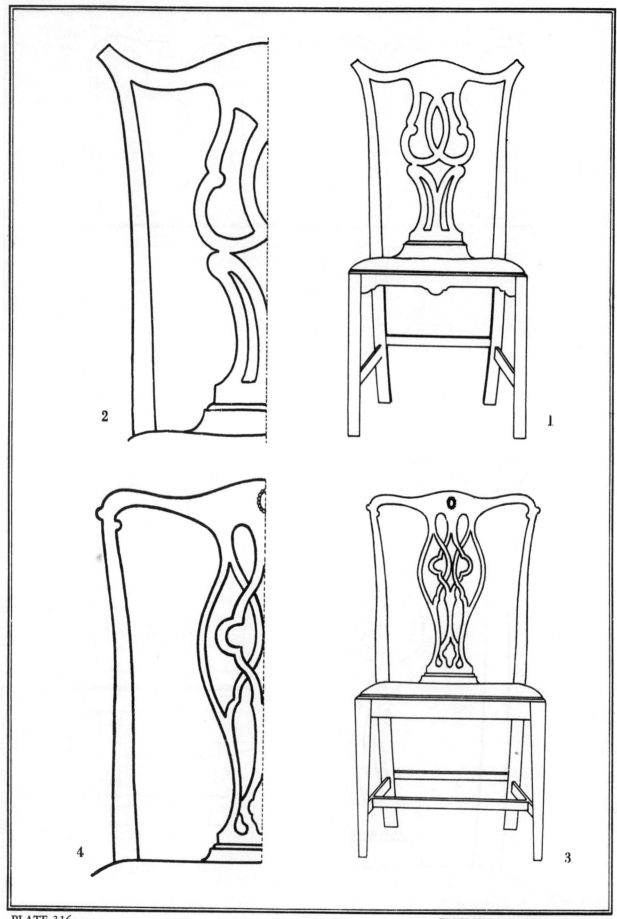

PLATE 316.   ENGLISH MINORCAN STYLE.
1. Chippendale style chair.   2. Detail of back.   3. Chippendale style chair.   4. Detail of back.
From the residences of Cosme Trebol Pons, Alayor and Juan de Salort de Salort, Alayor.

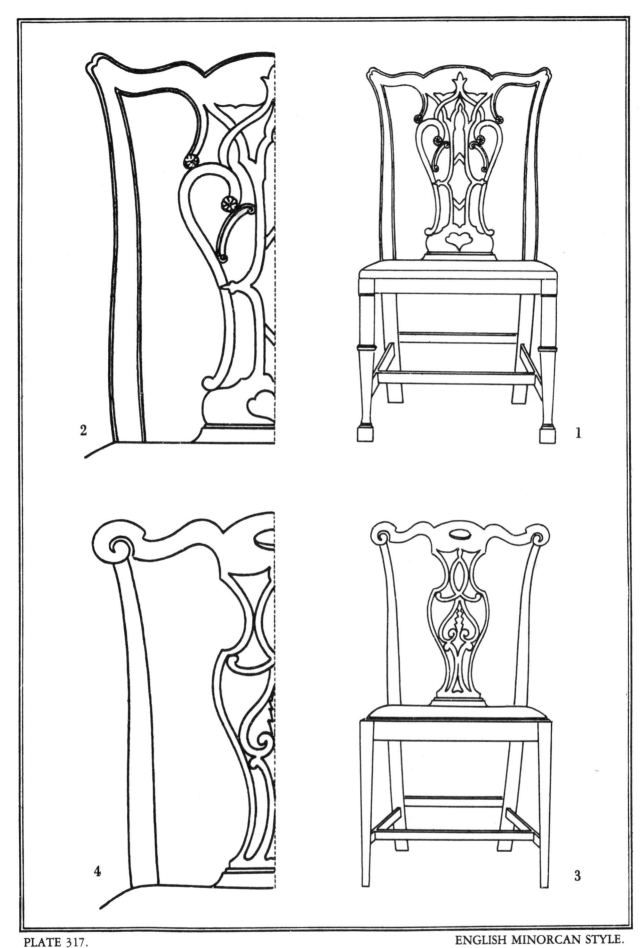

PLATE 317.

ENGLISH MINORCAN STYLE.

1 and 3. Chairs with Chippendale backs.   2 and 4. Details of backs.

From "Sa Cudia Cremada," the residence of Francisca Martorell, Mahon.

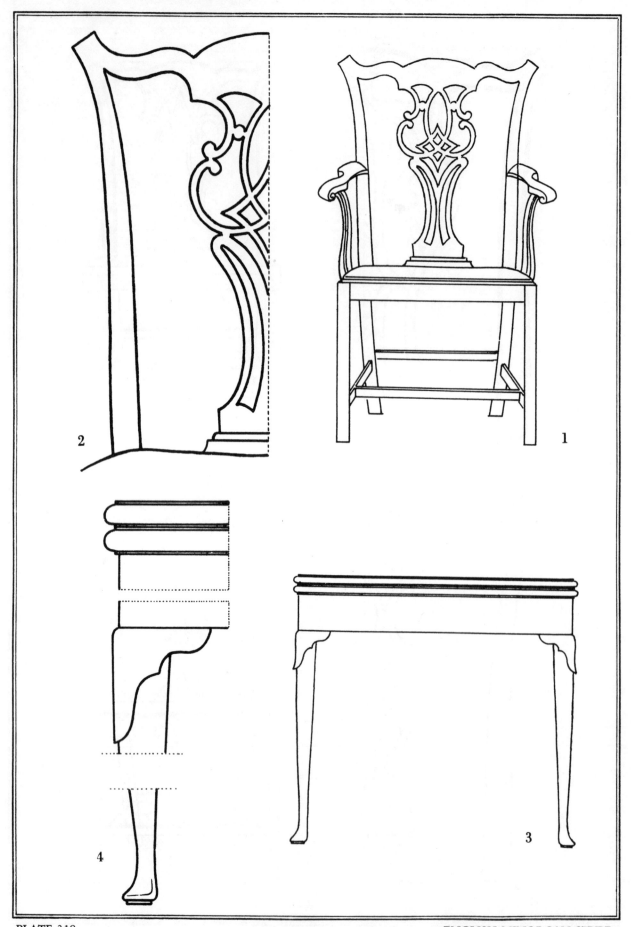

PLATE 318.   ENGLISH MINORCAN STYLE.
1. Chippendale style armchair.   2. Detail of back.   3. Queen Anne style table.   4. Detail of moulding and leg.
From the residence of Francisco Mercadal Montanari, Mahon.

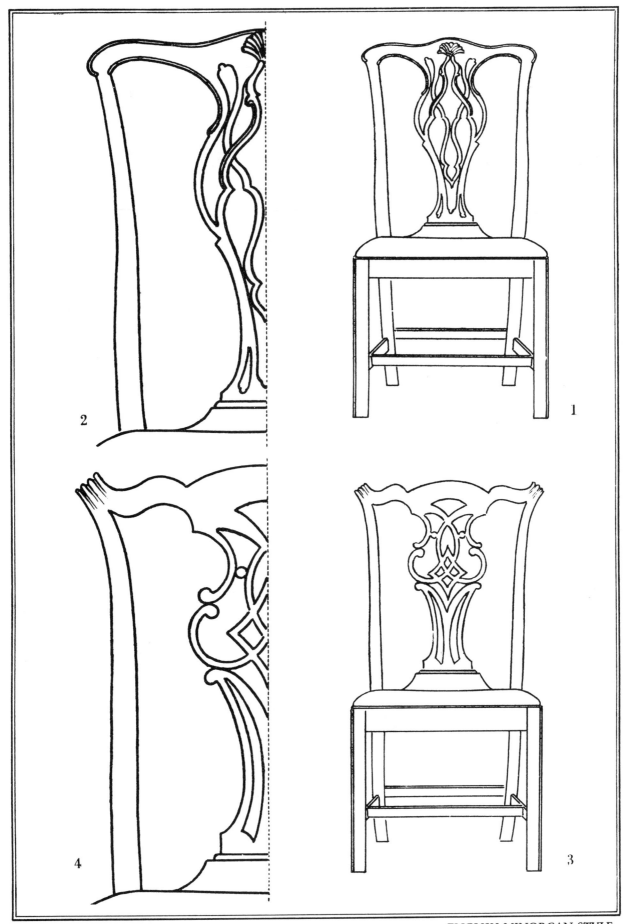

PLATE 319.

ENGLISH MINORCAN STYLE.

1 and 3. Chairs with Chippendale backs.   2 and 4. Detail of backs.

From the residence of Clotilde de Olivar, Vda, de Corral. Mahon.

323

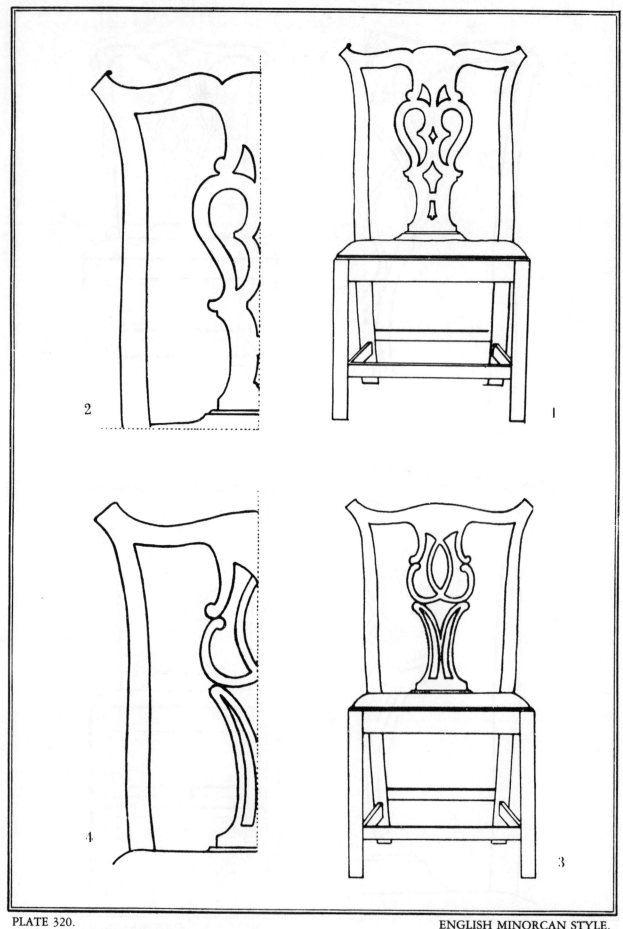

PLATE 320.

1 and 3. Chairs with Chippendale backs. 2 and 4. Details of backs.

ENGLISH MINORCAN STYLE.

From the residence of Francisco Vidal Sintas, Mahon.

PLATE 321.   ENGLISH MINORCAN STYLE.
1 and 3. Chairs with Chippendale backs.   2 and 4. Details of backs.   5. Another Chippendale back.
From the residence of Francisco Vidal Sintas, Mahon.

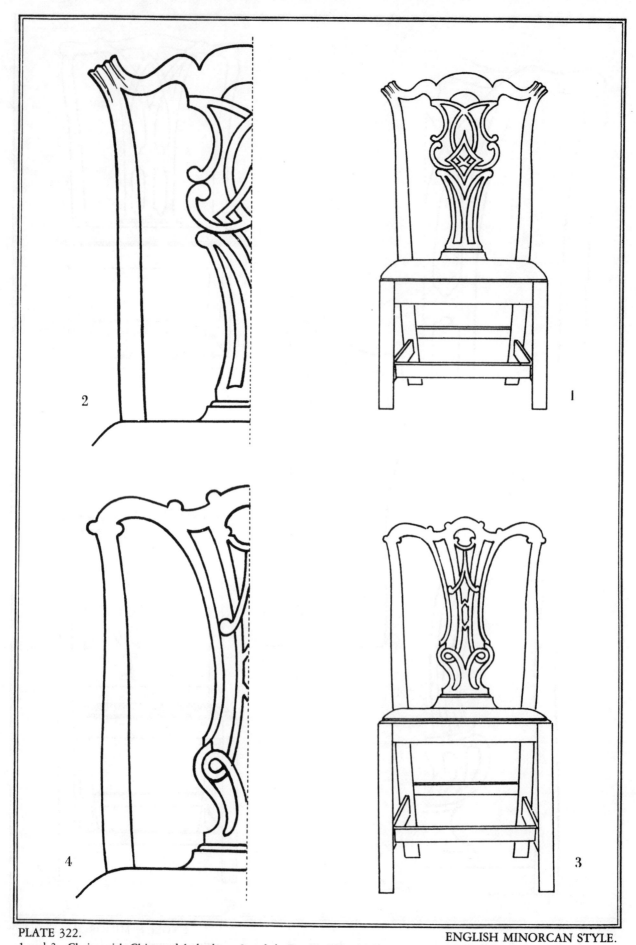

PLATE 322.
1 and 3. Chairs with Chippendale backs.   2 and 4. Details of backs.

ENGLISH MINORCAN STYLE.

From the residence of Juan Francisco and Jose Maria Andreu, Mahon.

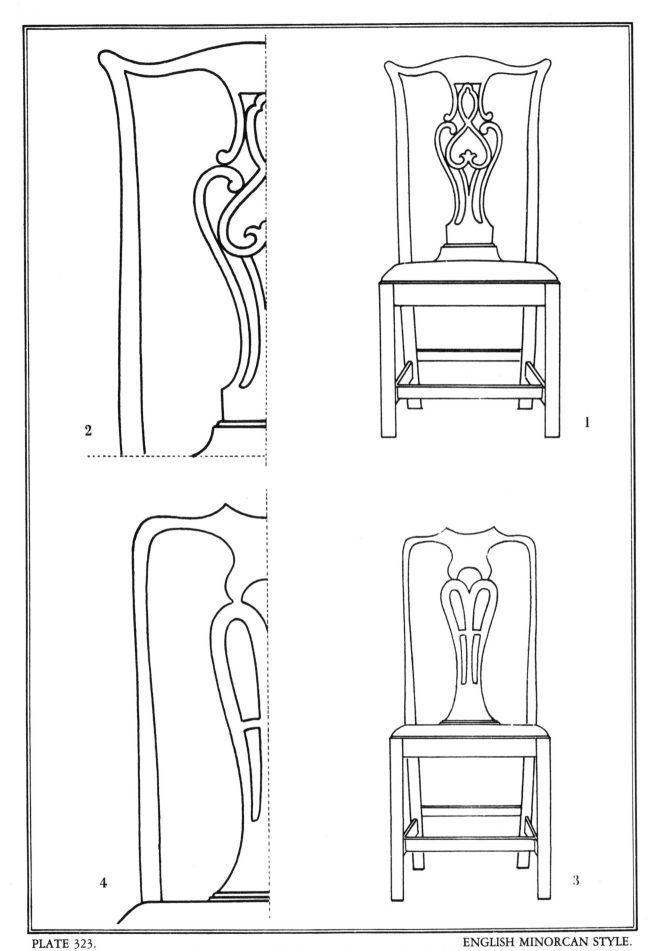

PLATE 323.   ENGLISH MINORCAN STYLE.

1. Chair with Chippendale back.   2. Detail of back.   3. Chair with whimsical back.   4. Detail of back.
From the residence of Antonia del Amo, Vda. de Alberti, Mahon.

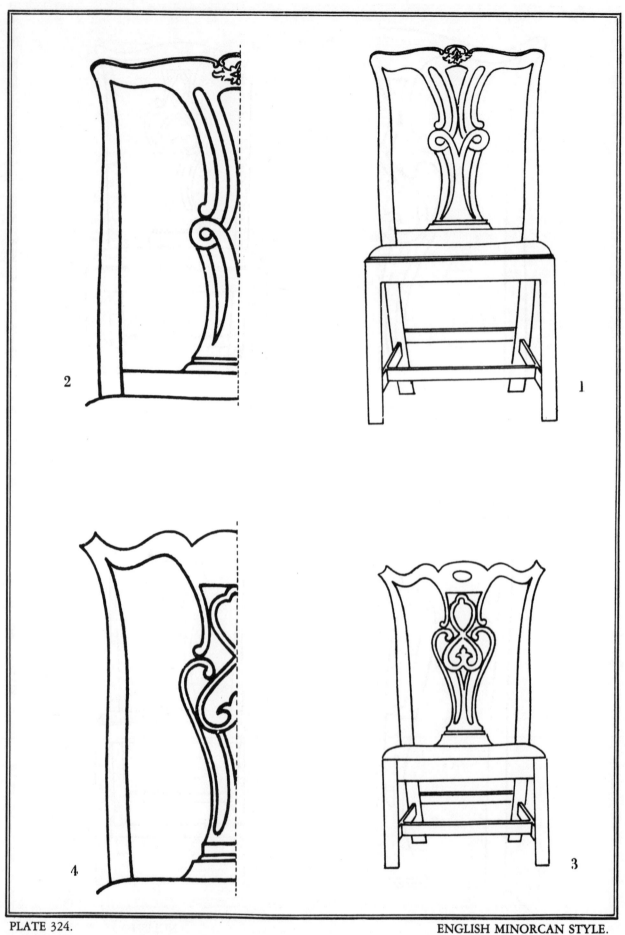

PLATE 324.

ENGLISH MINORCAN STYLE.

1 and 3. Chairs with Chippendale backs.   2 and 4. Details of backs.

From the residence of Luis Victory Manella, Mahon.

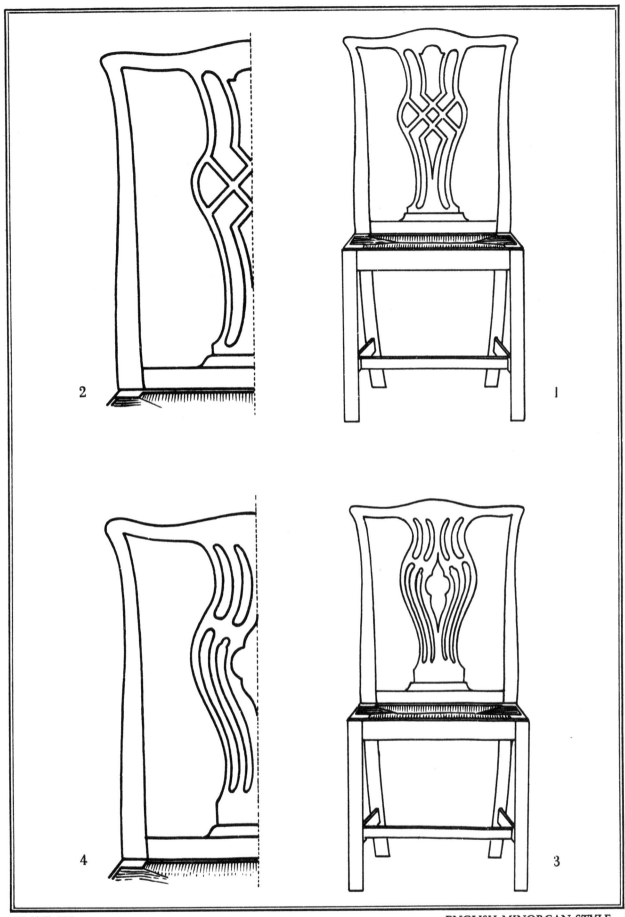

PLATE 325.

ENGLISH MINORCAN STYLE.

1 and 3. Chairs with vertical Chippendale backs.   2 and 4. Details of backs.

From the residence of Juan Campo, Mahon.

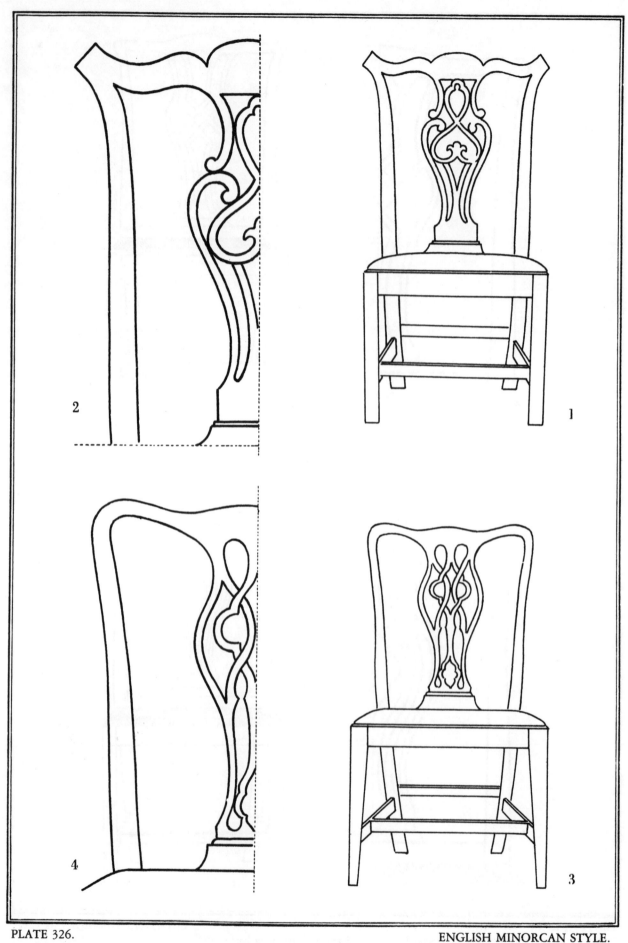

PLATE 326.
1 and 3. Chairs with Chippendale backs. 2 and 4. Detail of backs.

ENGLISH MINORCAN STYLE.

From the residence of Juan de Salort de Salort, Alayor.

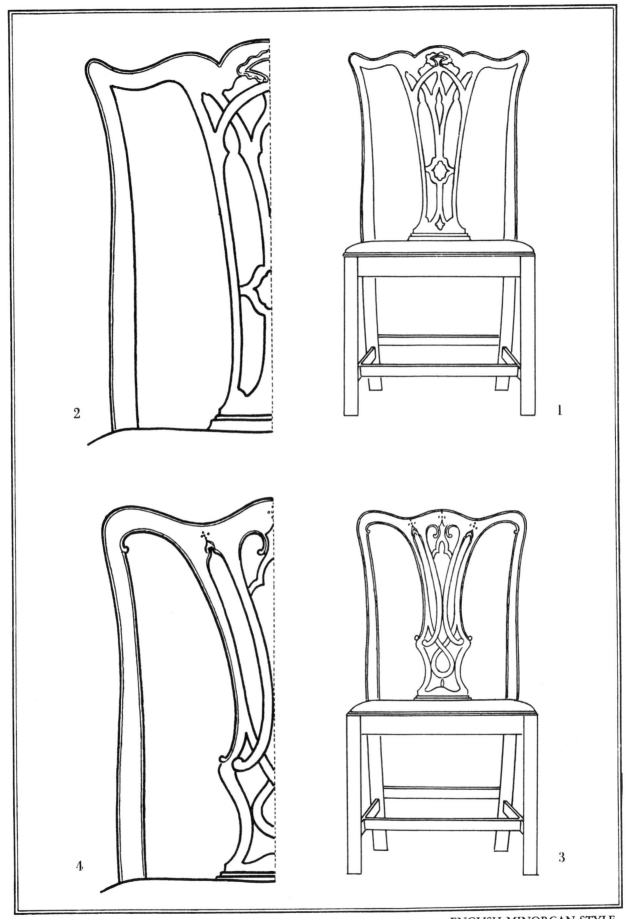

PLATE 327.

ENGLISH MINORCAN STYLE.

1 and 3. Chairs with Chippendale backs.　2 and 4. Detail of backs.

From the residence of Juan de Salort de Salort, Alayor.

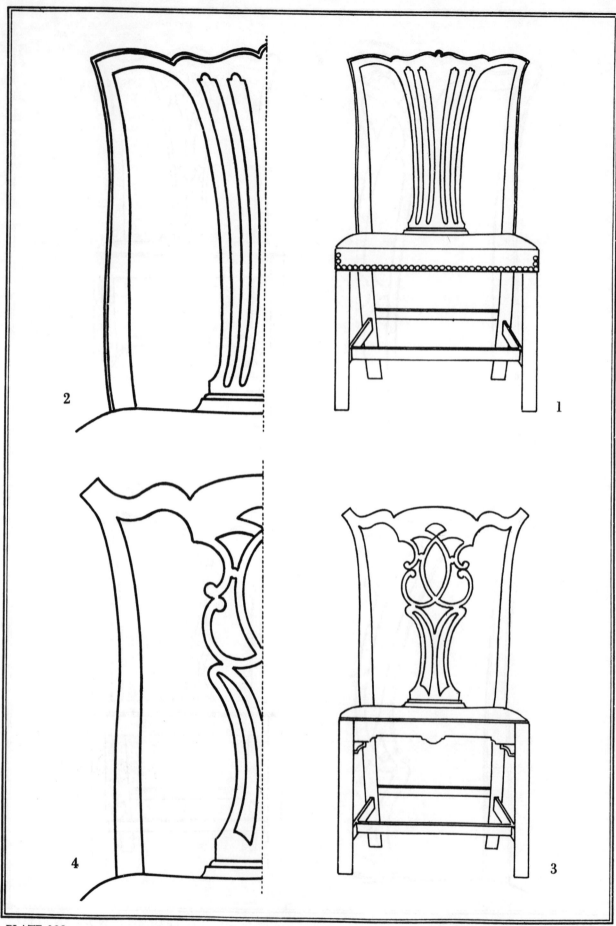

PLATE 328.
1 and 3. Chairs with Chippendale backs.   2 and 4. Details of backs.

ENGLISH MINORCAN STYLE.

From the residence of Dolores Vives, Vda. de Batione, Mahon.

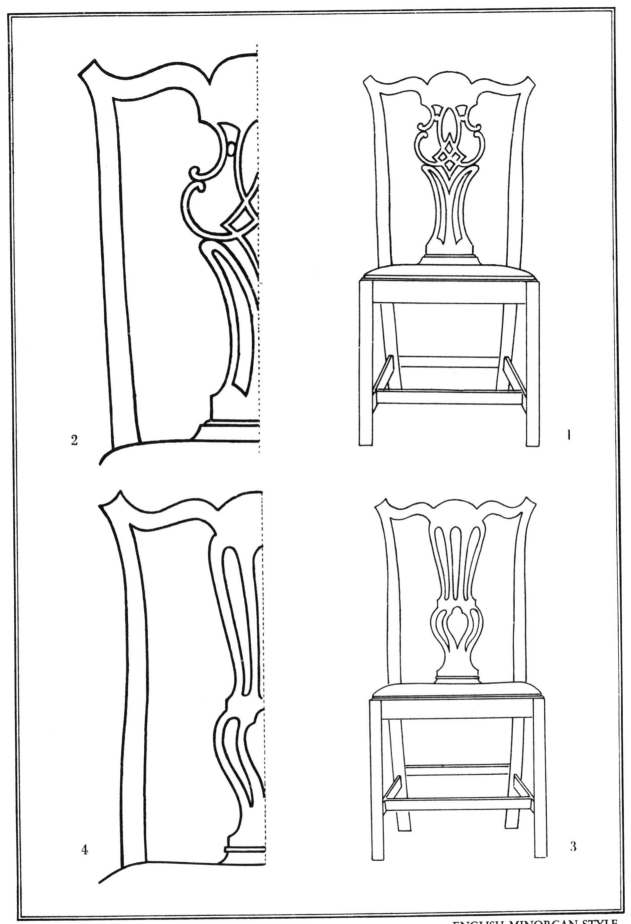

PLATE 329.   ENGLISH MINORCAN STYLE.
1. Chair with Chippendale back.   2. Detail of back.   3. Chair with Chippendale back.   4. Detail of back.
From the residences of Juan Vives Llull, Mahon and Simon Vidal Sintas. Mahon.

333

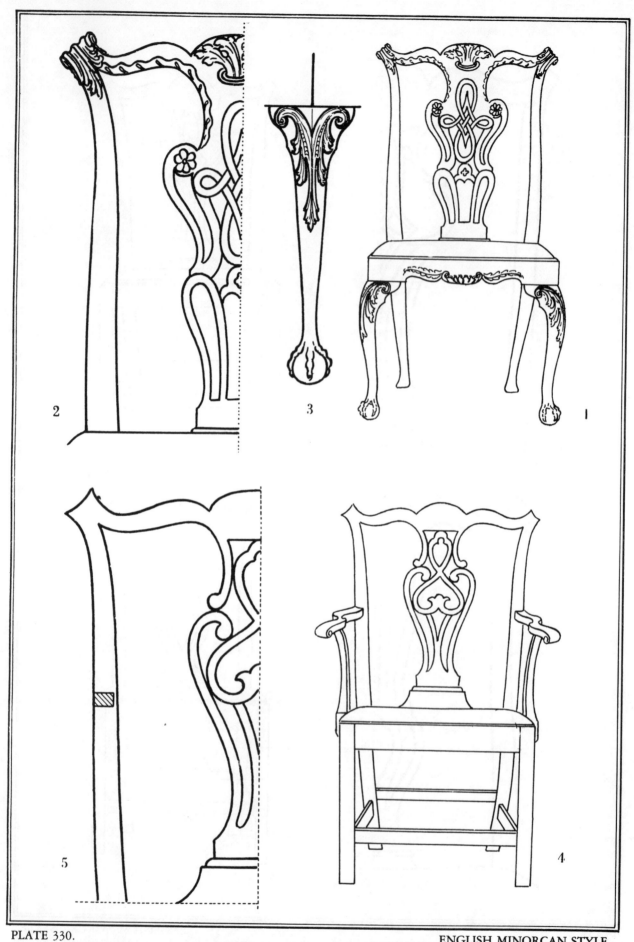

PLATE 330.   ENGLISH MINORCAN STYLE.
1. Chippendale style chair.   2. Detail of back.   3. Leg decoration.   4. Armchair with Chippendale back.   5. Detail
of back.

From the residence of Francisco Segui Poli Moncada, Mahon.

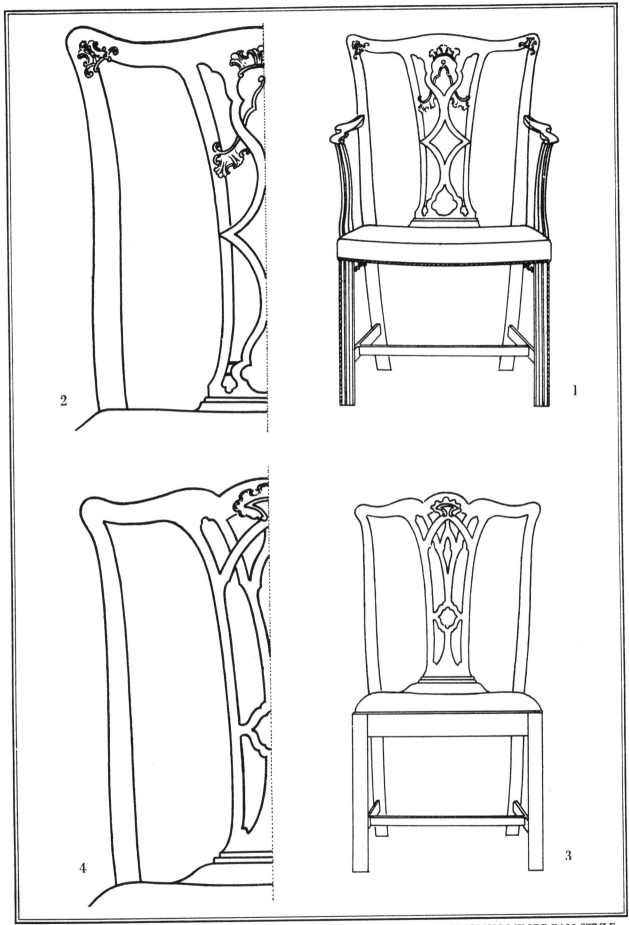

PLATE 331.

ENGLISH MINORCAN STYLE.

Armchair with Chippendale back.   3. Chair with Chippendale back.   2 and 4. Details of backs.

From the residence of Francisco Terres Coll, Mahon.

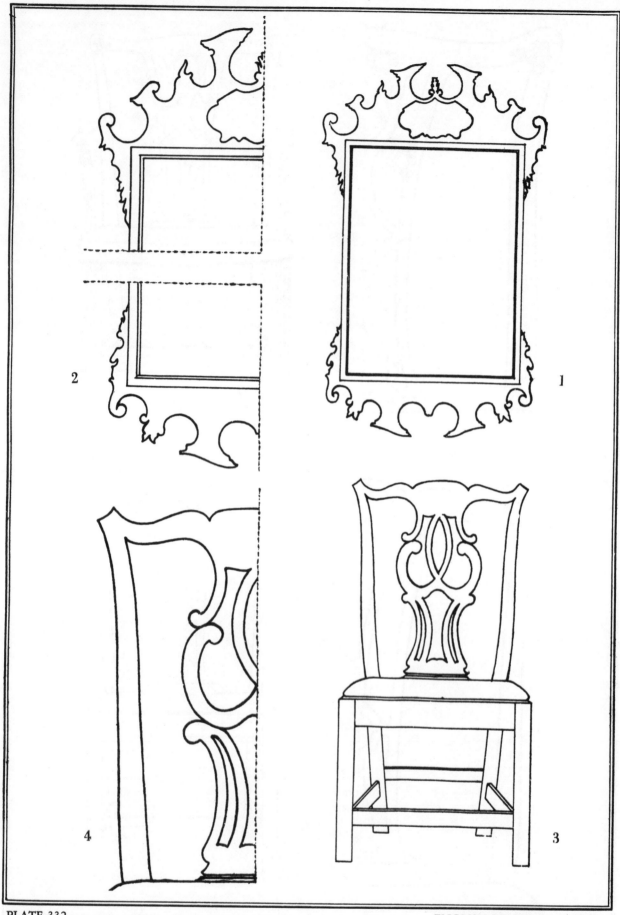

PLATE 332,

1. Mirror.   2. Detail of upper and lower frame.   3. Chair with Chippendale back.   4. Detail of back.

ENGLISH MINORCAN STYLE.

From the residence of Juan Victory Manella, Mahon.

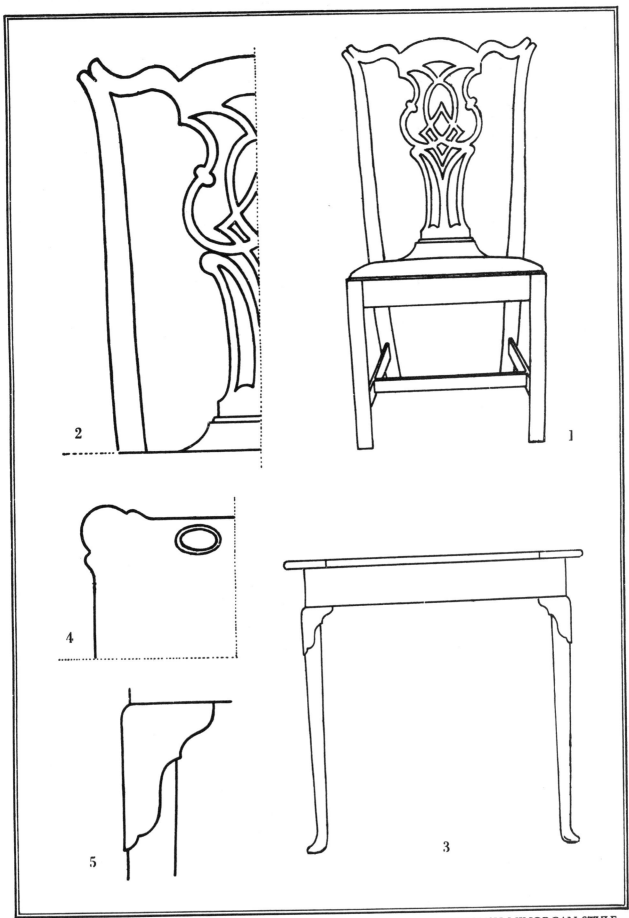

PLATE 333.

ENGLISH MINORCAN STYLE.

1. Chair with Chippendale back.   2. Detail of back. 3. Queen Anne style table.   4. Profile of table top.   5. Decoration at base of leg.

From the residence of Francisco Orfila Alberti, Mahon.

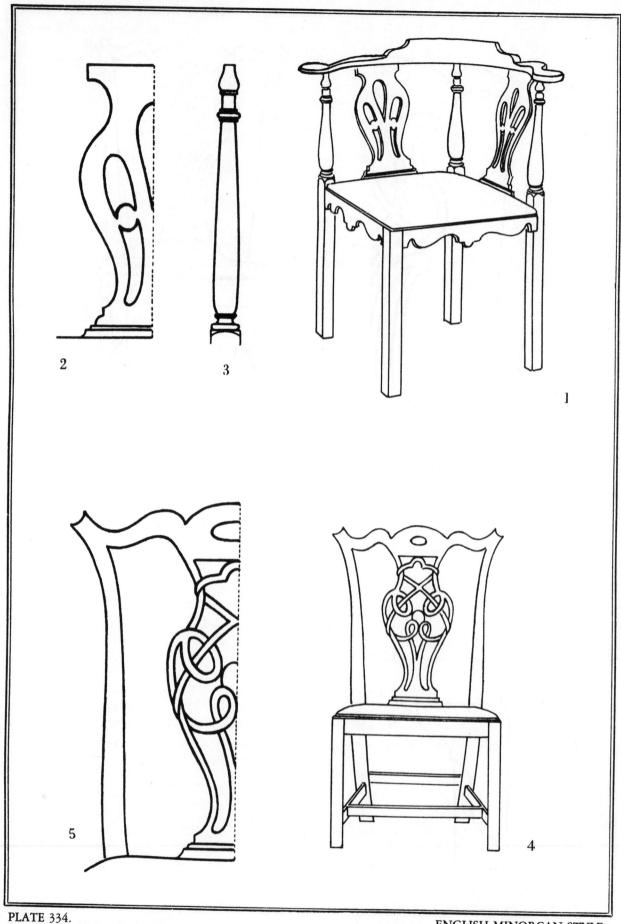

PLATE 334.

1. Corner armchair.   2 and 3. Details of back.   4. Chair with Chippendale back.   5. Detail of back.

ENGLISH MINORCAN STYLE.

From the residence of Juan de Salort de Salort, Alayor.

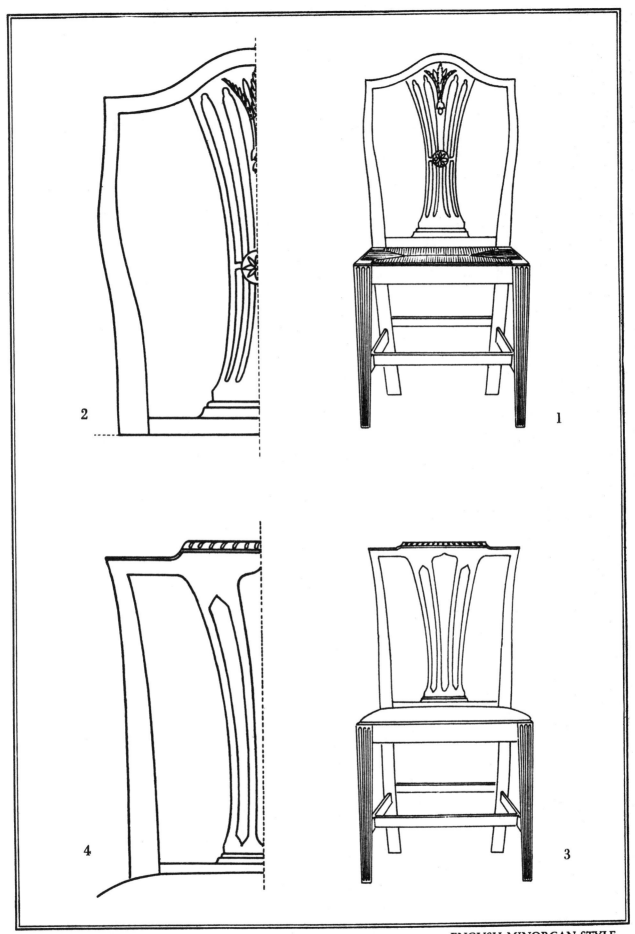

PLATE 335.   ENGLISH MINORCAN STYLE.
1. Chair with Hepplewhite back.   2. Detail of back.   3. Chair with Sheraton back.   4. Detail of back.
From the residence of D. Arnaldo Socias, Mahon.

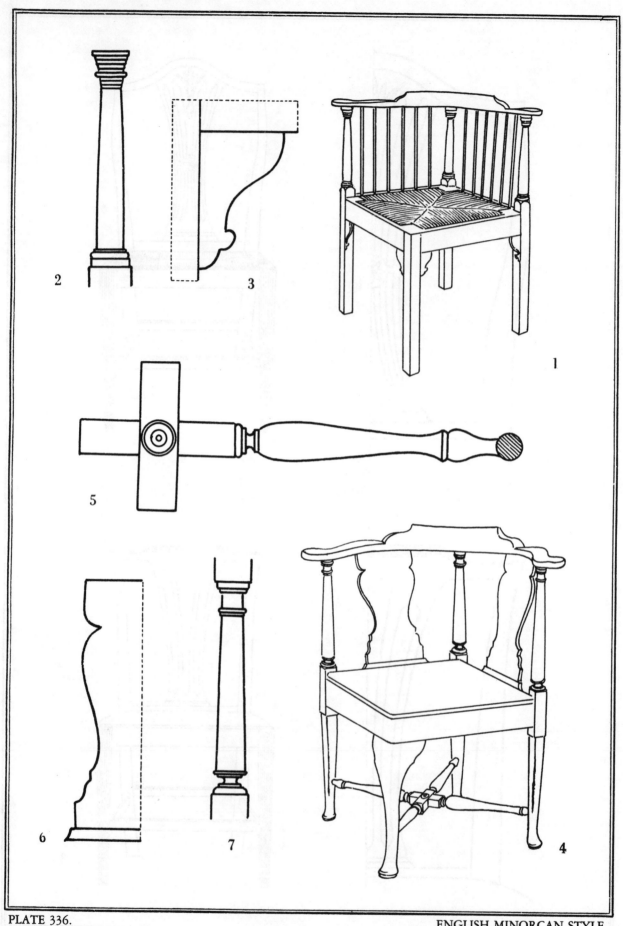

PLATE 336.

1. Corner armchair. 2. Small support column in back. 3. Bracket. 4. Corner armchair. 5. Detail of x-shaped crosspiece. 6 and 7. Details of back.

From the residence of Carlos de Olivar de Olives, Ciudadela.

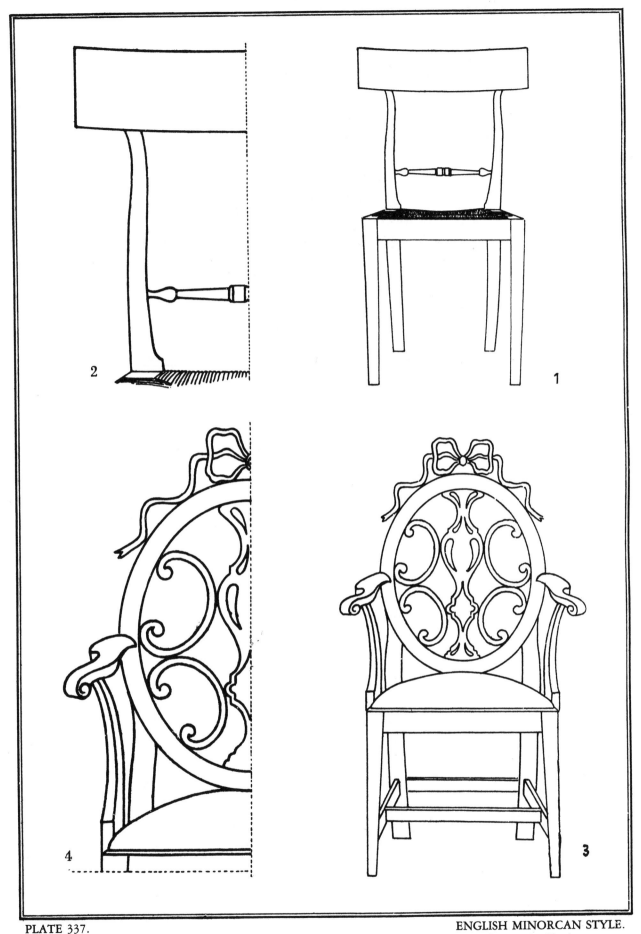

PLATE 337.

ENGLISH MINORCAN STYLE.

1. Very narrow chair.   2. Detail of back.   3. Armchair with original interlaced back.   4. Detail of back.
From the residences of Francisco Mercadal Montanari, Mahon and Mrs. Guillermo de Olives, Mahon.

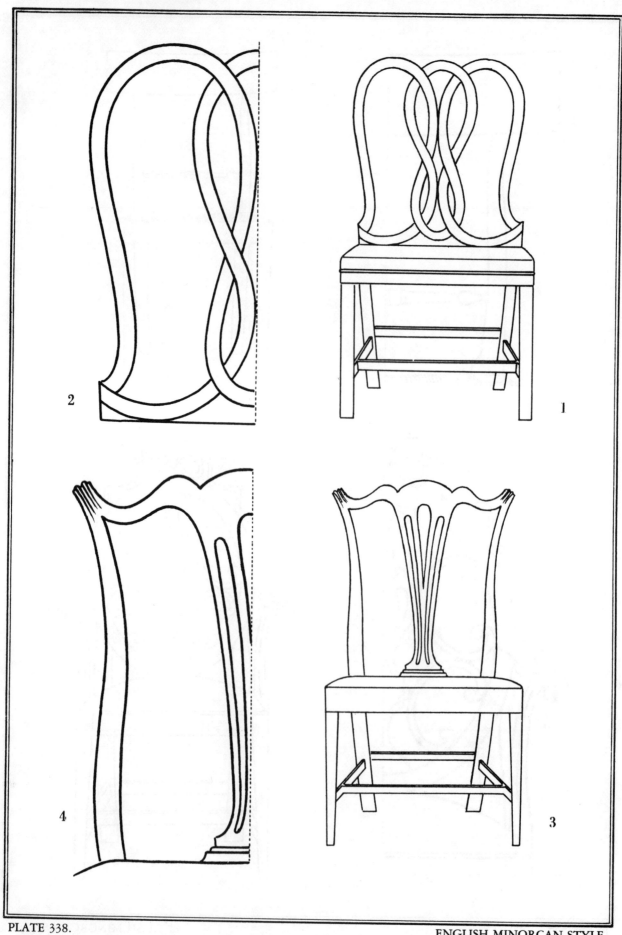

PLATE 338.   ENGLISH MINORCAN STYLE.
1. Chair showing French influence.   2. Detail of back.   3. Chair showing Dutch influence.   4. Detail of back.
From the residences of Antonia del Amo, Vda. de Alberti, Mahon and Juana Villalonga, Vda. de Alberti, Mahon.

PLATE 339.   ENGLISH MINORCAN STYLE.
1. Mirror.   2. Decoration on upper and lower frame.   3. Sheraton style chair.   4. Detail of back.
From "Sa Cudia Cremada," the residence of Francisca Martorell, Mahon.

PLATE 340

ENGLISH MINORCAN STYLE.

1. Mirror.   2. Decoration on upper and lower frame.   3. Corner armchair.   4. Small support column in back.
5. Detail of leg and bracket.

From the residence of Lorenzo de Salort y de Martorell, Ciudadela.

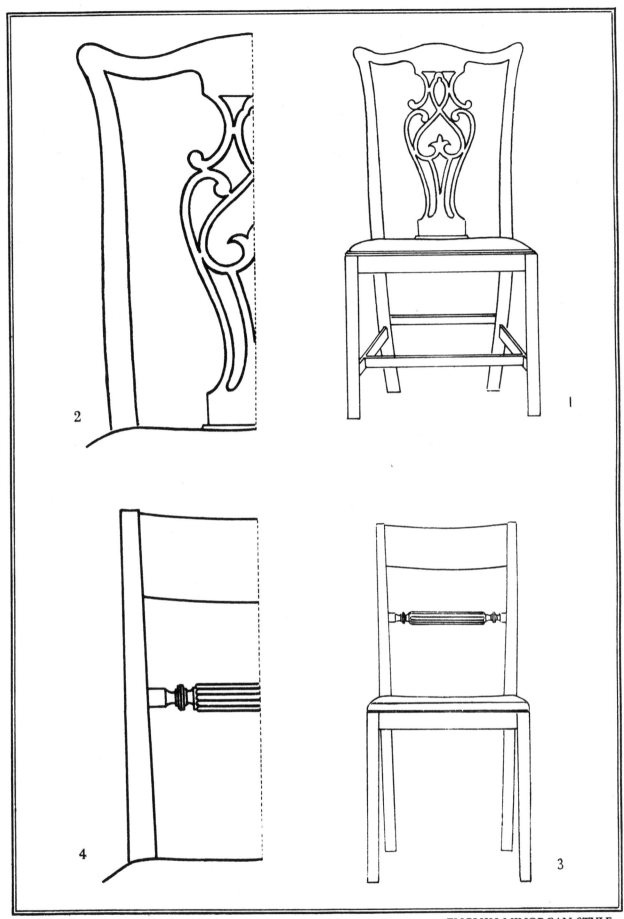

PLATE 341.
1 and 3. Chairs.   2 and 4. Detail of backs.

ENGLISH MINORCAN STYLE.

From residence of Juan Mir Llambias, Mahon.

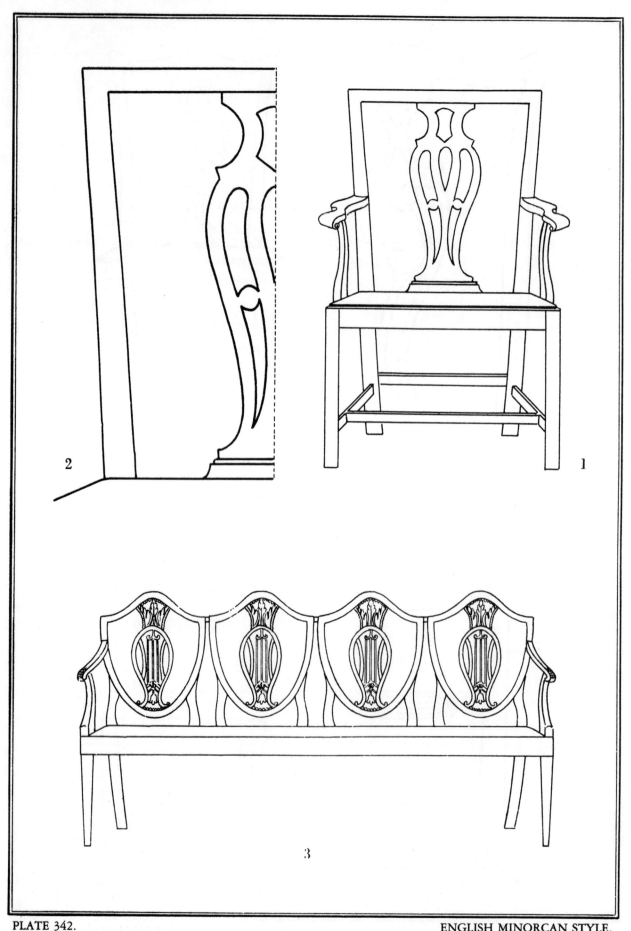

PLATE 342.   ENGLISH MINORCAN STYLE.
1. Armchair.   2. Detail of back.   3. Sofa with shield-shaped sections, characteristic of Hepplewhite style.
From the residence of Simon de Olivar Canet, Baron de Lluriach, Ciudadela.

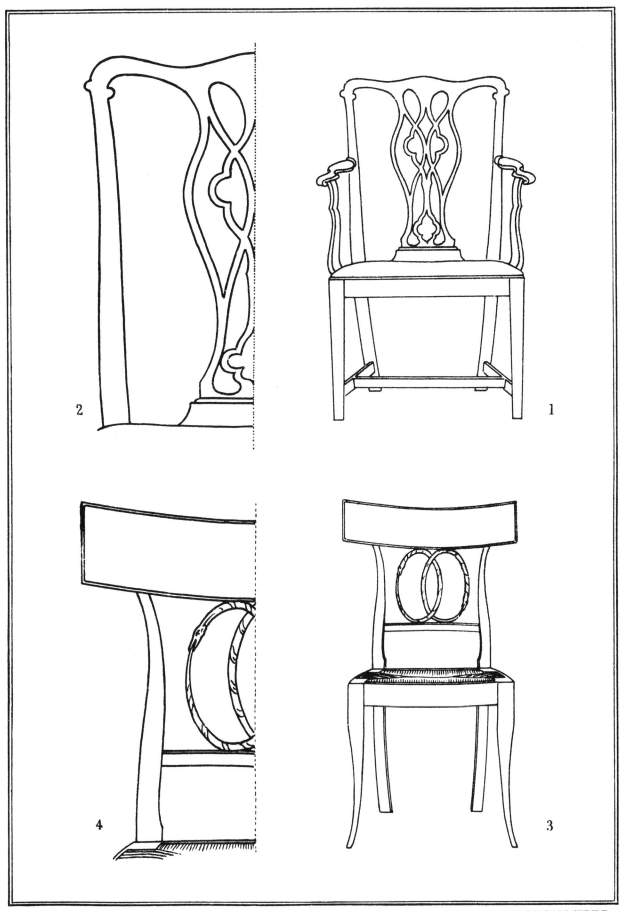

PLATE 343.   ENGLISH MINORCAN STYLE.

1. Armchair.   2. Detail of back.   3. Chair showing French influence.   4. Detail of back.

From the residence of Juan Campo, Mahon.

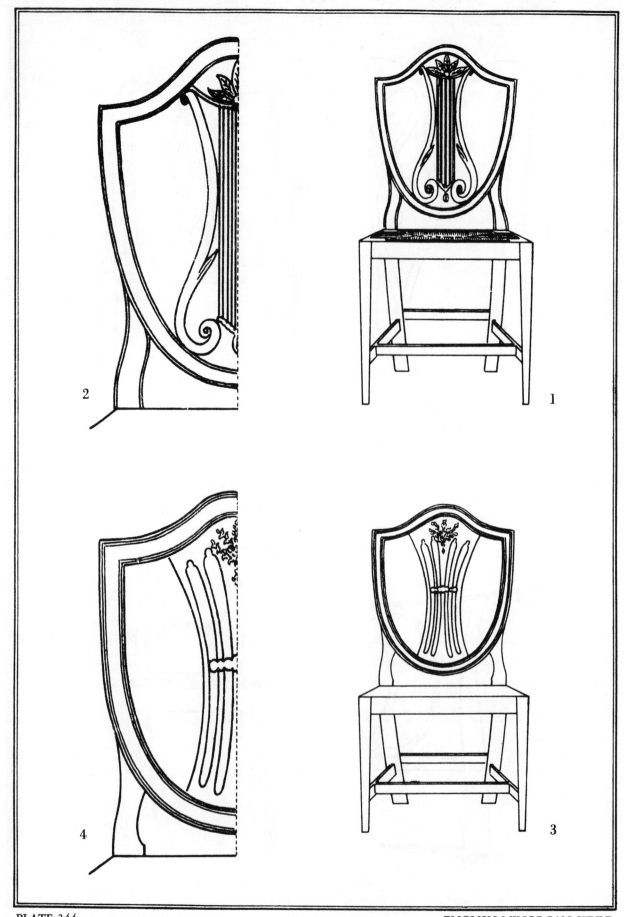

PLATE 344.

ENGLISH MINORCAN STYLE.

1 and 3. Chairs with Hepplewhite backs.   2 and 4. Details of backs.

From "Sa Cudia Cremada," the residence of Francisca Martorell, Mahon.

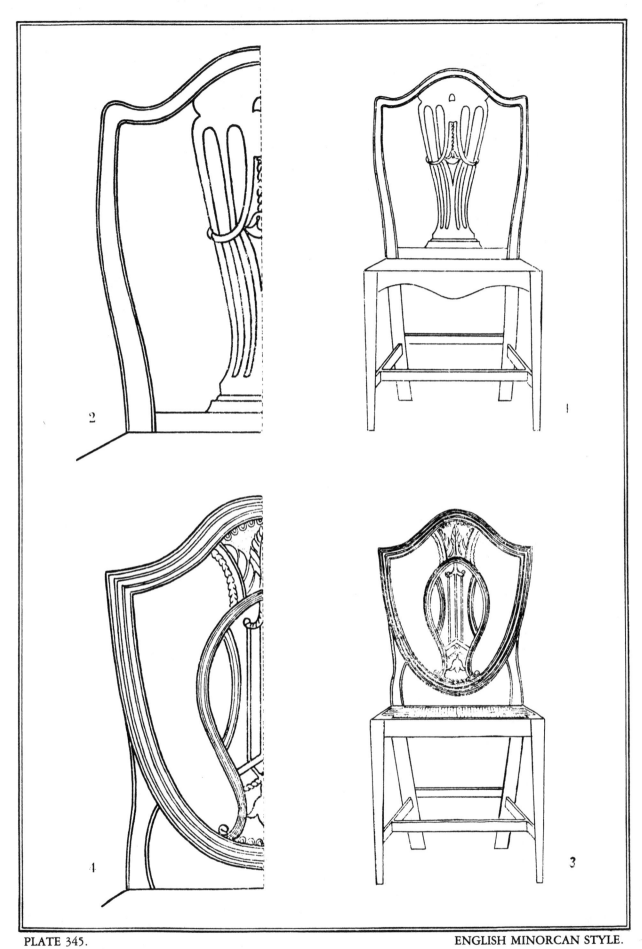

PLATE 345.

ENGLISH MINORCAN STYLE.

1 and 3. Hepplewhite style chairs.   2 and 4. Details of backs.

From the residence of Simon de Olivar Canet, Baron of Lluriach, Ciudadela.

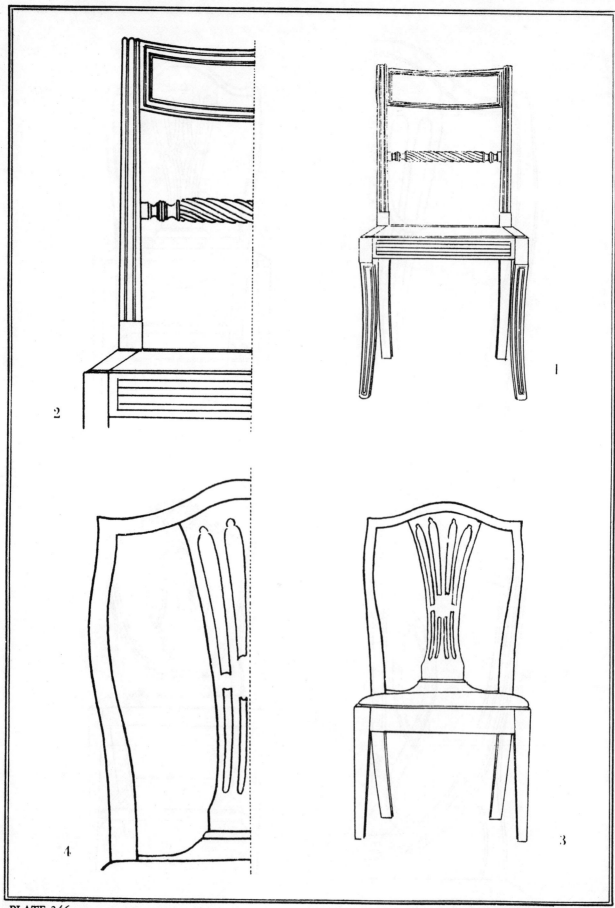

PLATE 346.
1 and 3. Chairs.   2 and 4. Details of backs.

ENGLISH MINORCAN STYLE.

From the residence of Juan Victory Manella, Mahon.

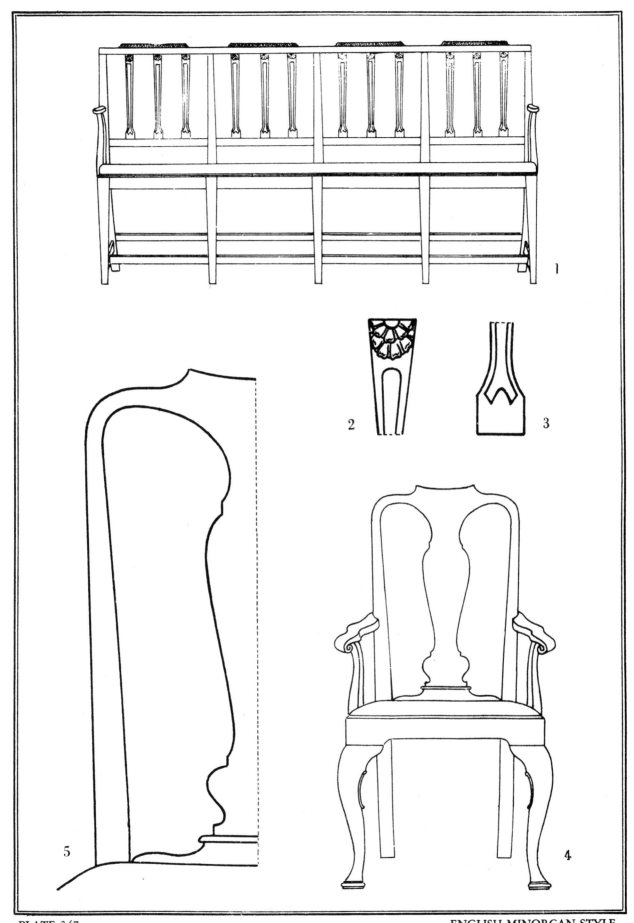

PLATE 347.   ENGLISH MINORCAN STYLE.
1. Sheraton style sofa.   2 and 3. Decorations on listels.   4. Queen Anne style armchair.   5. Detail of back.
From the residence of Alfonso Vivo Salort, Ciudadela.

INDEX